THE ROYAL NAVY'S FIRST

INVINCIBLE

BRIAN LAVERY

Published by

Invincible Conservations (1744–1758) Limited

© 1988, Invincible Conservations (1744–1758) Ltd.,
15/16 Hampshire Terrace, Portsmouth, Hampshire PO1 2QF

Printed in Great Britain by Burgess & Son (Abingdon) Ltd.

Contents

Acknowledgements

Although my name is the only one to appear on the title page, this book is in many ways a co-operative effort. In particular I have to acknowledge the work done by the members of the Invincible (1758) Committee, who have made publication possible. Apart from discovering, recording and excavating the ship, as recorded elsewhere in this book, I must thank them for asking me to write the book, for giving me all the volumes of information they have on the ship and for many helpful comments. Arthur Mack and John Bingeman have already carried out much research in the archives, and I must also thank Eddy Keough, who has tirelessly researched certain aspects of the *Invincible's* history.

I have also been helped by Jean Boudriot, author of *The Seventy Four Gun Ship*, who has opened several useful lines of enquiry and made many comments on French ships of this period; David Roberts, who is translating Boudriot's works into English, as well as carrying out work of his own; and Anne-Marie Poupon and Rachel Magowan who have supplemented my own meagre knowledge of French.

Thanks also go to the staff of the National Maritime Museum, in particular Roger Knight, David Lyon and Chris Ware; to Marc Fardet and the staff of the Archives du Port at Rochefort; and to the staffs of the Public Record Office at Kew and Chancery Lane, the Science Museum, British Library, London Library, the Archives Nationale in Paris and to Peter Hales for many of the photographs.

Sources for picture illustrations
National Maritime Museum, Greenwich – Pages 8, 11, 25, 32, 40, 43, 48, 59, 60, 61, 70, 73, 78, 79, 87, 88, 93, 94, 99.
Archives National, Paris – page 114.
Public Record Office, Kew – page 63.
British Library – page 66.

Finally, I must acknowledge the work of all those who have contributed to the *Invincible* project, as divers, researchers, conservators, administrators, experts, and in many other ways. I regret that there is not room to list them all.

BRIAN LAVERY
1987

Introduction

The Discovery of the Wreck

By normal standards 5 May 1979 was not a good day for the 27ft fishing boat *Vanessa* of Portsmouth. Melvin Gofton and Arthur Mack had taken her out into the Solent at 7.30 that morning. They had laid out trammel nets and left them for two hours while they went trawling for sole. When they came back and began to raise the nets there was plenty of weight in them, but it turned out to be seaweed. They went back to trawling. The net was put over the stern, along with the otter boards which held it open as it was pulled along, and the warps, the ropes and chain which were used for the towing. The boat proceeded eastwards along the Horse Tail bank, outside Langstone Harbour. After about 15 minutes it was brought to a stop by a tremendous jerk, which nearly knocked the fishermen off their feet. The nets had caught on an underwater obstruction.

Arthur Mack and John Bingeman in *Wishbone*

The fishermen tried to get the net free. The boat was taken back so that she was almost above the obstruction, and, with some slack in the net, they hauled in one of the warps and tried to lift one of the otter boards free. Having failed at that they decided to try to pull the obstruction away. The warps were tied around the boat's samson posts, and the engine was put in forward gear, the throttle was opened full and the boat moved ahead. The boat surged forward and the net came away suddenly, rather like a tooth being pulled. It was hauled in. Its head rope was torn off, the ground chain was broken and the net itself had been pulled to pieces. In the mesh was the cause of all the trouble – a piece of wood which had obviously broken off from something under the water.

It was time to end the day's fishing. They took the bearings of the obstruction so that they could avoid it for the future and set course for home. Melvin Gofton had had a bad day – he had caught nothing and he had done £150 of damage to his net.

Arthur Mack took the timber home with him. He had left school at 14, and by his own account his education was 'in the mud of Portsmouth Hard', but he always kept up an interest in maritime history and the piece of wood intrigued him. It had some iron fastenings, but it also contained a wooden peg known as a treenail. He knew this meant that it was old and its size suggested that it came from quite a large vessel. He put it under his dinghy at home, but he became obsessed with the idea that he had found something of great age and importance.

Two days later, on 7 May, he returned to the site in his own 17ft boat *Wishbone*. He put a chain between his otter boards instead of a net and towed it over the area where he had taken the fix on the obstruction. He found nothing. He tried again over the next few days, whenever he could spare time from his fishing, and he found it again on the 15th. In the meantime he had shown the piece of timber to several divers he knew, but none had shown any interest until he had spoken to an old friend and amateur diver, John Broomhead, who had often helped him to clear his nets from obstructions, and to Jim Boyle, the owner of a local diving shop. Arthur Mack, Jim Boyle and John Broomhead went out to the area the next day in *Wishbone*, but the divers found nothing for the marker buoy had drifted.

Arthur Mack would still not give up. On 28 May he found the wreck again and this time he was determined not to lose it. He left his chain tangled around the obstruction and attached a buoy to the warps. For good measure he dropped a spare anchor on the site to help hold the buoy in place. John Broomhead and Jim Boyle came back in the evening, freed the gear from the timbers below and took accurate bearings so that they could find it again. On 1 June John Broomhead and another diver went down to find the extent of the wreck. On board *Wishbone*, Arthur Mack was amazed to follow the divers' bubbles as they covered an area about 200ft long, following the line of visible timbers. Below, the divers' visibility was poor, but they saw enough to establish the importance of the site: 'Lots of old wooden beams found to be protruding from the sand at various angles, also very large planks held together by wooden pegs.' The first artefacts, apart from the original piece of timber, were brought up – part of a leather shoe, part of a steel shaft, and 'some old wood with some wooden pegs through it'. John Broomhead knew that this was the beginning of something extraordinary and for the first time in his life he began to keep a dive log and diary, recording the events surrounding the wreck.

Over the next few weeks the site was worked as much as possible on a strictly part-time basis. Arthur Mack found time from his fishing to take John Broomhead out after he had finished his day's work as a field service engineer with Goodyear, and other divers came along when possible. Many more artefacts were recovered. A small anchor, probably used for one of the ship's boats, was brought up. Several bottles were found and their shapes suggested a date of around 1750 or earlier. Bones were first thought to be human, but were later identified as sheep. Pottery was identified as sixteenth- or seventeenth-century German by the Portsmouth City Museum, where the artefacts were taken for conservation. Copper staples were brought up and these were found to be marked with what the divers at first called a 'crow's foot' – the broad arrow which had been used to mark the property of the British crown since the fourteenth century. Many musket shot and flints were discovered, along with several hand-grenades. Probably the most interesting early find was a sand-glass; many opinions were offered about its age, but eventually the Worshipful Company of Clockmakers pointed out that it was made in two halves and this indicated a date before 1800.

Naturally there was plenty of speculation about the identity of the wreck. After the early dives it was suggested that there were really two wrecks and this was an idea that was to recur several times. More experts were consulted and shown the appropriate artefacts. Visiting divers from other areas were consulted and they 'all thought the wreck to be very old and worth applying for some archaeological advice'. Arthur Mack contacted an old friend, David Houghton, a Ministry of Defence scientist and amateur historian, and asked him about some of the artefacts. He wrote to the National Maritime Museum for advice. In reply, Sean McGrail, the head of the Archaeological Research Centre, warned against the 'dustbin effect – contamination by artefacts not contemporary with the site being associated with it . . . This might possibly account for the range in dates (fifteenth century to mid-eighteenth century) suggested for the material from your site.' Alexander McKee, the discoverer of the *Mary Rose*, went down on his 61st birthday and it was reported that 'Alex considers the wreck to have been a vessel much larger than the *Mary Rose*, and possibly as large as *Victory*'. He suggested the *Impregnable*, a 98-gun, three-decked ship which was lost in 1799, and provided a copy of the court martial on the loss of that ship. John Broomhead examined it and concluded: 'I feel that the wreck which we have found is not only in the wrong place, but is also much older than 1799'. Two years later the wreck of the *Impregnable* was found, off Chichester, exactly where the court martial evidence had stated.

As the 1979 diving season came to an end, there was no doubt that the wreck was of great historical significance. The actual number of diving hours had not been great, and John Broomhead, the most active, had spent $22\frac{1}{4}$ hours underwater; but enough had been found to inspire interest and show that further work was worthwhile. There was a growing consensus that the ship was a British warship of the

A tankard before and after conservation

eighteenth century, but not much was known beyond that.

There was already much pillaging by other divers. It transpired that the wreck had been found by other fishermen and some divers had gone down to look at it, but they had shown no interest as it did not seem to contain any gold or treasure. Because of concern about the damage that unauthorised divers were doing to the site, the Royal Naval Museum in Portsmouth was consulted early in 1980 and shown photographs of some of the artefacts. The Curator,

Cdr Greg Clark, suggested that the divers contact John Bingeman, a Commander in the Royal Navy and Chairman and Diving Officer of Portsmouth Command Sub-Aqua Club. He had a great amount of experience underwater, having qualified as a naval diver in 1957 and led diving expeditions all over the world for eighteen years. He also had considerable knowledge of underwater archaeology for he had dived on sites at Cartagena, the Isles of Scilly, Kristiansand in Norway, as well as on the *Mary Rose* and *Pomone* nearer home. He was taken down to see the wreck on one of the first dives of 1980 and was impressed. 'John took me round the site and I was amazed at what I saw. The timbers just went on forever; in fact, the site turned out to be 59m long. Needless to say, we formed a partnership on the spot.' As well as his own experience, he brought with him the resources of the Portsmouth Command club, including many divers and much vital equipment. The diving programme of 1980 was to be considerably more extensive than that of the previous year.

For a time, the identity of the wreck seemed more obscure than ever. Army buttons belonging to several different regiments were found during the year. John Broomhead tried to find a battle at which all the units took part, but this proved fruitless. Moreover, the standard authorities claimed that buttons of this type were not in use until 1767, and this tended to conflict with the view that the wreck was earlier than that. Taking another tack, in September 1980 it was suggested that the ship was the *Great Charity*, which was sunk in the area on Christmas Eve 1656 while on a mission for Oliver Cromwell.

The letter from the Office of Ordnance, on the changing of the guns of the *Invincible* from 18 to 24 pounders

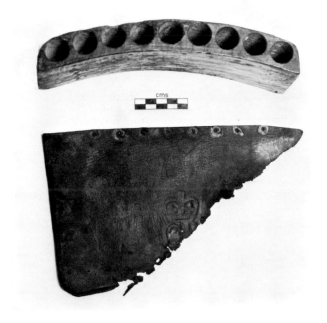

Part of a cartridge case cover and cartridge box

But already the evidence was beginning to point to a later period. On 10 April, the divers came up with 'the most important find so far in dating the wreck; this was a piece of leather which matched up to the musket shot dispenser found on a previous dive. The

leather had the crest of George the Second.' Since that king had reigned from 1727 to 1760, this gave a fairly clear indication of the date of the ship.

John Bingeman began a search through the available records. From a history of Portsmouth written by William G. Gates and published in 1931, he found that a 74-gun ship, the *Invincible*, had been wrecked on the Dean Sand in 1758. This ship had not been seriously considered before, largely because many secondary sources say that she was wrecked off Selsey Bill, some distance from the actual site, while others said 'near St Helens', on the other side of the Solent. The report of the court martial on the loss was consulted and it was perfectly clear: the ship had been lost on the Dean Sand, in an area which later became known as the Horse Tail. On 29 September,

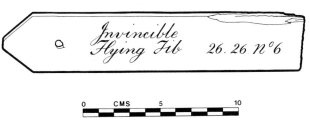

A sail tally, which gave the final identification of the wreck (*drawing by Peter Dawson*)

the first meeting was held between all the groups concerned with the wreck, and it was then that John Bingeman put forward his suggestion that the wreck was the *Invincible*. He believed that there was no other possibility, that no other ship of comparable size had been lost in the area within the period.

However, there remained one great difficulty. By this time, numerous items associated with the ship's guns had been recovered – shot, parts of gun carriages, tampions and rammers. Many of these were marked with the sizes of the cannon they were intended for, and there was no doubt about what sizes of guns the ship was carrying when she went down – 32, 24 and 9 pounders. All the lists consulted showed that the *Invincible* had carried 18, not 24 pounders.

John Bingeman and David Houghton went back to the original documents. They sorted through hundreds of gunnery records at the former ordnance depot at Priddy's Hard, Portsmouth. Eventually they found a letter dated 23 December 1755, from the Office of Ordnance to the 'Respective officers at Portsmouth':

I am commanded by the Board to acquaint you that His Majesty's Ship the *Invincible* is for the future to be gunned with 24 pounders on her upper deck, instead of 18 pounders as desired by the Lords of the Admiralty in their letter of the 17th Inst.

The identity of the wreck had been established 'beyond reasonable doubt'.

The final proof came during 1981. On 30 May John Bingeman brought up a piece of canvas which was found to be part of a sail. When it was unfolded it was discovered to contain a small flat wooden tally which was marked with the words '*Invincible* Flying jib 26 × 26 no. 6'. Despite immediate efforts at conservation the writing faded very rapidly after the tally was uncovered and attempts at special photography have not so far been successful; however, the writing can just be discerned today. It gave indisputable proof of the identity of the ship once known as the 'Horse Sand Spit Wreck Site'. She was the *Invincible* of 74 guns and 1,793 tons, captured from the French navy by the British in 1747 and wrecked under the command of Captain John Bentley on a dark windy morning in February 1758.

1 Building the Ship

The *Invincible* was built in the early 1740s, in the French dockyard at Rochefort. In August 1741 the Minister of the Marine, Maurepas, ordered that two ships, one of 74 guns and one of 64, were to be built side by side, the 74 by the senior constructor Geslain, and the 64 by his assistant Pierre Morineau. Plans were to be drawn up by the constructors and sent to Paris for approval. On 15 September the intendant in charge of the dockyard asked that both ships might be of 74 guns and this was approved by the minister. By a further order of 11 February 1742, the ship being built by Geslain was named *Magnanime*, and that of Morineau was to be called *Invincible*.[1] She would be the third ship of that name in the French navy, not counting galleys and privateers.

Pierre Morineau had been born around the turn of the century. He apparently spent his entire working life in the dockyard at Rochefort, unlike other naval architects in both Britain and France who tended to move from one yard to another to advance their careers. In 1720 he became an assistant constructor in the yard and in 1732 he was promoted constructor at a salary of 1,800 livres per annum. He had built a few small ships – the *Vipere* of 10 guns in 1739, the *Volage* of 26 guns in 1741 and the *Apollon* of 50 guns, his first two-decker, in 1738.[2] As a 74-gun ship, the *Invincible* was to be considerably larger than any of these.

The 74-gun ship was the classic sailing warship of the late eighteenth century in all the major navies. According to Falconer's Marine Dictionary of 1769, 'the ships of 74 cannon or thereabouts are generally esteemed the most useful in the line of battle, and indeed in almost every other purpose of war'. According to Stalkaart's textbook on naval architecture, published in 1781, the 74 united qualities which made her 'the principal object of maritime attention' and had given her 'so distinguished a pre-eminence in our line of battle'. On the French side, in 1791 the Comte de Luzerne had argued for 74s as the main backbone of the fleet on the grounds that 'these ships carry 36 pounder cannon in their first battery, 18 pounders on their second, can present a broadside as powerful as the strongest of ships', and that they used less of the very largest and most expensive timber than any of the larger ships.[3] Several hundred 74-gun ships served in the navies of Britain, France, Spain, Denmark, Holland, Venice, Turkey and the USA. They formed the backbone of all the largest fleets, with eighty-seven in the British navy in 1805. But in 1741, when the *Invincible* was begun, the type was almost unknown.

Obviously there was nothing magical about the number 74. It simply represented the optimum number of guns for a two-decked ship, and the two-decker was the optimum size for a general-purpose ship of war. Even in the second half of the eighteenth century, when the type was well recognised in both Britain and France, the two powers used slightly different gun arrangements. Later, after carronades were added to the armaments, the type was still called the 74, although it rarely carried precisely that number of guns. In the first half of the eighteenth century the French had many ships of 74 guns, although their arrangement was very different from that used later, to such an extent that the later ship must be called the 'true' 74 to distinguish it from earlier vessels.

The true 74 was evolved in France in the late 1730s and early 1740s, during a particularly creative period in French naval architecture. The French navy, unlike the British, did not have a continuous history. The British fleet was always the country's first line of defence and as such it was given priority. In France, with her vulnerable northern frontier, the army was regarded as much more important. In view of the numerical weakness of the British army, there was never any real danger of a large-scale invasion by sea and the very existence of the French navy, as more than a small collection of vessels, depended on having a minister with the vision and determination to argue the case at court and persuade the king that the vast sums needed for a modern fleet would be well spent.

In the late seventeenth century the navy had found such a minister in Jean Baptiste Colbert. He had persuaded Louis XIV to build a fleet which reached its peak in the 1690s with 131 *vaisseaux*, or ships of the line, 33 frigates and 101 other vessels. Its moment of glory came in 1690, when it defeated the combined forces of England and the Netherlands at Beachy Head. But the triumph was short-lived for, two years later, the British destroyed large parts of the French fleet at Barfleur and La Hogue. The French navy never really recovered from this and Beachy Head was its last clear-cut victory in a fleet battle. The British were soon outbuilding the French and in the first fifteen years of the eighteenth century, despite almost continuous warfare, the supremacy of the British fleet was never seriously tested.

Colbert's fleet had been intended to challenge the British on their own territory, the English Channel. It was an arm of the most powerful state in Europe, an instrument of the most populous and richest country in the West. It reflected the glory of the Sun King in its aims and also in its ships, which were often built like fortresses or palaces. Many had three decks, even when they had as few as 76 guns. Some were decorated by the greatest sculptors of the age, such as Pierre Puget. But this fleet was defeated in 1692 and had withered away to less than 150 ships and vessels, most of them old, by the death of Louis in 1715.

Fifteen years later it began a minor revival under the leadership of Maurepas. Much had changed since

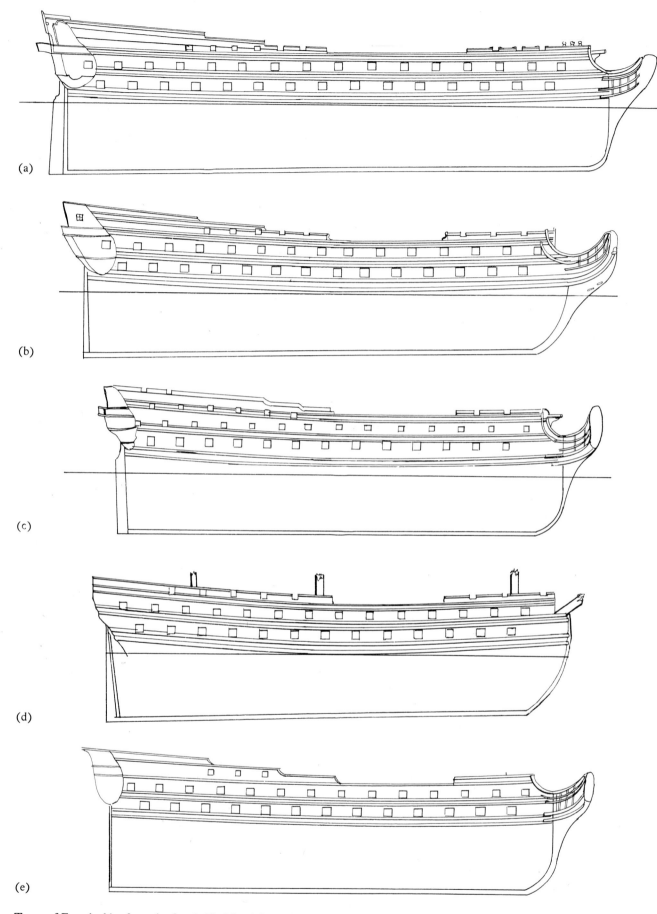

Types of French ship, from the first half of the eighteenth century:
a) two-decker 80-gun ship. This was the largest type in the fleet at that time
b) A 74, similar to the *Invincible*
c) The old type of 74-gun ship, *c*1720. It has less gunports on the lower and middle decks, and four guns on the poop
d) The 70-gun ship, as built around 1740, and superseded by the 74
e) A 64-gun ship. This type evolved around the same time as the 74, and remained common in the French navy until the 1780s

the heyday of Louis XIV. French power had been checked by the War of Spanish Succession and its relative position in Europe had declined. The British economy and population were expanding, while the French state was slowly heading for bankruptcy. There was no question of building a fleet which would take on the British on their own terms, for throughout the long peace they had maintained a fleet of about 240 ships and vessels, including 115 of the line, while the French navy could muster only 40 vessels of all types at its nadir in 1720.[4] Maurepas' fleet, reconstructed from such a narrow base, would be very different from that of Colbert.

Since 1700 the overseas possessions of the European powers had grown greatly in trade and importance. In the seventeenth century colonies had served to get rid of adventurers, religious fanatics and criminals. By 1730 they had become a vital and expanding sector in the economy. The French imported sugar from the West Indian islands, tea and spices from India, furs from Canada and fish from the Newfoundland banks. All this trade was highly profitable, but it depended on long-distance sea transport which would immediately be interrupted by a war with a major sea power, especially with Britain. Furthermore, the colonies themselves could easily be isolated. The French army, however great its strength, could not be everywhere at once, and without sea power it would be unable to reinforce an island or an outpost under attack. The first purpose of Maurepas' fleet was to defend the overseas empire.

Secondly, a fleet, even quite a small one, could be used to distract the British from their other efforts. It could make them fear an invasion of the homeland and force them to withdraw resources from elsewhere in order to prevent it. It could help exploit the biggest single weakness in the British position, the fact that a Jacobite revolt would threaten the very foundations of the state. It could threaten her isolated outposts throughout the world, such as Minorca and the West Indian islands; it could make the British government fear an attack which might come anywhere.

This was a new kind of war which would be fought all over the world. It demanded a new type of ship which could sail as well as it could fight, for the French squadrons had to be able to cross oceans without difficulty, to keep the seas in all weathers, to operate for months away from their bases and to evade the enemy squadrons when they were too strong. The classic ship of Louis XIV's day, the three-decker, would not fit the bill. It was generally high for its length, which made it a poor sailer. It carried its battery high out of the water, which might have given it an advantage in close action with an enemy, but tended to make it unstable and unable to carry sail in strong winds. It used a large number of small guns, rather than a small number of large ones, so its gun power was never quite as impressive as it sounded. It was not an economical use of timber for it tended to make disproportionate use of the largest and most expensive pieces.

Maurepas abandoned the three-decker almost entirely in favour of the two-decker. Only one three-decker was begun during his period in office and that was never completed, being destroyed accidentally by fire. The two-decker could carry heavy guns on her lower deck without any of the problems of stability and windage which were endemic in the three-decker. Apart from that, there was still no settled pattern in French shipbuilding. Two-deckers of many different types – of 80, 74, 72, 70, 66, 64, 60, 56 and 50 guns – were laid down during these years. There was no preconceived plan to develop the 74 as the mainstay of the line of battle and at this stage it was merely one of many types in use.

Even the gun arrangement of the 74 was not yet fully settled. The old type of 74 had been built since the beginning of the century. It carried twenty-six 24-pounder guns on its lower deck, twenty-eight 18 pounders on its upper deck and sixteen 8 pounders on the poop and forecastle. This made only 70 guns and the number of 74 was achieved by adding four very light guns to the poop. Because these guns were almost negligible in force, the type was often referred to as a 70, despite the existence of another class of 'true' 70, with no guns on the poop and only 12 pounders on the upper deck. The early 74 was about 152ft long.

In 1737, a new type of 74 was evolved at Toulon, by the constructor François Coulomb. The length of the hull was increased to 156ft and this allowed the fitting of an extra gunport on each side on the upper and lower decks so that 74 guns could be carried without fitting any on the poop.[5] Since the main deck guns were invariably heavier than those fitted on the upper works, this in itself caused a small increase in gun power, as well as lowering the centre of gravity. A greater increase was achieved by increasing the calibres of the lower-deck guns, from 24 to 36 pounds. This was possible because of an increase in the size of the hull, although subsequent events suggest that Coulomb's ship was over-armed and too small for her guns. But the 74-gun ship of this type was a very powerful vessel indeed, with a weight of broadside equal to any but the very largest British three-deckers. But she was longer and lower than such ships, and was a much better sailer.

Coulomb's ship the *Terrible* was launched in 1739. She did not immediately eliminate her rivals, and one of the old 74s, the *Duc d'Orleans*, was built in 1738. But several new 74s of the new type were begun during the 1740s: the *Invincible* and *Magnanime* in 1741, the *Conquerant, Intrepide, Monarque* and *Sceptre* in 1745, the *Florissant* in 1746, the *Magnifique* in 1747, the *Temeraire* in 1748, and the *Redoutable* and *Couronne* in 1748. In effect, the *Invincible* was the second ship of a type which was to dominate the seas of the world.

Morineau's plan of the new ship was completed by the end of September and sent to Paris for approval. He learnt his craft before the introduction of formal theoretical scientific training, although France led the world in such matters. The French national school of naval architecture was to be set up in 1741, for the

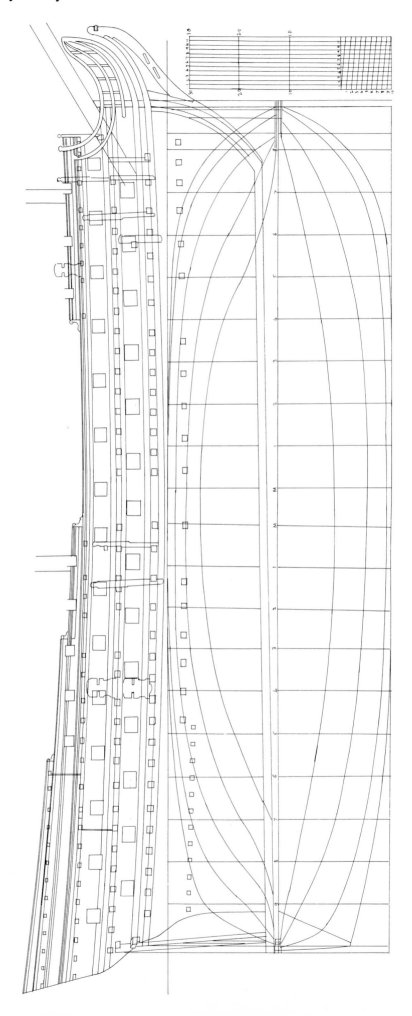

Morineau's plan for a ship 'similar to the *Invincible*', drawn some years later, and forming part of his manuscript book on naval architecture, now in the Archives National, Paris

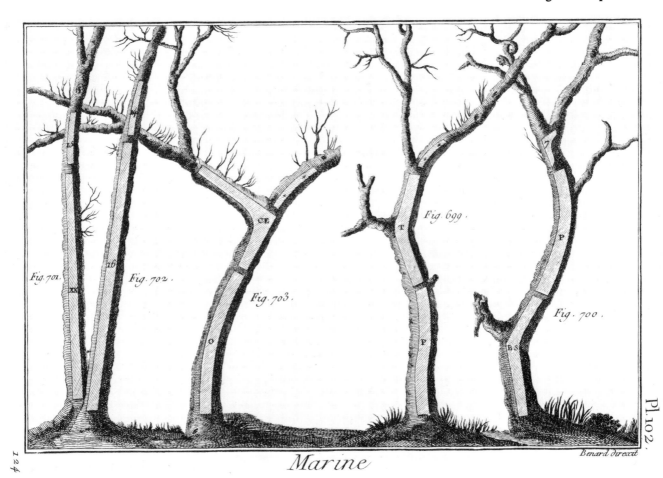

The method of selecting timbers from trees, from the French *Encyclopedia Methodique Marine*, of 1787.

training of royal ship designers; but clearly, this had no effect on the design of the *Invincible*. Before that, a few scientists had studied naval architecture, but their works were often in Latin and were not accessible to ordinary craftsmen. Morineau was more than a simple craftsman; he wrote at least two manuscript treatises in ship design.[6] These are confined entirely to technical matters and in particular to the geometrical methods used in drawing out the shape of a hull; but an old-fashioned craftsman would not have put his thoughts on paper in this way, even to pass them on to his children. Clearly, Morineau was an intelligent and literate man.

It seems that the individual shipwrights were given considerable scope in preparing their designs for the orders from Paris merely specified ships of a given number of guns and left the rest to the constructor. This worked very well when the French navy was small and standardisation was not a great advantage, and in a period when the navy had several excellent designers, such as Coulomb, Morineau and Blaise Olivier at Brest.

Morineau began by drawing out a sheer plan, or side view, of the ship. French shipwrights laid great stress on the distance between the guns, allowing space for the men who worked them. This was the main determinant of the gun-deck length for a given number of guns. Morineau chose a length of 162ft, 6ft longer than the *Terrible*. The keel of the ship was considerably shorter, with a rake at the stern and a greater one at the bows. The lines of the several decks

were drawn out and the gun-ports placed above them, equidistant from one another. The centres of the masts were drawn in position and some of the most important structural elements were also shown. Vertical lines were drawn along the hull, representing cross-sections. These were used to construct the lines plan of the ship, which was placed on the same sheet of paper as the sheer plan. A cross-section was drawn for every few yards, mostly based on circles and ellipses. Various horizontal, vertical and diagonal lines were drawn to show that the lines were smooth and fair, and the designer perhaps made a few calculations of displacement to prove that the ship would float at a suitable height out of the water and carry her guns high enough above the surface even when heeling in a wind. The complete plan would have been on a sheet of paper about 4ft long. Morineau preferred to roll his plans around a wooden cylinder for the journey to Paris, which might take a week. The same plan would be sent back to him, and he liked it to be in good condition when he got it.[7]

Morineau's plan for a 74 was sent to Paris by 19 September, very soon after permission was given to build a 74 instead of a 64. This haste suggests that he had prepared his plan well in advance and was looking for an opportunity to use it. Maurepas wrote back on the 28th, giving his approval for the plan, and his reply had been received at Rochefort by 14 October. Work on the *Invincible* began soon afterwards.

The *Invincible* was to be built with oak from local

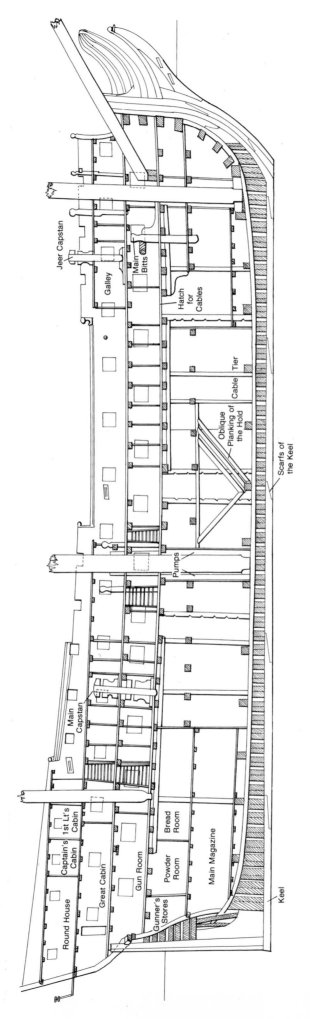

The interior of Morineau's 74, from a manuscript in the National Maritime Museum, Greenwich. It shows something of the layout of such a ship in the French service. After her capture, the capstans, powder magazine, cable tiers, and many other fittings would have been altered or re-arranged

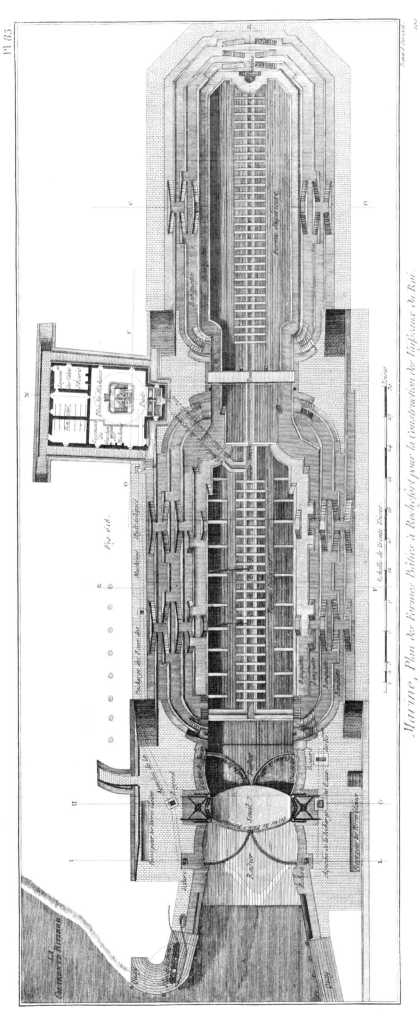

Marine, Plan des Formes Bâties à Rochefort pour la Construction des Ingénieurs du Roi.

One of the dry docks at Rochefort, from the French *Encyclopedia Methodique Marine*, of 1787

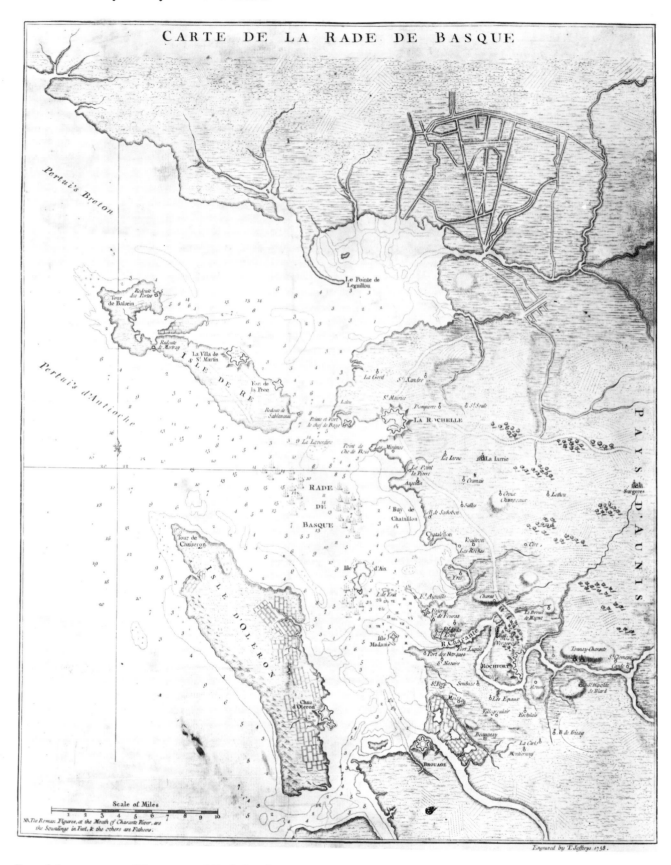

Part of the west coast of France around Rochefort, from a map dated 1758

sources, as far as possible. Rochefort seems to have been well stocked at this period, but more had to be bought to build such large ships as the *Invincible* and *Magnanime*. Purveyors were sent around the forests of the area to acquire the specialised sizes and shapes required by the navy. The king had considerable powers over the forests, especially near the seas and navigable rivers. The king's mark was put on suitable pieces and they were brought, usually by water transport, to the dockyard.

Meanwhile, Morineau was preparing the moulds of the ship. He needed a very large room for this and was given the use of the old sail-loft in the dockyard, while Geslain used half the mast store for his ship. A full-scale plan of the ship was drawn in chalk by scaling up from the paper plan. The shape of each individual timber was cut out on a thin piece of wood, and that would be used to guide the shape of the timber itself.

The first stage in the actual construction was to lay the keel. This was a long straight piece of timber, elm rather than oak. It was probably made in about six sections, linked together by means of complicated joints known as scarphs. It was laid so that its aftermost end was pointing towards the water of the River Charente and it was angled downward so that the ship would be in a suitable position for launching. At the bow was fitted the stem post and various other pieces attached to it. This was in the same plane as the keel, but it curved upwards to form the central part of the bow. At the stern the structure was slightly more complex. The stern post was straight and rose at a slight angle from the vertical. Above it was the structure of the upper stern, with a timber known as a fashion piece on each side; when it was assembled it resembled a lyre in shape. It was assembled on the ground and raised in position in one piece.

Each timber, or rib, of the ship was made up in six or eight sections, known as futtocks, as it was impossible to find a piece of wood whose grain followed the complex shape of the hull cross-section. Timbers usually formed pairs, with the joins at different positions on each. Each timber was 1ft wide and 1ft $\frac{1}{2}$in deep at its lower end, and it tapered until it was 6in square at its upper end, at the top of the side. At the bow and stern the timbers were canted, or angled, from the keel so that they would be more efficient in those areas where the hull narrowed. The timbers were very close together so that about two-thirds of the space under the planking was solid. They were held to one another, and to the keel, by either iron bolts which were driven right through and 'clenched' on the inside, or by round pieces of wood known as treenails. The timbers were arranged so that as few as possible were cut by the gun-ports. About half the timbers had to be cut by ports and the upper and lower edges of the ports were made up with horizontal timbers known as sills, while the sides were formed by the timbers themselves.

The deck beams were placed across the timbers. The largest ones, those of the lower gun-deck, were 16in square in cross-section and were supported from below by a thick piece of internal planking known as the clamp. The deck beams fulfilled two functions: to support the weight on the deck, including the guns, and to brace the timbers against the water pressure which would tend to collapse the hull. To give extra support and to prevent the hull from twisting out of shape, a kind of bracket known as a knee was placed between the beam and the hull timber. On most ships of the time these were made of wood, specially selected for its curved grain and thus very expensive. The French dockyards had been experimenting with wrought-iron knees since 1720, and this was a very early use of iron in ship construction. Such knees were fitted to the *Invincible* and have been found on the wreck off Portsmouth.

Rochefort was a purely naval town and an artificial creation.[8] Colbert and Louis XIV had wanted a dockyard on the Atlantic coast of France to match Brest, which controlled the entrance to the English Channel, and Toulon, which was the main base in the Mediterranean. A new town had been built from 1669, at first in wood and later in stone. It was laid out in a regular grid pattern and a rampart was built around it. It had a population of about twenty thousand in the 1740s and several thousand of these were employed in the dockyard and the other naval enterprises.

The dockyard and the other naval facilities stretched along the right bank of the River Charente. Rochefort was intended as a complete and self-contained naval base, able to produce and store all the needs of a fleet. It had a large dry dock, although that was not enough to cover all needs, and ships often had to be cleaned by other methods. It had several building slips and the *Invincible* and *Magnanime* were built side by side on two of these. The most impressive building was the 'corderie Royal', or ropeworks, which stretched for almost $\frac{1}{4}$ mile along the bank of the Charente. There was a large store for victuals, with a basin for loading and unloading supply ships. There was a foundry for making guns and other metal items, and a powder magazine. There was a barracks for marines, another for keeping seamen conscripted by the Inscription Maritime, large houses for the port admiral and the other officers, extensive storehouses and offices, and space for storing timber. Everything possible had been done to make Rochefort the complete naval dockyard. But nature had not been quite so kind to the yard.

Louis XIV and Colbert had chosen a site near the anchorages of Aix and Basque roads. This area of water was protected by the isles of Ré and Oléron. Like the Sound at Plymouth, or Spithead outside Portsmouth, this provided a place where fleets could assemble and ships could await a favourable wind while sheltered from the worst of the elements. This was the first requisite of a good naval base. It might have been possible to put the dockyard at the ancient harbour of La Rochelle, which also led out to the anchorage, but that town was dominated by Protestants and had a long history of conflict with the crown. Instead, a site was chosen several miles up the narrow winding River Charente. It was on the banks of this river that the *Invincible* was built.

There are no detailed reports on the progress made in the building of the *Invincible*, but it seems that the framing had been completed by the autumn of 1743, although not the planking. The shipwrights suggested that the hull should be covered for the winter by old sails and canvas to protect the frames from the rain, and this would suggest that much of the planking was not yet in place. (Eventually it was decided that it would be too expensive to cover the hull and it was not done.) In the same year, Morineau asked to be allowed to lengthen the forward part of the hull.

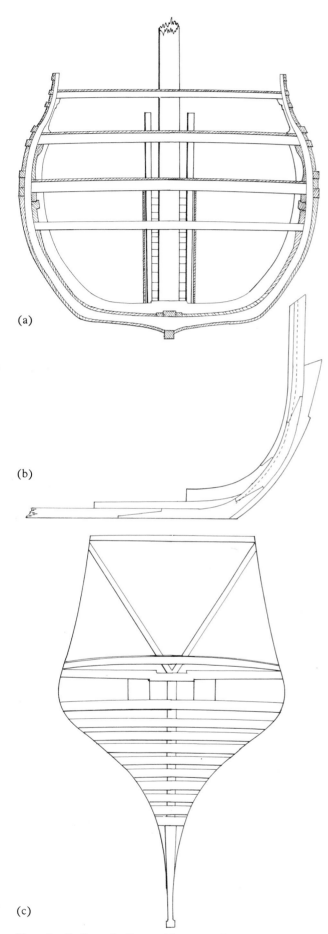

(a)

(b)

(c)

More details from the Greenwich manuscript:
a) A midship section, showing the arrangement of the timbers
b) The structure of the stem, built up of several pieces of timber
c) The structure of the stern, showing the cross pieces known as transoms

Presumably this meant the extreme foremost section, ahead of the first gun-port, for alterations anywhere else would disturb the careful arrangement of the gun-ports. It was evidently intended to alter the position of the bowsprit and its step, which was too close to the foremost gun on the lower deck and would interfere with its firing. The minister gave permission to do this, but only if it could be done quickly. Probably it was not done, as it was later reported that this very gun was obstructed by the position of the bowsprit step.

The hull was planked with Prussian timber. The wales were thicker planks, placed just below the gun-ports to give extra support. In accordance with the French custom of the time, each was a double row of plank, about 18in apart. The lower wales were approximately at the level of the gun-deck, but had a more pronounced curve than the deck. Likewise, the upper wales were at the level of the upper deck. The rest of the bottom and sides were covered with thinner plank, which was fastened with nails rather than bolts or treenails.

At first, construction of the *Invincible* and *Magnanime* proceeded rather slowly as funds were limited. France was involved in the War of Austrian Succession and Britain was at war with France's ally Spain, but as yet the two great sea powers were formally at peace with one another. By the end of 1743, tension between Britain and France was beginning to build up, and Maurepas was urging more haste in the construction of the two ships. In February 1744 the British and French fleets were involved in a battle off Toulon, and at the end of March war was formally declared.

By December 1743, the two ships had had 100,000 livres spent on them, and it was estimated that another 216,100 would be needed to get them ready to launch. Maurepas complained about this, as each ship would therefore cost more than 150,000 livres, whereas a ship of this class built at Brest or Toulon only cost 70,000. A further 26,000 would be needed for fitting out each ship. The *Invincible* and the *Magnanime* were rather bigger than any ship of this type launched before, even the *Terrible*. Their size alone made them expensive, as did the fact that they were built at Rochefort where labour and material costs were higher.

There were various delays throughout 1744, despite the minister's urgings, but the *Invincible* was ready for launching by the beginning of October. The hull was cleaned and caulked and all was prepared for the next full moon which would bring with it a high spring tide, absolutely necessary in the narrow shallow waters of the Charente. This came on 21 October and the dockyard intendant wrote to the minister that the launch had taken place without any accident – not something which could be taken for granted in such a confined space and with such a large ship. The *Magnanime* followed a few weeks later.

Despite the complaints about expense, the minister seems to have been well satisfied with the *Invincible*. Eight carpenters who had done extra work on the ship

An 80-gun ship being launched at Rochefort in 1768

were given a gratuity of 160 livres each, with an instruction that this was not to set a precedent. Later, Morineau was given a *gratification extraordinaire* for his work.

The figurehead and other carved works of the ship had not yet been fitted. Although the French fleet had left the glories of Louis XIV far behind, the government still took a great interest in the decorations of its ships. Back in August 1743, the minister had received plans of the bows and stern of the ship in order that the official artists could draw the designs of the carvings. These were sent to Rochefort at the end of January 1744 and work began on them. The figurehead was to be a full-length figure, of more than twice life-size. It apparently represented a classical warrior, with a shield and a cloak on his back. It was supported some way ahead of the main structure of the bow by the knee of the head and several curved rails, in a manner common to all the major ships of western Europe, but in a style that was peculiarly French. There was another carving, of abstract shape, on each side of the bow where the cat head projected from the hull.

Aft, there was an open stern gallery at the level of the quarterdeck, accessible from the captain's cabin. Below it there was a row of stern windows which gave light to the officers' cabins. There was a quarter gallery on each side at this level which served as toilet accommodation. Above, the stern gallery was merely continued around the sides and there was no enclosed space except for a tiny glazed portion in each corner of the gallery, which perhaps served for the captain's toilet needs. All this had a profusion of carvings. The highest part of the stern, below the taffrail, had fleur de lys and the royal coat-of-arms. The rail of the open gallery was covered with monograms and supported by knees carved with oak leaves. Other shapes carved in bas-relief filled the panels below the upper-deck windows. The name of the ship, *L'Invincible*, was carved in the centre of the stern. It was mid-1744 before serious work began on the sculptures, only a few months before the ships were launched. Some of them were not fitted until January 1745, well after the launch.

The cooking stoves were also installed after the launch. At that time it was normal to fit a pair of copper cylinders known as kettles, placed inside a brick furnace under the quarterdeck. In April 1745 the dockyard was still awaiting the copper kettles. Early in May they had not yet arrived from Brest where they were to be made, and Rochefort was instructed to make do with whatever was available in the yard stock. By this time the fitting out of the *Invincible* and *Magnanime* was well advanced.

Discussion on the armament of the two ships had begun before her launch. The total of 74 guns had, of course, been decided from the outset. Their arrangement was decided by the distribution of the gunports, which followed the precedent set by the *Terrible*. The calibre of the guns was probably decided at the same time for the weight of them played a large part in determining the total weight carried by the hull, and in particular the thickness of the deck beams would be decided according to the sizes of the guns intended for them. She was to have very heavy guns, 36 pounders, on her lower deck; the ball of 36 pounds' weight (39 pounds English) was almost as heavy as any that a man could handle efficiently in action. The guns on the upper deck were, of course, lighter, to help keep the centre of gravity low; 18 pounders were to be fitted there. Six 8 pounders were to be fitted on the forecastle and ten on the forward part of the quarterdeck. The after part of that deck was covered over by the poop deck and this formed the captain's cabin. This area was kept free of guns, although it had a row of five windows on each side.

It was necessary to decide what material the guns should be made of – bronze or iron. The former offered some advantages in strength and lightness, although it was much more expensive. The iron industry was improving its techniques and that metal was now much more efficient than it had been a century before. But bronze guns, with their extensive decorations and their better appearance, were regarded as more suitable for prestige ships. By August 1744 the minister decided that the *Invincible* and *Magnanime* should have a mixture of iron and bronze, with 16 bronze and 10 iron on the lower deck. This shows some confusion, for the ships were intended to carry 28 guns on the lower deck, not 26 like the old class of 74.

In any case, new guns were cast in the foundry at Rochefort to make up deficiencies in stocks. The *Invincible* ended up with 16 bronze 36 pounders on the lower deck and 12 iron; 16 bronze and 14 iron 18 pounders on the upper deck; and 16 iron 8 pounders. The bronze guns were of several different lengths, which suggests that some of them came from old stocks. The same numbers and types of guns were found aboard the ship when she was captured in 1747,[9] although some of them had been replaced in 1746. The guns were set aside for the ship when they were ready, but they were not to be put aboard for some time. Because the river was so shallow, they would not be loaded until she had been taken out to the anchorage off the Isle of Aix, which served as a depot for ships fitting out.

The masts and yards for the ship were constructed in the yard at Rochefort and work had begun on them by January 1744. Probably each of the lower masts was made in several pieces, joined together by means of 'tables' and 'coaks', in a very labour-intensive process. The masts were fitted to the ship at Rochefort. In most French yards this was done by hauling the ship alongside the dock and hoisting them in by crane, but the large rise and fall of the tides made this impossible at Rochefort. Ships were hauled alongside a floating *machine à mâter* (or sheer hulk, as the English would call it) to have their lower masts fitted. The upper masts and the yards would be fitted soon after, ready to help sail the ship down the river to Aix.

The size of the crew to be carried by the *Invincible* and *Magnanime* caused some controversy. The dockyard, recognising that they were bigger than any French ships afloat apart from the 80-gun two-decker *Tonnant*, proposed 720 men. Maurepas objected strongly to this, pointing out that precedent only allowed 620 men for a ship of this rate and that most had only 580. This was to be the established number for the *Invincible* and *Magnanime*. Later, while she was fitting out, this was increased to 650.

By the spring of 1745, the minister was urging yet more haste in the fitting out of the *Invincible* and several other new ships at Rochefort. They had already been chosen for an important service and they were to be taken down to Aix as soon as possible. This was not easy because of the shallowness of the river and its bends. To sail the ship down demanded the unlikely combination of a favourable wind and a spring tide. The alternative was to tow the ship out, and sometimes up to 500 men – soldiers, sailors, dockyard workers or convicts – were employed for this task. Owing to contrary winds and other difficulties, it was 1 July before the *Invincible* was able to get down to the Isle of Aix, along with the *Magnanime* and two smaller ships, the *Jason* and the *Ruby*. Captains had been appointed to them, crews were being raised and they had been ordered to escort an important convoy which was already assembling in Aix roads. The *Invincible*'s sea service was about to begin.

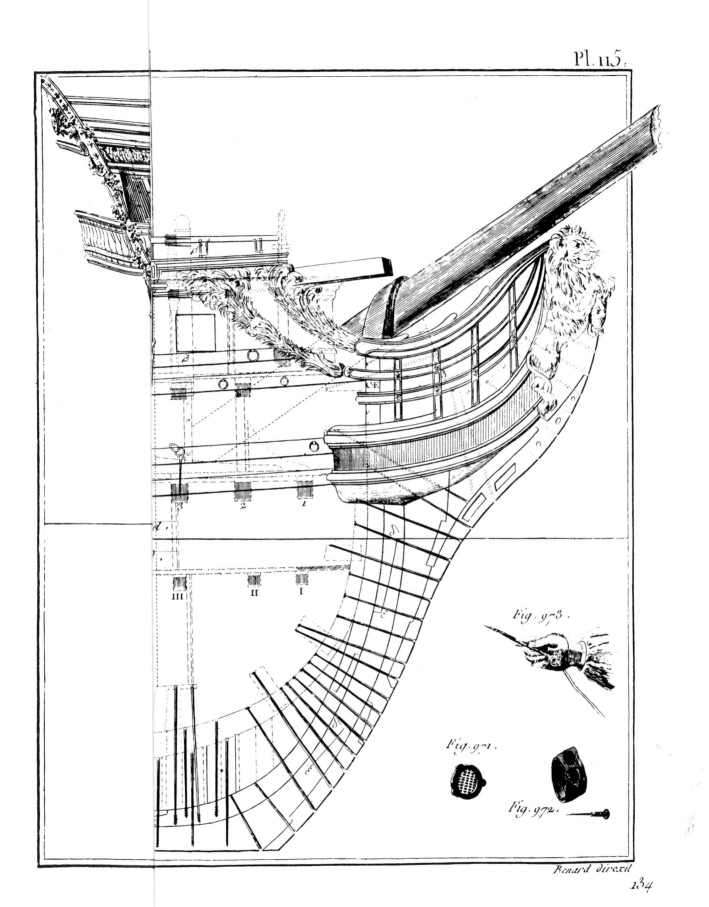

Pl. 115.

Fig. 973.

Fig. 971.

Fig. 972.

Benard direxit.

A French two-decker of the 1780s, showing some details of construction

MACHINE A MATTER DES VAISSEAVX DU ROY.
DU PORT DE ROCHEFORT

A sheer hulk used to fit masts to ships at Rochefort

the morning and took steps to protect their convoys. The French were close to their destination, so Macnemara ordered the merchant ships to set all sail and run for port. The British, under Captain Mitchell, ordered the convoy to lie to away from the enemy. Both sides cleared for action and ran out their guns.

By noon the British ships were drawing up for battle. The *Strafford* and *Lyme* hove to in order to wait for the *Plymouth* to join them from the other side of the convoy. The French ships were more dispersed and the wind was against them, so for a time the *Invincible* was isolated. At 3 pm the *Plymouth* had joined the others and the battle began an hour later. The *Invincible* was much more heavily armed than any of the British ships and was able to

The French colony of St Domingue, later Haiti

fight them off, although the combat was fierce. Eventually, the *Jason* and *L'Atalante* joined from the other side of the convoy, but night was beginning to fall and both sides were committed to protecting their convoys. The British broke off first, after three hours of engagement 'which was carried on very vigorously on both sides'.[5] At first the French, sensing their superiority in gun power, pursued them for about 15 minutes, but then returned to their own convoy.

Both sides had suffered casualties. The *Strafford* had 5 men killed and 8 wounded, and the *Plymouth* had 8 killed and 13 wounded. The captain of the *Strafford* was impressed with the size of the shot from the *Invincible*, one of which broke the spare anchor. He believed them to be 42 pounders. Later, one of them was found to weigh 38 pounds; this is reasonably accurate, since the French pound was heavier than the English. All the British warships had suffered much damage in their rigging and their progress was delayed.

The French had suffered casualties, too – 2 men had been killed and 29 wounded. The ships were damaged much lower down, with several holes close to the water-line which had to be plugged. This largely reflects the fact that the French usually fired into the rigging as a matter of policy, while the British aimed for the hulls. Moreover, since the French were firing to their windward side, the heel of the ship tended to cause the shot to fly higher.

By morning, the two fleets had lost sight of one another and Macnemara proceeded on his way. He dropped some of his ships at St Marc and on the last day of 1745 he anchored with the convoy and its escort at Petit Goave on the southern arm of St Domingue. His work was far from finished as the convoy was to divide and to be escorted to yet more destinations. Five ships had to go the southern side of the island, to St Louis, and to get there they would have to pass Cape Dame Marie, perilously close to the British stronghold of Jamaica. The three ships of war were to escort them and left on 2 January. Off Cape Dame Marie the three warships parted with the merchant ships and the warships remained there to meet a returning convoy which had been informed of the arrangement by land messenger. On the night of 14–15 January, before the new convoy had joined, a sudden gust of wind from the north struck the *Invincible* and seriously damaged her bowsprit. She went to St Louis for repairs, while the *Jason* and *L'Atalante* successfully met the convoy on the following day.

At St Louis, it was not easy to get a new bowsprit for the *Invincible*. The master carpenter of the *Jason* stayed to help the carpenter of the *Invincible* with the work, but the main difficulty was to find timber – three trees, 55ft long and 16in in diameter had to be found and brought to the ship. This had been done by 29 January and work began. The new bowsprit was ready by 21 February and was fitted that day. The rigging was set up, the *Invincible* sailed from St Louis on the 26th, with thirty-two more merchant ships, and was back at Petit Goave by 1 March. She rejoined the *Jason* and *L'Atalante* and collected more merchant ships for the homeward-bound convoy. Taking advantage of her large hold, she took on large quantities of indigo and sugar to carry it home on behalf of the local planters. Around the middle of March the ships sailed for Cape St Nicholas, successfully evading the British patrols which were fully informed of their presence, but had not expected them to sail so soon. They anchored in the harbour there, to await yet more ships for the convoy.

There the British found them. The *Strafford*, *Plymouth*, *Worcester* and *Seahorse* arrived off the Cape on 28 March. The *Seahorse* was sent to reconnoitre and came back two days later with 'an account of three French ships of war laid fast in the Cape, but no appearance of sailing'. Macnemara believed himself trapped and stayed in port for several weeks. The British, slightly puzzled by his behaviour, assumed that he was awaiting the out-ward-bound convoy to increase his strength. But the British fleet was rather less powerful than the French believed and Admiral Warren, the commander in chief, had to spread his resources very thinly to patrol all the colonies of France and Spain. He had no reserves to replace the four ships on station off St Nicholas. On 4 May, a blockade of five weeks, they were running out of victuals and were forced to withdraw to Jamaica.[6]

The three men-of-war set sail for Europe a few weeks later with a convoy of eighty-one ships. On the way back *L'Atalante* captured a British privateer. The convoy arrived at La Corunna, in Spain, on 14 August. It was reported, accurately, that a British fleet led by Admiral Anson was out and looking for the convoy and express messengers were sent out from Paris with warnings. The convoy evaded them successfully and anchored in Aix roads, after an absence of more than a year, at the end of the month. The merchant ships were sent on to their destinations, the ports of Nantes and Bordeaux, under the escort of other ships, and preparations were made to disarm and unrig the three warships for repairs after their long voyage.

None of Macnemara's reports on the performance of the *Invincible* seem to have survived, but in 1772 some time after her demise, one French naval architect, Clairin-Deslauriers, a nephew of Morineau, wrote of her:

> This ship carried sail well, steered well, and had a fine battery. But as far as the other qualities are concerned, which are also essential, such as good sailing close to the wind and gentleness of movement, it must be said that other vessels of the same rate were superior to her.[7]

Probably this was based on reports from her first captain, Macnemara, for her second captain had had rather less time at sea in the ship and no time to make a considered report. If so, the defects mentioned must have caused some reconsideration of her design, and as early as September 1746, very soon after her return from the West Indies, there was discussion about the *doublage* of her hull. This was an ambiguous term and often meant merely a thin coating of plank intended to keep out the ship-worm. This was normally done before a voyage to the West Indies, not after it, but she was now on her way to tropical waters again, and sheathing would have been needed for a voyage to India. On the other hand, it is clear that the doubling applied to the *Invincible* was much thicker than that. Possibly it was intended to remedy the defects mentioned by Clairin-Deslauriers, for it was perhaps believed that it would have increased both her breadth and displacement, and allowed her to stay more upright when sailing close to the wind. Certainly in later years Admiral Boscawen was to hint that this was the case. Modern research, however, suggests that the contribution of such a doubling would have been minimal. Possibly the doubling also helped to remedy the damage done to her hull near the water-line in the battle of 26 December 1745, or to strengthen her structure. But on the whole the purpose of her doubling remains something of a mystery.

Originally it had been intended to send the *Invincible* and *Jason* to Port Louis, further up the coast near the East India Company port of L'Orient, to be doubled and refitted. It was also intended that the doubling should cover the whole underwater hull, owing to pressure of time and delays caused by unfavourable winds, the work was carried out at Rochefort during November. It was decided to carry the doubling down only ten strakes of plank below the water-line. When the ship was surveyed at Portsmouth in 1747, it was found to be 'girdled from 2ft 7ins below the upper edge of the wale 14 feet down, which is $2\frac{1}{2}$ins thick at the upper edge, and 2ins at the lower edge'.

By this time the *Invincible* had been chosen for another mission. The French position in India was declining rapidly, largely owing to lack of naval power. The various settlements along the Coromandel coast were isolated because French ships were unable to sail without harassment from the British Squadron. The French East India Company, the Compagnie des Indies, asked the king for help, and eventually it was allowed three naval ships, including the *Invincible*, which were to be put under the command of the company's officers and were to escort a convoy to the East.

It was an unusual and rather complicated arrangement. The navy was to provide the ships themselves, including their masts, anchors, guns and ammunition. Everything else was to be at the expense of the company. They were to provide the officers and pay the crew's wages, and to supply victuals and all the other stores, such as cordage and spare parts, which would be necessary. Careful accounts were to be kept of the stores issued at Rochefort in order that there would be no dispute later.

The *Invincible's* captain was to be Jacques-François Grout, Chevalier de St Georges. He was an experienced East India captain who had been born in 1704 and had entered the company's service at the age of 16. He had become a captain at the age of 30 and had made eight voyages to India in that capacity

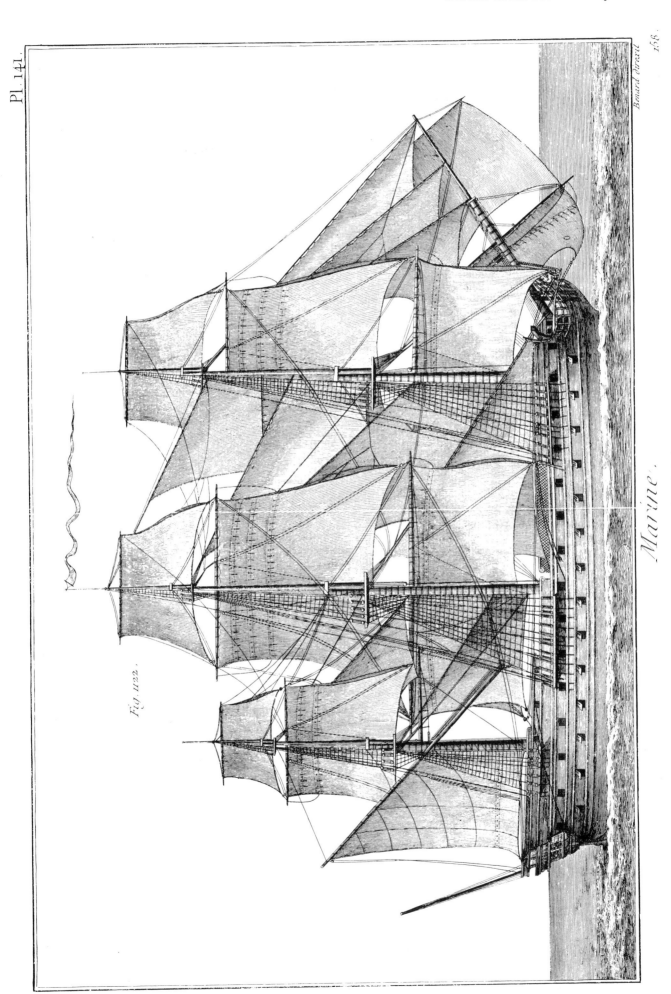

A ship of the line, from the French *Encyclopedia*. The *Invincible* would have carried similar sails and rigging by 1744.[9] On 1 November, in his palace at Fontainebleau, the king granted him a commission as temporary 'Capitaine de Vaisseau'. On 7 December he arrived at Rochefort and registered his commission in the port office.[10]

Under the laws of the *Inscription Maritime*, crews were normally only conscripted for one year so that of the *Invincible* was due for replacement. The old crew was kept on to help with the careening in November, but after that another one was substituted. The arrangement caused some difficulties. The company did not have the power to impose naval discipline on the men and found it very difficult to stop desertion. The dockyard intendant complained of the crew's *libertinage*, and St Georges had a list of forty-one men who had deserted.[11] Deserters who were caught could not be court martialled in the usual way, but were kept in prison while the authorities decided what to do. While the *Invincible* was still in Rochefort, St Georges was obliged to have one of the boats row guard around the ship all night to prevent men from swimming ashore. The minister urged him to act with severity, but he did not specify what to do. One man, Jacques Reou, had already deserted from the *Arc-en-Ciel* at Aix and been caught and pardoned. He deserted again from the *Invincible*.

By December, after she had been taken down the Charente to Aix roads, the *Invincible* was listed as having a crew of 631 men, not including the *officiers major* who would have numbered about 16, and the *garde marine*, or midshipmen, of whom she would have carried about a dozen. She had 92 *officiers mariniers*, or petty and warrant officers. These would have included several master's mates and quartermasters, a gunner and carpenter and their mates, two *bossemans*, or boatswain's mates, about 40 *aides cannoniers*, or quarter gunners, armourers, surgeon's mates, caulkers and sailmakers. There were 409 *matelots* and their number would have included a butcher and a baker, and 60 *mousses*, or ship's boys. She had 10 servants and 2 pilots, but her complement of soldiers was not yet complete, for she had only 6 *officiers soldats*, or NCOs, and 52 soldiers.[12] She was under orders to carry 100 soldiers to India, in addition to her crew of 620 men. In effect, her complement had been increased to the level demanded by the dockyard two years before.

Victuals were supplied from the great storehouse at Rochefort, but charged to the Compagnie des Indies. While at Aix she was supplied with 64 quintals of flour, 60 of mutton, 100 of chickens, 534 of rice, 712 of plums, 190 of sugar, 190 of butter, 142 of bran, the same amount of barley, and 20 quintals of hay (for the live animals). This was harbour victuals, of better quality and variety than what the men would have to consume at sea.

The *Invincible* and *Jason* were to escort the East India convoy. They were to sail to L'Orient, the port of the Compagnie des Indies, where they would meet the third royal ship, the 64-gun *Lys* (which was fitting out at Brest), and where the convoy was to assemble. On 10 January 1747 it was reported that the *Invincible* and *Jason* were ready to sail, but winds from the south-west delayed their departure for some time, and it was the beginning of February before they left Aix roads. On the 11th they arrived at Port Louis, opposite L'Orient, and waited for the convoy to assemble. The *Invincible* took on more victuals from the East India company stores, including 542 quintals of biscuit, 190 of Bordeaux wine, 48 of codfish, 39 of rice and 89 of sardines.[13] She also took on quantities of gold to finance the company's operations in India.

St Georges was called to Paris for his instructions from the Compagnie des Indies and arrived back at L'Orient on 4 March. The convoy was still assembling from various ports, including Nantes. The anchorages off L'Orient and Port Louis were full of ships, to such an extent that the *Lys* and some of the merchantmen had to move to Groix to make room. Finally, on 28 March the three men-of-war sailed with eighteen East Indiamen.

St Georges had already received intelligence that several British warships were cruising nearby, between Penmarcks and Les Saintes. At daybreak on the morning of the 29th, the look-outs sighted five warships making straight for them; it could only be the enemy.

East Indiamen were large ships, which looked like men-of-war from a distance, although they were not nearly so heavily manned or armed. St Georges decided to try an old but effective trick – to attempt to convince the enemy that his larger Indiamen were warships. He formed a line of battle, with five of the larger Indiamen disposed between the three king's ships. He watched as the enemy came within about 2 miles of him and then formed a line parallel to his own. He saw the British ships hoist out their boats and row towards their flagship to consult with their commander.

The leader of the British squadron was Captain Savage Mostyn. He was not the most daring of King George's officers, and two years before he had failed to press home an engagement with two French ships. He was court martialled for that and acquitted; but the charge still stuck in the popular mind, and as he made his way back to his ship he was barracked by a crowd of seamen and dockyard workers who shouted 'All's well, there's no Frenchman in the way'.[14]

Mostyn had indeed called his captains together for a council of war. He was fully convinced that the French had eight warships, of 50–74 guns. His own squadron had only five ships, a 70, a 50, a 40 and two 24s. Aboard Mostyn's ship, the *Hampton Court*, the captains were asked 'whether it is possible with our strength to attack the fleet of 18 sail to leeward'. Their opinion was 'unanimously no'. They correctly identified the *Invincible* as a 74-gun ship and also believed they saw a 64- and several 50-gun ships. Mostyn believed that one of the ships was a three-decker and another was the 70-gun *Northumberland*, captured from the British three years before. The council of war was convinced that 'this must be the

Port Louis East India fleet, under convoy of eight sail of men-of-war and two frigates'.[15]

While the council was in progress one of the ships in St Georges' convoy, a small brig from Nantes, lost her foremast and began drifting towards the enemy. The East India company frigate *La Légère* was signalled to go to her rescue, and did so. The British ships did not attempt to intervene, but set sail for home. They had never come closer than 2 miles and by Mostyn's own account the visibility was less than perfect; had he come a little nearer he might have discovered that the enemy was not of overwhelming force and a well-conducted attack would have damaged or even defeated him.

St George's luck was not to hold much longer. A favourable wind would have carried the squadron clear of danger, but the wind now dropped to a calm, which lasted all night. On the morning of the 30th it began to blow again, but it was coming from the west so that the ships could not make any progress away from the land.

At 1.30 pm St Georges saw a sight which he later described as the most shocking he had ever seen at sea.[16] The frigate *La Légère*, which had rescued the brig from Nantes the day before, was carrying a suitable amount of sail for the wind and was only a few hundred yards from the *Invincible*. She was struck with a sudden gust of wind. The frigate, which was carrying 20 guns and 120 men, capsized immediately, and the crews of the other ships were horrified by the cries of the drowning sailors. St Georges had his barge hoisted into the water and went with it himself in an attempt at rescue. The *Jason* also sent a boat, but only thirteen men were saved and two of these died later.

The storm continued and the crews, especially those of the East Indiamen, were dispirited by the loss of the *La Légère*. Many ships suffered damage to their sails and during the night they were dispersed over a distance of about 12 or 15 miles. It was the morning of 1 April before St Georges had reassembled his convoy and spoken to most of his captains. Nearly all of them urged him to give the order to anchor so that their ships could be repaired. But St Georges was made of sterner stuff and hoped that a more favourable wind would come soon.

Instead, there was a calm that night, followed by a renewal of the storm. This lasted for several days and did more damage. By 5 April the wind had moderated, but it was still unfavourable, so the fleet had made little distance from the French coast. On the 8th, after twelve days of danger and gales, a violent wind again struck the fleet and lasted for about two hours. There was no suitable anchorage to hand and the fleet was in danger of being blown on to the rocky coast of Poitou. St Georges was at last convinced of the need to abandon the voyage and decided to return to Aix roads.

Early that morning the crew of the *Invincible* heard gunfire not far away. It was the British 40-gun ship *Ambuscade* (captured from the French a year earlier) commanded by Captain Montague. He had parted from the fleet two days before with orders to seek out the French convoy. At 4 am he had seen several sails to the north-west and to the south. Before he knew what was happening, he found himself very close to a 36-gun frigate, which was the East Indiaman *Auguste*, carrying gold for the company. The two ships fought until 8 o'clock, when the *Invincible* and the *Jason* were seen approaching. They pursued the *Ambuscade* for several hours and Montague

> found that the large ship came up with me on a wind, so that at ten I put my ship right before it. He then showed his broadside and fired a gun, under French jack, ensign and pendant, and steered after me again. About 11 he fired another gun at me. I found I went from him. He soon after left off chase and stood with his head to the northward, and I with mine to the southward, so that in a short time lost sight of him.[17]

Montague believed that the *Auguste* 'was much disabled, my fire being so hot upon her, and so near, that the men could not stand to their quarters'. He was correct about the damage and the *Auguste* had to put back to Nantes under the escort of another East Indiaman, the *St Antoine*. The convoy was dispersed again and in the poor visibility St Georges could only see eight of his ships.

The rain continued all day, as did St Georges' anxiety. The ships were dangerously close to the rocks of Belleisle and there was no possibility of anchoring for some time. By evening, when the *Invincible* had at last found a place to anchor between Belleisle and the mainland, she had only three ships in company, and two of these had damaged masts. The ships took on some provisions, then sailed south. Off the Ile d'Yeu they encountered another ship, the Indiaman *Le Petit Chasseur* which had been abandoned by her crew during the storm, but was still afloat and relatively undamaged. St Georges put men aboard her and she went with the others. Soon afterwards they arrived back at the anchorage at Aix, where they found the *Jason* and three of the East Indiamen. Later, two more were found between the Ile d'Yeu and the mainland, having lost anchors and cables and not knowing where they were. They too, were rescued and brought to safety at Aix roads.

At Aix roads St Georges found another squadron, with its own convoy. This was intended to reinforce the French position in Canada, as St George's was intended to reinforce India. There were twenty-four merchant ships, escorted by five warships, the largest of which was a 66-gun ship the *Serieux*. It was commanded by Chef d'Escadre (Rear Admiral) de la Jonquière, an admiral of considerable experience.

Soon it was suggested that the two squadrons should travel together for part of the way until clear of the immediate danger from British blockading squadrons and patrols. Although their destinations were different, it was quite common for ships crossing to Canada to go as far south as Madeira to pick up a favourable wind for the crossing, and this would fit in well with St Georges' plans. The idea was obvious enough and seems to have occurred almost

Part of the Bay of Biscay, showing the places visited by the *Invincible* in 1747

simultaneously to Maurepas, to the Compagnie des Indies and to La Jonquière. The latter suggested it to St Georges who soon consented. Since La Jonquière was the senior officer, the joint force came under his command.

The ships stayed at Aix for a few weeks, as some of the missing Indiamen came back and repairs were made. The *Invincible* had a crew of 711 men and was re-equipped with seven months of victuals. By the beginning of May the fleet was ready to sail. On the 10th the wind was from the north-north-east and would serve to carry the ships out of the roads. Anchors were raised and the *Invincible* set sail on her last voyage under French colours. The squadron consisted of 37 ships, including 2 warships and 7 Indiamen under St Georges, and 4 men-of-war under La Jonquière.

La Jonquière had been informed that a privateer had sighted fourteen British warships off the Brittany coast and this reinforced his resolve to take the southerly route. He set course for the north-west corner of Spain, where he intended to pass Capes Ortegal and Finisterre and then head south for Madeira, where the two fleets would go their separate ways. On 12 May the Spanish coast was in sight, 15 miles away, and the following afternoon the fleet was 12 miles north of Cape Finisterre.

It had already been sighted by the enemy. At 4 o'clock on the afternoon of the 13th, the British sloop *Falcon* had seen some sails south-east of him, 12 or 15 miles away. He counted thirty-eight, 'nine of which were large ships and had the appearance of men-of-war.[18] He hurried back to join his main fleet for the departure of the Rochefort convoys had long been expected and the British were waiting for them. At 7 o'clock on the following morning he rejoined Admiral Anson's fleet which was spread out in line abreast with each ship a mile apart from her neighbour in order to search the widest possible area of sea. On receiving the news from Captain Gwyn of the *Falcon*, Anson immediately made the signal to call his ships together and made sail to the south-west where he hoped to cut off the enemy.

Vice Admiral Anson was Britain's leading naval commander of the age. He was a member of the Admiralty Board, so he had considerable influence on the formation of British naval strategy. His present force had been formed as a kind of flying squadron, with orders to

cruise on such station or stations you shall judge proper (according to the intelligence you have, or may receive) for intercepting and destroying the ships of the enemy, their convoys outward and homeward bound, and for suppressing their privateers, and annoying their trade, and for protecting the trade of His Majesty's subjects.[19]

The French reinforcement for Canada had been much in mind when Anson set sail on 17 April and this had led him to search the Bay of Biscay. His force was a strong one. He had fourteen ships of the line, including his flagship the *Prince George*, a 90-gun three-decker, the *Namur*, 74, the *Devonshire*, 66, three 64-gun ships, five 60s, and three 50s. A 40-gun ship (the same *Ambuscade* which had attacked St Georges' convoy a few weeks before), a sloop and a fireship were in support. It was a much larger force than that commanded by La Jonquière and in gun power it outnumbered him by nearly three to one.

At 7 am on the 14th, the masthead look-outs in La Jonquière's ships sighted some sails to the north-east. By 8 o'clock seventeen had been counted and over the next hour concern began to increase as it was noted that the sails were very white, which suggested that they belonged to warships, and that the topsails were quite small, which suggested that they were British. Anson's look-outs were a little slower than La Jonquière's, but at 8.30 his leading ship, the *Namur*, signalled that she had seen a fleet bearing south-west by south. Almost immediately the men at the *Prince George's* masthead also sighted it and Anson made the signal for his fleet to chase.

The French warships could not use their superior sailing qualities to escape from this; they had to protect their convoy. La Jonquière ordered the merchantmen to crowd on all sail to escape, while he formed up his fleet to resist. But the merchant captains were cautious and slow in executing the order, and the enemy was gaining. Clearly, the British force was far stronger than the one St Georges had evaded six weeks before and his own fleet was relatively weaker; he had more warships, but the ships of the Canada convoy were much smaller than East Indiamen and would not pass for warships. Nevertheless, he decided to attempt the same stratagem: to form a line of battle with both warships and East Indiamen in the hope that at least he would gain some time for the convoy to escape.

St Georges advised him that three of the East India ships, the *Apollon*, *Philibert* and *Thetis*, were considered to have the appearance of 50-gun ships, and

these were put in line with the six warships. The fleet was drawn up across the path of the approaching enemy. This was done around noon while the British were still several miles away; but Anson noticed it immediately and observed that three of the ships in the line seemed to be smaller than the others.

Nevertheless, Anson remained cautious. He ended the head-long chase and formed his fleet in line of battle abreast. Half an hour later he formed them in line ahead, with the flagship in the middle of the fleet and the *Namur* leading it towards the enemy. This took some time and his critics said that it allowed more of the convoy to escape. According to some reports, Warren, the second in command, objected and advocated a more direct approach without any particular formation. But custom forbade a British fleet to attack an enemy which was still in good order, unless it was in line of battle, and Anson was not yet ready to abandon the rule-book.

By 2 pm the fleets were quite close together and Anson signalled for the leading ships to alter course and head for the centre of the French line. At this point the nerve of two of the French East India captains failed. The *Apollon* and *Thetis* broke ranks and began to manoeuvre out of the line. La Jonquière ordered St Georges to stop them and the latter fired his guns in an attempt to bring them back. It was too late; the order of battle was disarranged and the leading ships of the French fleet were too weak to make much resistance. The British saw that 'the French fleet seemed to be in great confusion, some standing one way and one another'. La Jonquière hoisted the signal for a retreat. The ships abandoned their line and set sail to the south-west. Anson saw this and he, too, abandoned the line of battle. He ordered his ships to chase the enemy to the best of their ability.

At 4pm the leading British ships had come up with the French rearguard, including the *Invincible*. The British had overall superiority, but at this stage of the battle, as their ships came into action in small numbers against a fleet which was still coherent, the French had a certain advantage. The first British ship to come up was the *Centurion*, 50 guns, under Captain Peter Denis. She was caught between the fire of the *Invincible* and the *Serieux* for ten minutes until the *Namur* and *Defiance* could come to her aid. The *Namur* engaged the *Invincible* on the other side and drew her fire. The British fire was faster and more accurate for Anson had taken much trouble to train his gun crews. The *Namur* engaged the *Invincible* for about an hour, knocking down her mainmast, before passing on to attack La Jonquière in the *Serieux*.

By about 5pm the main British strength was beginning to come into action. The *Invincible* was the largest French ship, and there seems to have been some rivalry among the British captains for the honour of capturing her. According to one account published soon afterwards,

It was pleasant enough to observe a laudable contention between the commanders of the *Bristol* and *Pembroke*,

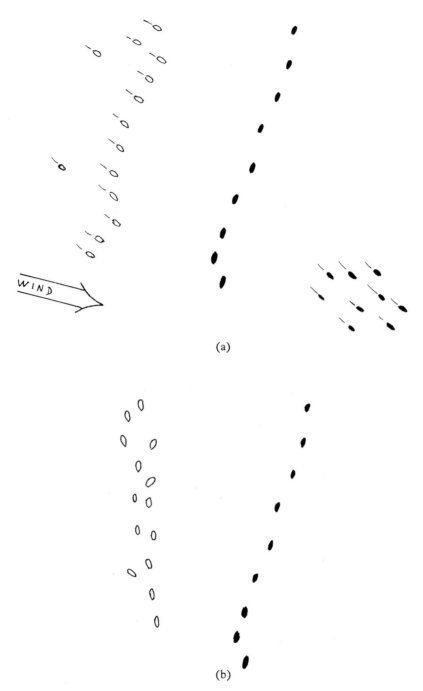

(a)

(b)

The First Battle of Finisterre, 3/14 May 1747:
a) Noon. The British fleet (white ships) approaches the French (in black) The British are approximately in line abreast, while the French are forming line ahead, and the convoy is attempting to escape
b) 12.30. The British begin to form line of battle, taking some time to get the fleet in order

which should engage the *Invincible*. The *Pembroke* attempted to get between the *Bristol* and the enemy, but there not being room enough, the commander of the *Pembroke* hailed the *Bristol*, and bid her put her helm a-starboard, or his ship would run foul of her. To which Captain Montague replied, 'Sir, run foul of me and be damned; neither you nor any other man in the World, shall come between me and my enemy.'[20]

The same account claims that the *Bristol* shot away the *Invincible's* mainmast long before the flagship had arrived. This conflicts with the ship's log which merely records: 'Half past three, the admiral made the signal to engage the enemy. At half past seven, seven French ships of war had struck, and three others. The last was the *Diamond* of 54 guns, who

struck to us.[21] In fact, the *Bristol* was one of the last ships in action and her surgeon's mate later recorded: 'The *Bristol* was not up in time, had only one broadside at the commodore, a near wreck from many other ships.'[22] Montague (no relation to the captain of the *Ambuscade*) was the brother of the First Lord of the Admiralty and a constant embarrassment to him. He was known in the service as 'Mad Montague' for fairly good reasons.

At 5.30 the *Devonshire* of 66 guns was engaging the *Invincible* 'within half pistol shot'. Her captain, Temple West, believed that she had struck to him and that the *Bristol's* broadside was fired after that. In fact, the *Invincible's* pendant had merely been shot away and she had not surrendered.

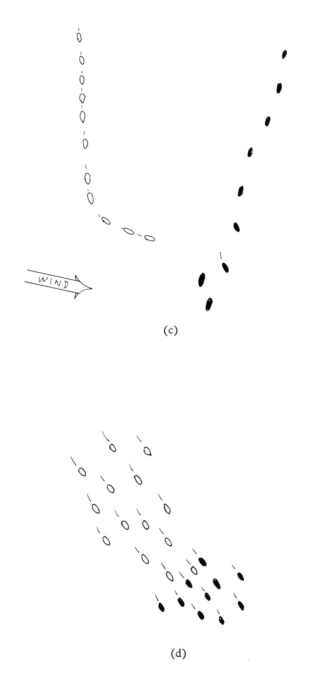

WIND

(c)

(d)

c) 2.15. Anson signals his leading ships to sail 'more large', ie with the wind behind them, causing a more direct approach to the French line. Some of the French East India captains begin to break the line, and the French fleet falls into disorder
d) 4pm. After a general chase in which neither fleet is in any particular order, the first British ships are beginning to come among the French, and the battle begins.

The general British tactic was to attack the rearmost ships as they came up with them and disable them by destroying their masts and rigging. After that, each ship moved forward to attack the next Frenchman, cutting off the van ships and preventing them from escaping. As a result, the *Invincible* was engaged by several ships in turn, often more than one at a time. The *Windsor* was engaged with her for an hour and a half, along with several other ships. As evening came on, ships were surrendering all round her. Several of the Indiamen had hauled down their flags by 5 o'clock and at 6 the *Serieux* was besieged by the *Namur* and another ship. La Jonquière was forced to surrender. The *Invincible* now had a ship on each side. The *Pembroke* fired her starboard broadside into her at close range, while the *Namur* was engaging her on the other side. Her mainmast had already fallen and taken much of the other rigging with it. She had suffered damage to the hull and there was 6ft of water in the hold. Her second captain, de Buisson, had been wounded in the leg, and she was running out of ammunition. According to legend, St Georges put his own silverware into one of the guns and fired it at the enemy. This sounds far-fetched, but after the battle St Georges reported that he had lost none of his personal possessions in the fight 'except his table furniture'.[23] St Georges asked the surgeon for a report on casualties and was told that 125 men had been killed and 80 wounded out of a crew of 711. (A later, more sober, report gave 80 killed and 170 wounded.)

At 6pm, Anson finally joined the battle. The *Prince George* was a three-decker, slower than the other ships, and had not done well in chasing. The *Diamant* had fled, the other ships had surrendered, and the *Invincible* was the last to stand her ground, although she had an enemy ship on each side. The *Prince George* came up astern of her, within 200yd. She turned her broadside at the *Invincible's* vulnerable stern windows and galleries, ran out her guns and prepared to fire at the crippled ship. It was enough for St Georges who hauled down his flag and surrendered.

It had been a spirited and brave defence, although doomed from the first. Anson wrote:

To do justice to the French officers, they did their duty well, and lost their ships with honour; scarce any of them striking their colours till their ships were dismasted. M. St Georges kept his colours flying some time after the general had struck.[24]

Anson hailed the *Pembroke*, which was one of the other ships engaged with the *Invincible*. He ordered her to send an officer and some men on board the *Invincible* to take possession.[25] A midshipman, William Cocklin, was ordered to find any secret papers which might be on board, but St Georges made sure that everything of importance was thrown overboard in time.[26] One hundred seamen and all the *Invincible's* officers were rowed on board the *Pembroke*. Admiral Anson had won a considerable victory, which was to enhance his reputation and augment British sea power. And the *Invincible* was in the hands of the British navy.

3 Purchase and Fitting Out

George Anson has a unique place in British naval history. He was as important in the development of the fleet as Pepys, Nelson or Fisher, but, unlike the other three, he had absolutely no desire for self publicity. He was the link between the navy of Pepys and that of Nelson, in more senses than one. Not only did he carry through the essential reforms in all aspects of the navy, which allowed Nelson his victories forty years later, he was also both a great fighting admiral and an administrative reformer. Pepys carried out all his work as a civilian as part of the central administration. Nelson, on the other hand, spent all his career at sea and never had to prove himself in the London offices. Anson was the only figure in British naval history who excelled at both fighting and administrative reform.

George Anson, captor of the Invincible, and the leading British sea commander and naval administrator of the age

The battle of 3 May 1747,* known to the British as the First Battle of Finisterre and to the French as the Battle of Cape Ortegal, was the climax and the conclusion of Anson's fighting career. He had already become a national hero in 1744, when he returned from his famous circumnavigation after four years. He had set out in 1740 with a fleet of eight ships and 1,900 men. Storms or poor design had wrecked the ships or forced them to turn back. Scurvy or old age

* Note the change in date. Until 1751 the British calendar was eleven days behind the French one.

had decimated the men, some of whom were veteran soldiers taken out of retirement at the Royal Hospital, Chelsea. Anson persevered, raided the Spanish possessions in the Pacific and eventually captured a treasure galleon, seriously damaging the Spanish finances as well as making himself into a rich man. On his return in 1744, he had entered parliament, been promoted rear admiral and appointed a member of the Board of Admiralty. He was to remain on the Board until his death seventeen years later, with only a short break, becoming First Lord in 1751. Throughout this period he strove constantly to reform the navy, which had fallen into complacency, corruption and ultra-conservatism since the end of its last war in 1714. Every aspect of the navy – manning, victualling, tactics, training, equipment and ship design – felt the effect of Anson's zeal, although, as one recent historian has put it,

> the presence of his own guiding hand is easier to sense than to prove. He effectively covered his tracks from the historian not only by not keeping papers, but by not creating them. He hated correspondence, and conducted the inescapable minimum by the hand of his secretary.[1]

Far more than a mere administrative reformer, he created a new fighting spirit in the navy. The over-cautious tactics of the first half of the century were replaced as younger and more daring officers, often Anson's own protegés, took command of the fleets at sea. The First Battle of Finisterre, when Anson abandoned the rigid line of battle to order a head-long attack on the French, was an important stage in this process.

As night fell on 3 May 1747, Anson had more immediate tasks to attend to. He had won a significant victory, albeit with the numerical odds greatly in his favour. The capture of six major warships did more than weaken the French fleet; they would eventually be added to the British navy to increase its strength. Since the value of prize ships and their cargoes was divided among their captors (with the greatest share going to the senior officers) there was jubilation among the seamen, especially when it was discovered that the *Invincible* was carrying gold for the French East India Company. One seaman wrote ecstatically to his brother, 'In one of the ships was found three million of money, in the other about 16 million ... If we have justice done us, we shall have a thousand pounds a man.' But his information about the money was wildly exaggerated, as was the rest of his letter: 'Such a battle was never known in all the whole world ... there is ten thousand prisoners, five ships of the line, two of them are like towers, great ships of 90 guns ... This will crush the French for ever.'[2] In all these expectations, he was to be disappointed.

But much had to be done before the crews could go home to enjoy what prize money they might get. The fleet was 500 miles from its base and had suffered some battle damage. The later ships to reach action, including Anson's *Prince George*, were untouched, but the *Centurion* had her main topmast shot away and several feet of water in her hold so that it was necessary to keep the pumps going continuously. The *Namur* had her boats destroyed to such an extent that she was unable to take possession of her prizes for some time; her lower masts shot through, and her 'sails and rigging all shot to pieces'.[3] The French ships, of course, had suffered much more and most were dismasted. The *Invincible* had only her mizzen and bowsprit standing, although other parts of her rigging were recovered and brought back. Clearly none of the prizes could be sailed home on her own.

The *Pembroke* took responsibility for the *Invincible*, as did the *Centurion* for the *Gloire*, the *Bristol* for the *Diamond*, and the *Namur* for the *Serieux*. The crews of the *Prince George* and *Pembroke* spent the night after the victory ferrying prisoners from the *Invincible* into their ships, while other ships returned to the fleet with ships they had captured from the convoy. It was not until 4am on the 6th, nearly $2\frac{1}{2}$ days after her capture, that the *Invincible* was taken in tow by the *Pembroke*. The damaged British ships were repaired as much as possible, the *Bristol* being given a spare topmast from the *Pembroke*, while the *Namur* had one from the *Prince George*. The next week was spent putting the ships into a condition to sail, especially the *Centurion* which had suffered the worst. By the 10th, a week after the battle, she was setting up her main topmast shrouds and was almost ready to sail. The fleet was still 350 miles from Scilly and had moved only a few miles from the scene of the battle.

Even here, Anson's aversion to writing showed itself. His dispatch to the Admiralty was dated 11 May, more than a week after the battle. Having completed it, he called the *Centurion* alongside and gave it to her captain, Peter Dennis, with instructions to make all speed to Portsmouth and then to convey the letter to the Admiralty in London. This was a post of considerable honour and there can be little doubt why Dennis was chosen for it. He was one of Anson's innermost circle of protegés, having been with him on the circumnavigation, and his ship had distinguished itself in the battle, perhaps more than any other. Her prize, the *Gloire*, was transferred to the *Pembroke*, while the *Prince George* took the *Invincible* and the *Centurion* set sail for home. The rest of the fleet, towing prizes, proceeded at a more stately pace.

Anson was already impressed with the *Invincible*, despite her battered condition. With his dispatch to the Admiralty he enclosed a table comparing the dimensions of the *Invincible* with those of his flagship, the *Prince George*. Since the ships were at sea it was only possible to measure them internally, but it was shown that the gun-deck of the *Invincible* was 167ft 4in long, while that of the *Prince George* was only 160ft; the breadth of the *Prince George* at the main hatchway was 38ft 7in, while that of the

Invincible was over 40ft. This was despite the fact that the *Prince George* was a three-decker of 90 guns, while the *Invincible* was a two-decker of only 74. To the First Lord of the Admiralty he wrote, 'She is a prodigious fine ship, and vastly large. I think she is longer than any ship in our fleet, and quite new.'[4]

Anson was well aware that the British fleet needed larger and better ships. During his circumnavigation, only the largest ship, the *Centurion*, had completed the voyage. In 1741 three British 70-gun ships had battled for hours to subdue a single Spanish ship, the *Princessa*, of nominally equal force but considerably greater dimensions. At the Battle of Toulon in 1744 the British had their first encounter with the new French fleet, including the *Terrible*, the first new type 74. They were impressed and one admiral noted: 'The general discharge of a French 74-gun ship is $1,705\frac{25}{63}$ lbs', which was compared with 1,606 of an English 90-gun ship, 1,312 of an 80, and 1,044 of a 70.[5] Admiral Knowles had written to Anson in 1745, that 'our ships of 70 guns are little superior to their ships of 52 guns', and recommended that the 'dimensions for a ship of each rank' should be 'as near as possible to those of our enemies (the French and Spaniards)'.[6] During Anson's first year on the Admiralty he had attempted to cause the building of 74-gun ships. A committee of sea officers, supported by master shipwrights in the dockyards, 'was directed to propose ships carrying 74 guns, with two decks and a half', in place of the old 80-gun ships of three decks, already coming under fierce criticism. The conservative element had prevailed on the committee and they were

> sorry to differ in opinion with your lordships therein, but we having observed on many occasions the advantage 80-gun ships with three decks had over those with two and a half, judged it for the benefit of the service that so useful a class of ships should be continued'.[7]

The fleet acquired a few 74-gun ships over the next two years, but only by cutting down 80- and 90-gun ships. A few 66-gun ships were also added to the list by reducing some other 80s – hence the guns carried by the *Namur* and *Devonshire* at Finisterre.

The British navy of 1747 shared a common technology with the French, but its recent history had differed greatly. Whereas the French fleet had largely collapsed after the end of the last war, the British one was popular with public and parliament, who demanded that its numbers be kept up even in peacetime. However, the taxpayers were not willing to pay great amounts of money for this, while the politicians were afraid to ask for more in case it sparked an enquiry which might probe too deeply into their affairs. The great majority of ships were laid up in ordinary, slowly decaying at their moorings in the great naval dockyards. When necessary, they were put into dock for repair. When decay had gone too far, a ship was 'rebuilt'. This ambiguous term concealed the fact that almost no timber from the old ship was used in the new one. It also committed the shipbuilders to making the new ship in a form close to that of the old one so that their natural conservatism was reinforced.

The system of rebuilding was only part of the restriction which stifled any initiative in the British dockyards. While the French master shipwrights had almost a free hand, and thus came up with many new ideas on shipbuilding, their British counterparts were bound by the 'Establishments of Dimensions'. By 1719, the dimensions of every part of a ship of each class were laid down by standing order and the shipwright was left only to draw out the shape of her hull. The establishment was not immutable, but the Admiralty could only alter it with the co-operation of the Navy Board, which was responsible for technical matters. This body was made up of aged and very conservative men, inclined to reminisce about the days of Charles II. In fact, the dimensions were increased in 1733 and 1741, but only slightly and grudgingly, and not nearly enough to make the ships as big as the latest French and Spanish ones. The committee of 1745 caused slightly greater increases, but still not enough; the largest British two decker, the 70-gun ship, was to be 160 ft long, whereas the *Invincible* was 171 ft long, by English measurement, and in France she was now regarded as too short for a 74-gun ship.

But an increase in dimensions would not, in itself, have been enough. The British fleet relied too heavily on three-deckers instead of the two-deckers, which sailed better and gave greater gun power for a given expense. Until 1741 ships which were lost or decayed were invariably replaced by others with the same number of guns. As a result, gun arrangement and general lay-out were frozen, even more than the dimensions. There were six classes of ship regarded as capable of standing in the line of battle. The largest were the three-decker first rates of 100 guns. They were expensive to build and man, clumsy to handle and could only operate from the deepest harbours. Because of this, they had seen little service during the war of 1739. The second rates of 90 guns were also three-deckers. They had been conceived in the 1670s as a slightly cheaper version of the 100-gun ship, while still retaining her advantage of height of battery. They shared most of the disadvantages of the larger ships to a lesser degree; additionally, they were shorter in proportion to their height which made them notably poor sailers. Admiral Vernon wrote that:

> These great ships . . . are in my apprehension little or no service at all to prevent invasion, as there is no harbour from this open road not even safe for them to ride in, in the winter season between here and Edinburgh Firth, which a three-decked ship can go into.[8]

The third rates of 80 guns, with three decks, were probably the worst ships in the fleet. They had been first built in the 1690s as two-deckers, but had been found too weak because too much of their armament was concentrated on the quarterdeck and forecastle. Over the next twenty years all of them were rebuilt as three-deckers. This policy was no more successful for the ships were top heavy and too high for their length. They were the smallest ships to carry 32-pounder guns, and in that sense they were the nearest equivalent to the French 74s; but in other respects they were a complete contrast – short and high (while the French ships were long and sleek), poor sailers and designed for height of battery rather than good sailing. In all aspects they were a relic of the 1690s when they had first been built as three-deckers. When the sea was high or the wind strong they were often unable to open their lower ports and could only use the 18 and 9 pounders on their middle and upper decks. Admiral Mathews wrote:

> I have now but two ships of 90 and three of 80 guns that can make use of their lower tiers if it blow a cap full of wind. Admiral Rowley in the *Barfleur* was obliged to run out his weather guns, to lash 30 tuns of water to windward, and to cut away his lee anchor before he could do it . . . As for the rest of them, they can scarce haul up a port; the *Chichester* hauled up but her two aftermost, but was soon obliged to lower them.[9]

Vernon believed that

> most of the 80-gun ships . . . were not the men-of-war they ought to be, their lower batteries lying too low, and that they were crank ships, and believes that the *Chichester* and *Torbay* may be the worst of them, so that with anything of a fresh gale, they are put by the use of their lower tier, in which their principal defence lies.[10]

It is probably no coincidence that Anson, who as a member of the Admiralty had a relatively free choice of his ships, had none of the 80s in his fleet at Finisterre. The small three-decker was a relic of a past age, when fleets had rarely ventured outside the Channel and the North Sea. They were 'floating fortresses' rather than good fighting ships. The new age of colonial warfare demanded ships which could sail much better, and contemporary thinking on gunnery demanded heavy guns mounted low in the ship rather than light ones on the upper works.

The 70-gun ships carried their guns on two decks and in lay-out they were closer to the French 74s. The main problem was that they were too small to carry a heavy gun armament. Those built before 1741 had only 24-pounder guns, which made them considerably inferior to the 39 pounds (English) of a French 74's lower deck. Since the new dimensions of 1741 there had been an attempt to make them carry 32 pounders, first in the guise of 64-gun ships and then as 70s after 1745. But they were still much smaller than the French 74 and their sailing qualities were severely criticised. Savage Mostyn wrote to Anson about his ship the *Hampton Court*:

> This ship has a great deal to be done to her, for her weight of metal tears her to pieces. I believe your lordship is of opinion they are not of proper dimensions for this metal, and I hope I may be excused for saying so, after four years experience in the crankest and worst ship in England.[11]

The other ships in the line of battle, the 60s and the 50s, were even smaller. They carried only 24 pounders, even in their post-1741 versions.

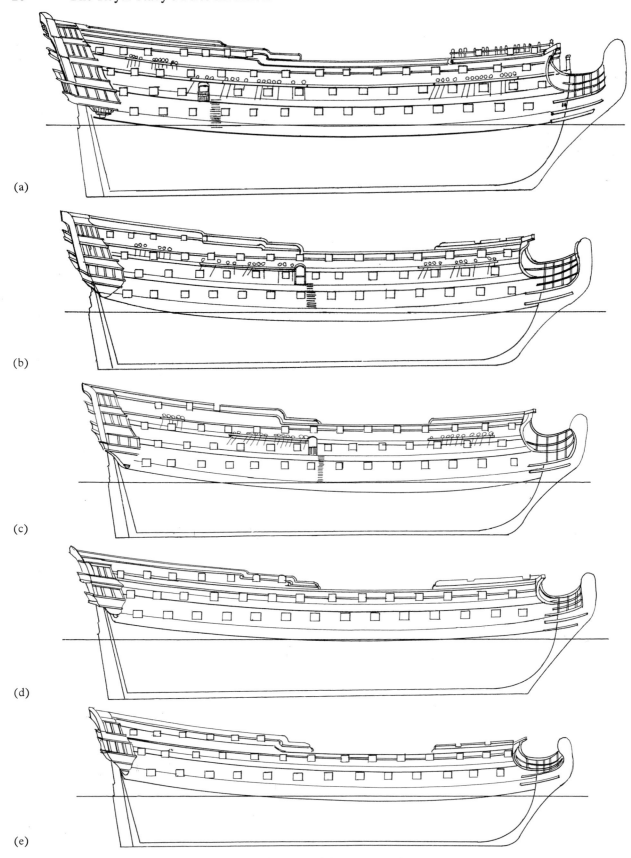

(a)

(b)

(c)

(d)

(e)

The *Invincible* compared with typical British ships of the line of the same period:

a) The *Victory* of 1737. She was lost off the Casquets at almost the same time as the *Invincible* was launched, and represented the extreme of the 'floating fortress' concept of shipbuilding. She was very little longer than the *Invincible*, but carried 100 guns on three decks, and had four galleries at the stern, compared with the *Invincible's* two. As a result, she was 15ft higher out of the water at the stern, and was a poor sailer

b) A 90-gun ship of the 1719 establishment, similar to Anson's flagship at Finisterre

c) An 80-gun ship on the 1719 establishment. This type was considerably smaller than the *Invincible*, but had three decks

d) The *Culloden*, the first British 74, launched in 1747. Built on the hull of an 80-gun ship, she was nevertheless considerably smaller than the *Invincible*

e) The typical ship of the British line of battle at the beginning of the war, a 70-gun ship of 1719. With only 24-pounder guns, she had much less gun power than a 74

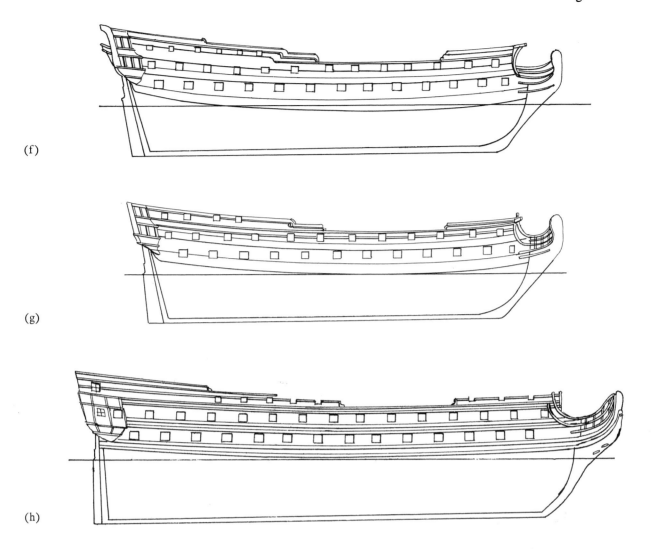

(f)

(g)

(h)

f) A 60-gun ship of 1719, and
g) a 50-gun ship of the 1730s. Neither class was really large enough for the line of battle, but both had to be used in view of the lack of anything else
h) The *Invincible* to the same scale

In the circumstances, the French 74 as represented by the *Invincible* must have been close to Anson's ideal ship. He had already tried to introduce the 74 into the British navy in 1745; he singled the ship out for special attention immediately after her capture for she was the only prize which he had measured, and, apart from a list of the ships engaged in the battle, the table of measurements was the only enclosure with his dispatch to the Admiralty, which must have emphasised his point strongly. And, as we shall see, he was to favour the *Invincible* during her career with the British navy.

The news of Anson's victory was carried home by Dennis in the *Centurion*, who arrived at Spithead just before midday on 15 May. He took the dispatch to London and was given the traditional reward for the bearer of good tidings – a gift of £500 from the king. The public, which had expected great things from the war but had been starved of sea victories since 1744, was jubilant. According to the Duke of Bedford, the joy was 'universal' and he had just come home 'through illuminated streets and bonfires'.[12] Horace Walpole wrote of 'the great naval victory that Anson has *gained* over the French off Cape Finisterre'. It

was 'a very big event, and by far one of the most considerable that has happened during this war. By it he has defeated two expeditions at once, for the fleet he has demolished was to have split, part for the recovery of Cape Breton, part for the East Indies.'[13] A few weeks later, the king would wind up the current session of parliament with a speech which referred to:

The signal success which has, by the blessing of God, already attended my fleet, has happily disappointed some very pernicious projects of our enemies, and given a considerable blow to their naval strength, as well as to their commerce.[14]

Anson's fleet proceeded homewards. On the way back he had sent off detachments to pursue and identify ships sighted. In the afternoon of the 13th, the cable towing the *Invincible* had broken and the ship was adrift until 4am the next morning, when another cable was put aboard her. Otherwise the voyage was uneventful. The *Pembroke* put into Plymouth with her prize the *Gloire*, and her prize crew was taken off and replaced with men from the *Prince George*. She was still carrying prisoners from

A contemporary print, somewhat out of scale, of Anson's fleet arriving back at Spithead with its prizes. In the right middle ground is Portchester Castle, where the prisoners were taken

the *Invincible* and they were taken ashore to begin their captivity at Plymouth. On the afternoon of the 16th, only eighteen hours after the *Centurion's* arrival, the rest of the fleet rounded the eastern corner of the Isle of Wight, and the *Invincible*, still under tow, entered the Solent for the first time. The French ships carried the white flag of France under the blue ensign which Anson, as Vice Admiral of the Blue squadron, flew from the ships under his command. Pilots and sailing masters were sent out from Portsmouth dockyard to help convey the prizes to their anchorage and at 9.30 the *Prince George* cast off the tow and came to anchor at St Helens roads with the fleet and its prizes.

Still there was no rest for the seamen. Next morning, all the ships were taken further up the Solent to Spithead, where they were closer to Portsmouth Harbour and dockyard. That afternoon, 176 seamen prisoners from the *Invincible* were put into ships' boats and dockyard craft and rowed 5 miles to the nearest prison, Portchester Castle on the north side of Portsmouth Harbour. Later, 56 seamen were sent to hospital. Possibly these were also prisoners from the *Invincible*, for the *Prince George* had suffered few casualties in the battle, but they could also have been seamen who had fallen sick, as many did after a long voyage. On the following day, the 19th, the yacht used by the commissioner of the dockyard came alongside and took out the treasure found in the *Invincible* – thirty casks and nine chests of money. On the 20th, the first two of the prizes, the *Invincible* and the *Jason*, were taken into Portsmouth harbour, presumably towed by boats. On the 21st, the officer prisoners were sent to Fareham.

As soon as the fleet had anchored, Anson struck his flag and left the *Prince George*. He took horse to London and arrived there in time to attend an Admiralty Board meeting on the morning of the 19th. Rewards and honours soon followed. On 13 June he was raised to the peerage as Lord Anson, Baron Soberton. As his share of the prize money, he gained £62,991, although the treasure was found to amount to only £300,000 and the seaman on the *Centurion* must have been disappointed to find that his share was only about £35. Almost a year after the battle, Anson consolidated his social and political position by marrying Elizabeth Yorke, daughter of Lord Hardwicke, the Lord Chancellor.

The Admiralty had no great wish to hang on to the prisoners from the *Invincible* and the other ships, for the capture of 2,500 men in Anson's victory was straining their resources. Summer was approaching and overcrowding could cause deaths in warm weather. A week after their arrival at Portsmouth many of the prisoners were still aboard their old ships for lack of accommodation. A proposal to reopen an old prison at Southampton was rejected after St Georges, on a visit to his men at Portchester, pointed out how ill-ventilated it was. Plans were made to erect more buildings at Portchester, while some of the men were to be sent to Dover, and about 100 of the *Invincible's* men were already at Plymouth.[15]

At the beginning of June it was decided to give all the officers parole, with half being sent to Salisbury, half to Winchester – both inland towns where they would not be able to spy on British war preparations. Each had to sign a declaration that 'I will behave myself decently, and with due regard to the laws of the kingdom, and also that I will not directly or indirectly hold any correspondence with either France or with Spain'. One contingent, including St Georges, arrived at Salisbury on the evening of 28 June and the populace turned out to gaze at them from windows and streets, although without any show of hostility.[16]

The prisoners were exchanged quite early. At the end of July the Admiralty arranged for the transport *Charming Molly* to take the officers and some of the seamen, to a total of about 180, to St Malo, where many of them had their homes. St Georges was not with them for he had struck up a life-long friendship with Anson. During the voyage home after the battle he had impressed the officers of the *Prince George* with his wit and with his stoical acceptance of defeat. Anson invited him to London and later had him presented to the king. He was sent home in mid-August, via Deal and Calais. He kept up a correspondence with Anson in which he called him 'the dearest of friends and most generous of captors'.[17]

The soldiers who had been aboard the *Invincible* were not so lucky. After the war it was discovered that only 38 out of 100 had returned to France; 4 were known to be ill and it was not known whether the remaining 58 had died in captivity or had deserted.[18]

French prizes were not yet a common sight in the British dockyards. In the second half of the eighteenth century the British were to capture dozens of enemy ships and incorporate them in their fleet. In the French Revolutionary War, 1793–1801, they were to capture thirty-seven ships of the line alone, although not all of these were good enough to be taken into the navy as fighting ships. In fleet battles and in single ship actions, warfare was intense, and the British navy's superiority in fighting skills was enough to give it victory in the great majority of cases. But in 1747 the situation was very different. Anson's victory was the first fleet battle of the century to result in captures from the French. Single ship actions were still indecisive, and two years previously Knowles had written, 'I have never seen or heard, since my knowledge of things, that one of our ships alone or singly opposed to one of the enemy ships of equal force has taken her'.[19]

Therefore, the new ships attracted considerable attention. They, and the other ships captured later in the year, were featured in a series of prints published by Short and Boydell in 1748. Another print, published by Christopher Seton in 1747, showed Anson's fleet returning to Spithead with its prizes, while yet another print by Boydell showed the *Invincible*, with some other ships, fitting out at Portsmouth. More important, the captured ships

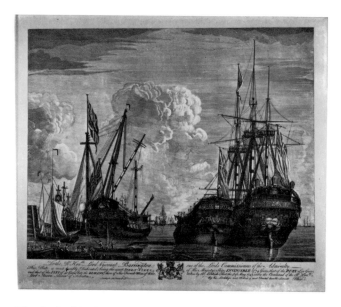

The *Invincible*, *Ruby* and *Isis* fitting out in Portsmouth Harbour, 1747–8

were to have considerable influence on future British ship design, in particular the *Invincible*.

The hull of the *Invincible*, dismasted and battle damaged, had been taken into Portsmouth Harbour on 19 May and transferred to the care of the dockyard officers. So it remained for several months, virtually untouched. On 20 May, two days after Anson's return, the Admiralty had ordered that the *Invincible* and *Serieux* be surveyed 'with all dispatch' and then purchased for the navy, but it was not easy. First of all, the stores had to be taken out of the ship to lighten her and to allow the surveyors to look closely at her timbers. Then she had to be put into a dry dock so that her bottom could be inspected. A large ship like the *Invincible* needed a spring tide, which occurred every two weeks. But there were plenty of other large ships damaged in the Battle of Finisterre or simply in need of a routine cleaning which had greater priority. On 3 July, two months after the battle, the Admiralty became impatient at the lack of progress in surveying the *Invincible*, but the Portsmouth officers replied that they had gone as far as they could in surveying the ship afloat, that they had also surveyed her anchors, stores, etc, but they were now awaiting a suitable opportunity to put her in a dry dock.

This occurred on 14 August, after she had lain at Portsmouth for nearly three months. The Portsmouth officers produced a long report on her condition. It was not intended to assess her importance as a fighting ship, but to give details of her scantlings and report any deficiencies or damage. There was much shot damage to the hull.

> Two planks in the deck, and two planks between the ports, cut by shot, require shifting . . . The quickwork on each side and the bulkheads of the great cabin, being damaged by shot, want repair . . . One piece of channel wales, two planks on the side, and three planks between the ports, cut by shot, require shifting.

About forty major timbers needed to be replaced and many less important parts of the hull structure needed some repair. The rigging was almost totally destroyed, and 'all the masts and yards except the bowsprit require to be new'.[20]

Other comments illustrated the differences between British and French shipbuilding practice: 'There are no sailrooms, carpenters' or boatswains store-rooms, nor cabins for the purser and surgeon. Some better conveniences are wanting in the steward's room.' In fact, all these items were almost certainly fitted, but the comment in the survey merely reflects that the below-decks lay-out of a French ship was very different from a British one. French ships stowed their cables forward in the hold, British midships on the orlop deck. On a British ship the main magazine was forward in the hold, while it was aft in French ships. British ships had a very elaborate arrangement of cabins and store-rooms both forward and aft on the orlop deck. The French arrangement was different, and less sophisticated.

The survey also claimed that there was no 'furnace for dressing provisions'. This is unlikely and it must have been damaged beyond recognition in the battle. The coamings around the hatchways on deck were said to be too low and had to be raised. The ladders and grating were in need of repair, but whether from battle damage or ordinary wear and tear was not made clear. The Portsmouth officers objected to the arrangement of the hatchways:

> As the fore hatchway on the gun-deck is in the wake of the forecastle, and no fore hatchway on the upper deck, it is necessary to remove it further aft between the next beams, which will occasion all the beams on the orlop, lower and upper deck to be altered.

Two features of the structure attracted some attention. The use of iron knees was almost unknown in England and was not to become common for at least half a century. The survey merely recorded the facts without comment: 'Quarterdeck, kneed alternately with one wood or iron knee, except in the wardroom; there all iron.' (Possibly this gave more comfort for the officers, as an iron knee took up much less space, even though it was covered with a wooden casing.) The upper deck was 'kneed with one iron knee to each beam except against the main- and mizzen-masts, which are wood'. The gun-deck was also kneed with iron, but the orlop had wooden knees, but iron standards at the end of each beam. The British shipbuilders were evidently not particularly impressed with this use of iron, for there is no sign that they attempted to copy it, or even that they had much debate on it. On the other hand, they were not totally opposed to it, for the *Invincible*'s iron knees survived all her extensive repairs in British yards, and have been found on the wreck.

It was assumed in Portsmouth that the extra layer of planking, the *doublage*, had been put on to increase the breadth and therefore the sailing qualities of the ship. This practice, known as girdling, had been common in England in the 1660s and '70s, when ships had been badly designed from the outset, or had

their armaments increased so that they did not carry
sail well. Some of the most famous ships of Charles
II's fleet, such as the *Prince*, the *Royal Charles* and
the *Britannia*, had been girdled, but the practice had
fallen into disfavour in the '90s, and was now very
unusual. Evidently, her girdling was kept on until her
'great repair' of 1753–6.

The survey concluded with a complete list of the
ship's dimensions, from the 'length on the gun-deck
from the rabbet of the stern to the rabbet of the post'
(171ft 3in) to the thickness of the plank on the
roundhouse ($2\frac{1}{2}$in). The general tenor of the report
was favourable, and it was agreed that the bottom
'appears to be in good condition, but fastened mostly
with nails' – meaning, presumably, that these were
used instead of wooden treenails, or iron bolts which
went all the way through the timbers. By the usual
formula for calculating tonnage, which gave no real
indication of displacement, she was registered as
1826 tons – bigger than a 90-gun ship on the current
establishment and only 50 tons less than the *Royal
Sovereign*, the biggest ship in the fleet.

Within a week, the ship was bought from her
captors at a price of £13 per ton. The Admiralty
therefore paid £23,738, a very large sum in the
circumstances. In contrast, a new 70-gun ship would
have cost about £16,000, while the *Serieux*, captured
alongside the *Invincible*, cost less than half as much.
The *Terrible*, 74, was also captured later in the year,
but only £11,211 was paid for her. All this suggests
that the *Invincible* was held in very high regard by the
Admiralty. We can rule out any suggestion that
Anson used his influence at the Admiralty to raise the
price. After his capture of Spanish and French gold,
such sums were insignificant to him. Moreover, it
would have been just as easy to increase the prices of
the other Finisterre prizes, such as the *Serieux*.

Thus the *Invincible* became part of the British
navy. Her name needed no translation into English
and it had not been used for any other ship. On 21
August, the Admiralty issued an order to 'register her
in the name of the *Invincible* and to be fitted for the
sea'. But much had to be done before she would be
ready to take part in the war against France and
Spain.

Her guns were not suitable for service in the
British fleet. They were partly of brass, but such guns
were extremely rare in the British navy by this time,
mainly because brass was about eight times as
expensive as iron, and the British iron industry had
developed to such an extent that brass offered no
compensating advantages. Only two ships in the
British fleet, both first rates, had brass guns by this
time. Furthermore, the calibres of the French guns
were inappropriate. There was no British equivalent
of the 36 pounder, the nearest being the 42 pounder
and the 32 pounder. It might have been possible to fit
the *Invincible* with the larger guns on the lower deck,
but these would have been somewhat heavier than the
French 36s and would have put extra strain on the
decks. 42 pounders were rare and generally reserved
for first rates. In later years their efficiency was

The bow and stern of the *Invincible*, from Charnock's *History of
Marine Architecture*, published 1800–2. Charnock was a great
admirer of the *Triumph* and *Valiant*, which were copied from the
Invincible.

questioned as the ball was too heavy for a man to
handle easily in action, although there is no evidence
that this was a factor in 1747. There was never any
serious proposal to arm the ship with 42 pounders
and on 22 August, the day after the ship was taken
into the navy, the Portsmouth officers were propos-
ing that her lower deck should carry 32 pounders.
This recommendation was soon accepted by the
Admiralty. This disposes of one common myth about
the eighteenth-century British navy – that it always

increased the gun power of ships captured from the French. The two-decker with 32 pounders on its lower deck was the kind of ship Anson favoured most. It is notable that all his ships of the line at Finisterre, except for his flagship which was a three-decker, fell into this category. Such ships were not yet common in the British navy and it seems likely that he had gone to some trouble to assemble such a force.

The upper deck was to carry 18 pounders. This was the nearest calibre to those taken out of the ship, although of course it was slightly smaller than the French 18 pounder. The quarterdeck and forecastle were to have 9 pounders, also similar to her old guns. The total gun power of the *Invincible* was to be 1,562lb. This was considerably more than one of the latest British 70s, with 1,480lb and was slightly more than an 80-gun ship, with 1,540lb. A three-decker 90 was somewhat more powerful, with 1,684lb. However, the *Invincible* was a better sailer than any of these.

The Ordnance Board, which was a part of the army administration but was also responsible for the supply of guns to the navy, was asked to find the appropriate weapons. There was a general shortage of both 18 and 32 pounders, mainly because they were needed for the new ships of the 1745 establishment. The Ordnance Board planned to take most of the *Invincible*'s guns out of old ships. In October they proposed 'To have the *Royal William*'s 32-pounder guns and carriages of 10ft, which carriages are already of appropriate height, but that they should be surveyed, and if in want, repaired before they are put on board'. The *Invincible* was also to have twenty 18 pounders, 9½ft long, from the 90-gun *Blenheim*. Some of the *Blenheim*'s guns, however, were defective and had to be discarded, so ten more were 'wanting to complete the set for the *Invincible*'. They were to be sent from the Ordnance depot at Woolwich. It had been proposed to cut down some of the *Blenheim*'s 18-pounder carriages so that they would fit the *Invincible*'s gun-ports, but this was found to be impracticable with the ten new guns, for which new carriages had to be made. It was late in November before all this had been done, and the *Invincible*'s guns and carriages were ready, although not yet installed aboard the ship.[21]

Another question had to be considered: how many men the *Invincible* was to carry. The main factor here was to provide enough to man all the guns in time of action, with some left over to handle the small arms, trim the sails and man the helm. A pair of 32 pounders, for example, one on each side of the ship, had a crew of fourteen men who would have to operate both guns if the ship was engaged on both sides. Portsmouth proposed that the *Invincible* should have 650 men – the same number as a three-decker 80, and 100 less than a 90-gun ship. This was soon accepted by the Admiralty, but it was eventually found not to be enough. Although the *Invincible* had less guns than an 80, they were considerably heavier and needed more men to operate them, and her masts and sails were much bigger.

It was decided to class the *Invincible* as a third rate, and it is useful to examine the implications of this. The main object of rating a ship was simply to fix the numbers and pay of her officers. Some officers, such as lieutenants and masters' mates, had constant pay in any type of ship, but the number carried varied according to the size of the ship. Other officers – the captain and master, and the heads of departments such as the surgeon and carpenter – were considered to have more responsibility in a larger ship and were given greater pay accordingly. Certainly, it would have been possible to include the *Invincible* in a higher rate on account of her size alone. But the second rates were a relatively homogeneous group, all being three-deckers of 90 guns. The *Invincible* would not have fitted in well with such clumsy ships. The third rate was much more mixed, for it already included ships of 80, 74, 70, 66 and 64 guns. It also included all the large two-deckers, in particular the *Culloden* and *Namur*, the navy's only 74-gun ships. As a third rate, the *Invincible* could in a sense be regarded as the precursor of a breed of standard ships, whereas in the second rate she would have been considered mainly as a flagship and not something to be copied generally. In practice, the *Invincible* was to spend much of her career as a flagship, but she also set the pattern for dozens of ships to come. As a second rate, she might have had slightly less influence on ship design. On the other hand, her low rating almost certainly influenced the decision to keep her crew down to 650 men. There was no provision in the regulations for a third rate to carry more than that.

The hull itself was repaired by the dockyard. All the damage mentioned in the survey was made good, and the lay-out was partly rearranged so that the internal fittings conformed to British practice. Storerooms were built in the orlop, a magazine in the hold, and two double capstans were fitted in the British manner, both extending between the lower and the upper deck and both of the same size so that they could be interchanged in an emergency. Her decorations do not seem to have been much altered for several prints and drawings show her flying the British flag, but still with French-style quarter galleries, stern and head. The dockyard spent a total of £3,400 in preparing the hull for sea. Evidently, there was no underwater damage for the ship was not put into dock until the spring tide of 3 February 1748, when she was graved and tallowed overnight.

Other fittings were decided in consultation with the Admiralty, for the established rules did not cover such a ship. She was to have two anchors of 60cwt, another of 56¼cwt, a stream anchor of 17¾cwt and a kedge of 16¼cwt. Her cables were to be 22–24 inches in circumference. She was issued with a standard set of ship's boats, presumably a longboat for heavy work such as moving anchors and fetching water; a 10-oared barge for the captain's personal use; a pinnace to row the lieutenants and other officers ashore or to other ships; and a 6-oared deal cutter, which was the best sailing boat of the four.

Her masts, like her guns, had to be replaced

entirely, and, like the guns, they were partly taken out of old stocks. Discussion about the dimensions of the masts had begun in August, soon after the purchase of the ship. Admiral Warren had been asked his opinion on the matter, but replied that he did not understand the rules for masting and would be satisfied with what the master shipwright and master attendant of the dockyard decided. These two drew up a list and sent it to the Navy Board on 4 September. The masts and yards were to be slightly smaller than those of a 100-gun ship of the 1745 establishment and rather larger than those of a 90-gun ship. The foremast was 'a stick that lay many years at [Port] Mahon, and then made a mainmast for the *Marlborough*, and since that lengthened by the heel to make a foremast for this ship'.[22] This mast was to cause problems later, and it was soon to be shown that the whole principle on which her masts were planned was erroneous.

All these items – guns, carriages, masts, anchors, boats and other stores – were ready by the end of 1747 and laid aside for the ship. But, following the usual custom, they were not fitted in the ship until her crew was aboard and she was made ready for sea. This procedure began on 12 January when the Admiralty ordered her to be fitted out as a flagship.

4 Service in 1748

William Lloyd, the first British captain of the *Invincible*, was appointed on 12 January 1748. By any standards this was a meteoric rise. Not much is known about the early career of Captain Lloyd, but he had been promoted lieutenant in March 1744 and commander in July 1747. Since then he had been in charge of one of the smallest vessels in the fleet, the *Otter* sloop of 14 guns and 247 tons. Now, after less than five months as a commander, he was promoted to captain and put in charge of one of the navy's largest ships, the *Invincible* of 74 guns and 1,823 tons.

Probably the explanation can be found in the order to fit out the *Invincible* as a flagship. Almost certainly she was intended for Sir Peter Warren, second in command at the First Battle of Finisterre and now in command of the Channel Fleet. In those days a flag captain was a relatively junior captain for he was constantly under the eye of the admiral. 'The flag captain who actually commanded the flagship was generally newly promoted and less experienced than the captains of smaller ships.'[1] When a two-decker like the *Invincible* was serving as a flagship, the captain did not even have the privilege of a large cabin to himself. The admiral took over the 'great cabin' on the quarterdeck, and the captain usually had two junior officers' cabins run together in the wardroom. Such cabins were separated off only by canvas curtains which were normally taken up in the daytime, so the captain had no real privacy.

Presumably, Lloyd was chosen for the post because he was a protegé of Warren. Likewise, three of the four lieutenants appointed to the *Invincible*, John Lockhart, Henry Page and Richard Norbury, had served aboard Warren's flagships, the *Devonshire* and *Prince George*, during the previous year.

Captain Lloyd came on board on the 22nd and took command by reading his commission to the ship's company (although only about thirty men, including the third lieutenant, carpenter, boatswain and purser, were actually on board by that time). The ship, which was alongside the Jetty Head in Portsmouth dockyard, was an empty shell without guns, stores or masts.

Much of the labour of fitting a ship for sea devolved on her own crew rather than on the dockyard workers, and the raising of men was largely the responsibility of the captain. At this stage in the war, after nine years of conflict, it was not easy. Captains were not yet ready to stoop to taking on large numbers of raw landsmen or prisoners, as they were to do forty or fifty years later. The patriotic fervour of the beginning of the war had long since evaporated and volunteers were hard to find by 1748. The press gangs, whether employed ashore or afloat, had taken up any surplus in the merchant fleet and

those now afloat were in ships and vessels which carried protections from impressment. Captain Lloyd had to rely on other sources to man his ship.

His quick promotion carried its disadvantages. On transferring from one ship to another, a captain was allowed to take a certain number of men with him, according to the rate of the ship he was leaving. Thus, from a first rate he was allowed eighty, from a third rate, fifty. These men would often be personal followers of the captain, some of whom would be made petty officers and would create a core around which the captain could build his crew. But the regulations only allowed ten men to be taken from a sixth rate, and Lloyd's ship was even smaller than that. Only eight men from the *Otter* were taken on board the *Invincible*.

The most fruitful source of skilled seamen was from other ships which were being taken out of service or were likely to spend a considerable time in dock. Thus, on the 23 January the *Invincible* received thirty-one men from the *Intrepid* and seventy-four from the *St George*. More men were taken on over the next few weeks, but manning was to remain Captain Lloyd's biggest problem.

The marines did not come fully under Admiralty control until 1755, and until then it was the duty of the army to supply the ships with soldiers. Their main function was to provide a force of small-arms men and a core of disciplined men aboard the ship; but, day to day, they could be used for many of the more laboursome tasks and as such they could be useful in fitting out. Unlike seamen they could not be ordered to work aloft, but they could pull on ropes and capstan bars, and this was useful in the circumstances. The soldiers for the *Invincible* were taken from General Richbell's Regiment (later the 39th Foot, and later still to become the Dorset Regiment). Ninety of them arrived on board on 23 January and eventually their number was to be made up to 124.

By now Lloyd had enough men to start the heavy work of fitting out. On the 27th, the ship was hauled over to a sheer hulk so that her lower masts could be fitted. The sheer hulk was an old ship permanently moored in the harbour and fitted with 'legs' to lift the masts into place. The mast, which might weigh up to 14 tons, was slowly lowered into the ship, through the holes provided for it in each deck. Its lower end, known as the heel, was fitted into a solid block of wood, the step, placed above the keelson of the ship (or on the gun-deck in the case of the *Invincible*'s mizzen). The mast was tenoned into the step. The spaces where it passed through each deck were filled in with wedges to hold it tightly in position. By the 28th, after two days alongside the sheer hulk, the *Invincible*'s three masts and bowsprit were in place.

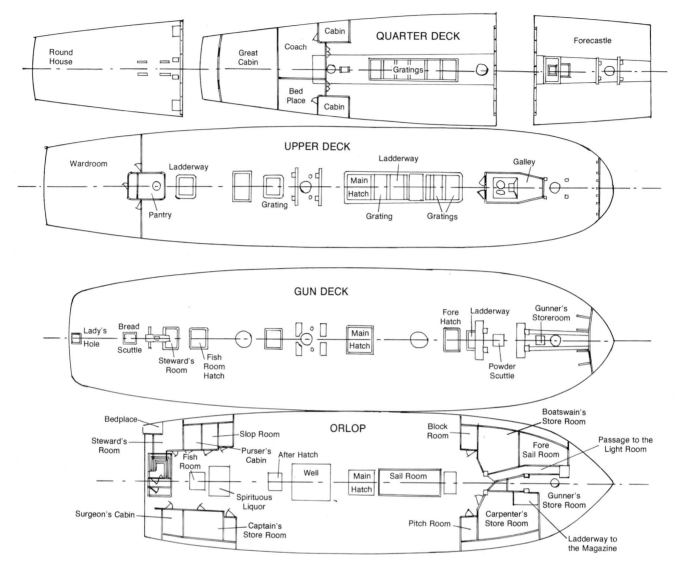

The deck plans of a British 74-gun ship of the eighteenth century. The *Invincible* would have been fitted in a similar way after her capture

For the next few days the seamen were 'employed rigging, watering and heaving out the ballast'. She could not be stored or fully rigged yet for she had to be kept light until she was put into dock. Again, this had to await a spring tide, which occurred on 2 February. The ship was hauled into a dry dock at high water and the dock was emptied, partly by the effect of the tide going out and partly by pumping. That night she was graved, almost certainly with 'brown stuff'. This was a compound of tar, pitch, brimstone, oil and rosin, which was intended to prevent the two dangers which threatened the underwater hull of a wooden ship, weed and barnacles, which stuck to the bottom and slowed it down, and worm which ate its way through the plank and eventually destroyed the ship. Brown stuff, like all the other compositions tried on ships of the period, was not very effective, and the problem was only solved with the introduction of copper sheathing around 1780. (The *Invincible* was to play her part in this story, too.) After graving, the bottom of the ship was covered with tallow. This had little effect as a preservative, but it helped to make the surface smoother and reduced friction with the water. It was not often applied to

ships of the line and this may indicate that the *Invincible* was intended for special missions which would use her sailing qualities fully. The crew of the ship and the dockyard workers had to labour through the night to get the ship finished in time, for the level of each successive high tide would soon begin to decline and any slight delay could cause her to be stuck in the dock for a fortnight. None occurred and she was refloated at 11.30am on the 3rd.

It was now possible to start stowing the hold. Iron ballast was not in regular use at this time, so the first item to be put in was shingle ballast. As well as keeping the ship upright in a wind, this was spread to create a flat surface on which the other provisions could be stowed. On the day after she left the dock, the *Invincible* received her first 143 tons of shingle out of her total complement of 350 tons. Every part of this had to be shovelled into baskets, hoisted aboard ship and then lowered into the hold through the hatchways and spread about the hold by the seamen working there.

Above the ballast were three layers of casks of food and drink. The first layer, known as the ground tier, consisted entirely of water, stowed mainly in the largest casks, with a few smaller ones to fill up the spaces around the edges. In the case of the *Invincible*, this consisted of 145 butts (108gal each), 20 puncheons (72gal) and 7 hogsheads (54gal). This had been stowed by 10 February.

Water would not keep an eighteenth-century seaman contented for long, nor was it clean enough, after weeks in the cask, to drink alone. Diluted rum was a relatively new addition to naval life, for Admiral 'grogram' Vernon had introduced it only eight years before. Nor was it a universal drink, as the orders for the *Invincible* make clear. The captain was to 'take care that the malt spirits supplied to your ship's company be good and wholesome, and to cause the same to be issued with a proportion of water when all the beer is expended, but not to issue any of it while the beer lasts'.[2] Thus the ship took on 337 butts of beer, in addition to its 350 tons of water.

The stowage of the hold was completed with casks of food, mostly beef and pork. Biscuit served instead of bread. It was kept in bags and stored in the aftermost part of the hold, the bread-room, where it was raised slightly above the bilge water. The stowage of the hold was labour intensive, as the casks had to be taken out to the ship by dockyard craft and each one was raised by block and tackle and lowered into the hold. It was also skilled work, for the casks and the ballast had to be distributed in such a way as to give the ship her best trim – which usually meant that she floated a few feet deeper at the stern than forward. The stowage of the hold was the duty of the master, who was in charge of the sailing of the ship, rather than the purser, who was responsible for the provisions themselves.

Meanwhile, the rigging of the ship had to be completed. A top was a broad flat structure which was placed near the head of the lower mast. It served to spread the shrouds of the topmast, as a platform for the men working in the rigging and as part of the system which bound the topmast and the lower mast together. The top was got into place after the shrouds of the lower mast had been fitted, by lifting it over the head of the mast and then lowering it slightly. After that, the topmast was hauled up through the hole in the centre of the top and through another hole in the cap of the mast, and wedged in position with a fid. The cross-trees, at the head of the topmast, was less solid than the top at the head of the lower mast, but it, too, was fitted, and the highest mast of all, the topgallant, was hoisted through it. Then the yards were crossed: three each for the fore and main masts, two for the mizzen, plus a lateen yard which ran diagonally fore and aft.

Getting the guns aboard was perhaps the heaviest task of all, for there were 74 of them and 28 of these weighed 55cwt each. This had to await the crossing of the lower yards, for a tackle to lift the gun was rigged from the end of the yard. Furthermore, several days were lost in the middle of February because high winds made work impossible. The task began on 16 February when a dockyard hoy (a small cargo vessel)

arrived alongside carrying twenty-eight lower-deck and four upper-deck guns. Each one of these was lifted out of the hoy by the tackle at the end of one of the yards and then swung inwards until it reached one of the gun-ports on the side of the ship. After it had been hauled in through the port, its weight was transferred to a tackle slung from the deck above and it was lowered into place on its carriage, which had already been hoisted on board. Two days later the task was completed and the ship's sails were taken on board. These were tied or 'bent' to the yards by the skilled seamen who were distributed along the yards, while the sail was hoisted up by the less skilled men below. On 19 February, Captain Lloyd wrote to the Admiralty that he was 'ready for sea in all respects, except men'.

His efforts to find a crew had not been very successful. His log books give no sign that he sent out press gangs from his own ship, but it could be assumed that in a naval port like Portsmouth any suitable men would have been taken up long ago. He relied mainly on drafts from other ships, but these were not enough. By the 22nd his effective crew consisted of only 164 officers and seamen, plus 119 soldiers. The deficiency was largely made up by other ships lending 242 men. By the end of February there were 625 men on board, out of a nominal complement of 650. Few ships in those days sailed with a completely full complement, and this was judged sufficient for her to set sail.

In the meantime, her intended duties had changed. Admiral Warren had not been able to wait for his new flagship to be fitted and he had sailed on 5 February aboard his old one, the *Devonshire*. He took with him two more British ships and three belonging to the Dutch allies. Since then, the Admiralty had issued several different orders for the *Invincible*. On 18 February she was to convoy two East Indiamen 600 miles out to sea, if no other ship was available. Lloyd reported that the *Glorioso*, a Spanish prize, was on hand, and she was given the task. On 22nd, the *Invincible* was to go to sea to join Warren's fleet without waiting for the *Chichester* as had originally been intended. And on 26 February, she was ordered, at the request of the Secret Committee of the East India Company, to escort one of their ships, the *Orford*, until she was 600 miles out to sea, where she would be relatively safe from French and Spanish raiders. After that she was to make all haste to join Warren at a rendezvous which was transmitted to the captain within a sealed envelope, not to be opened until the ship was well out to sea.

On 1 March, the *Invincible* left Portsmouth harbour for the first time and anchored just outside at Spithead, where she met the *Orford*. The following day the two ships moved down the Solent to another anchorage at St Helens, where they would be ready to get out into the English Channel at the first sign of a favourable wind. This occurred on the 4th, with a north-north-easter, which would have served to carry the ships out of the Channel. But no sooner had they set sail than the wind 'flew round south-south-west

The *Invincible* after her capture

and blowed very hard off the Isle of Wight, which obliged us to put back here' (St Helens).

Even on this brief voyage, Lloyd had begun to see that all was not well with the fitting and manning of his ship.

Please to acquaint their lordships that 'tis with great difficulty we work the ship, not having but 625 men on board, and our masts and yards are much superior to any of the first rates, and I am afraid that the first bad weather we meet with we shall lose the masts, she being greatly overmasted.

Possibly the Admiralty had recognised the difficulty of sailing the ship with such a small crew, for on 1 February they had given Lloyd permission to carry extra men above the complement if he could find them. But in the general manning situation, and in the absence of any special effort to find men for *Invincible*, such an instruction was pointless.

Finally, on 9 March, the anchor was raised, the sails unfurled and the *Invincible* began her first voyage under her adopted flag. She got out into the Channel with her consort and met a group of ten English and American merchant ships. They requested to be escorted out of the Channel and Lloyd agreed. The ships ranged from the *Duke of Bedford* of 575 tons, 61 men and 26 guns, to the *Margaret* of 100 tons, 12 men and 4 guns. They were carrying cargoes of corn and 'bale goods' to Leghorn, Jamaica and Madeira. One ship, the *Chester*, of 120 tons, was on the way to Africa, presumably to take part in the slave trade. Again, Lloyd was not lucky with the weather. The next day the wind increased, so Lloyd and his convoy sought shelter in Torbay. They sailed soon afterwards, but on the 13th they ran into more gales. One of the smallest ships in the convoy made the signal of distress. The *Invincible*'s cutter was hoisted out and a carpenter's mate was put on board the merchant ship to see if anything could be done.

He discovered she had sprung a leak and had 3ft of water in the hold. As the *Invincible*'s log recorded: 'They finding she gained [water] so fast, they were obliged to quit her, the master and men came on board.'

By the 16th, the *Invincible* was 183 leagues from the Lizard in Cornwall, and this meant she had carried out her orders in escorting the Indiaman out to sea and the other ships had parted company already. Therefore she set course for the rendezvous with Warren. On the same day she sprung her jib-boom, but this was not serious enough to impede her progress greatly. On her way to the rendezvous, she considered it her duty to prosecute the war against France and Spain. This meant that any strange ship had to be investigated. Since the wearing of false colours was common and acceptable, provided the ship did not open fire while flying them, this was not a simple task. The *Invincible* usually had to get close enough to a ship to speak to her captain and even to board her in doubtful cases. Since any British or allied ships encountered would be suspicious of her, particularly when her hull still retained some of the hallmarks of French construction, she often had to chase ships to ascertain their true identity. Thus, on the 17th she chased one ship, but lost it in a squall. On the 19th, she caught up with another and fired a shot across her bows to stop her, but she proved to be an Irish brig bound from Waterford to Barbados. On the 22nd, another ship turned out to be a Portuguese ally, bound from Lisbon to Antigua. On the following day she found a fleet of seven ships, but these proved to be a convoy of six merchantmen, bound from Kinsale to the West Indies, under the escort of His Majesty's ship the *Dover*.

On the 24th, the weather worsened again, to what the log described as 'hard gales with a large sea'. At this point Lloyd's predictions about the masts almost came true, for it was found that the foremast, the same 'old stick that lay many years at Mahon', was badly rotten and in imminent danger of being blown down. It was 'sprung in many places, rotten, and entirely decayed, so as not to be trusted with the weight of the fore yard'. According to John Vivion, the *Invincible*'s carpenter, it was 'sprung on the larboard side three feet above the upper deck, and about two feet round, deep in; and about ten feet higher, found it rotten in several places, and likewise sprung on the starboard side above the deck'.

This was a serious crisis, for the breaking of the mast would do considerable damage to the rest of the rigging and perhaps even the hull of the ship. The only option, as the weather continued rough, was to take the pressure off the mast. The sails on the foremast were quickly taken in. The three yards, fore, fore-topsail and fore-topgallant were got down. On the 25th, the topgallant yard was lowered down to the deck and lashed. On the following day, the foretop was lowered down to the forecastle deck and the topmast was taken down. The sea was still heavy and either the wind or the rolling of the ship forced the topmast over the side, where it was lost. The ship would be very difficult to handle without any sail at all on the foremast, so the fore-topsail yard, considerably lighter than the foreyard, was hoisted, and the fore-topsail set on it. On the 29th, the ship limped back to Spithead.

The officers of Portsmouth dockyard must bear most of the responsibility for this near disaster on the *Invincible*'s first British voyage. In the first place, it was found that the defects in the foremast had been deliberately concealed from the officers of the *Invincible*. The defects had been payed over so that they were not apparent without close inspection. Someone in the dockyard had been guilty of more than negligence.

Secondly, the officers of Portsmouth had recommended the number of men and the sizes of masts to be borne by the *Invincible*. In both, they had shown a distinct lack of imagination and a reluctance to depart from established practices. The *Invincible* was not the kind of ship they were used to and it did not fit into their preconceived ideas. They had decided that the *Invincible* was larger than a standard 90-gun ship and masted her accordingly. But, as Lloyd pointed out, she was only a two-decker, whereas a 90 was a three-decker. The actual length of mast above the deck was 7ft more in the *Invincible* because she had one deck less. According to Lloyd, she was

> greatly overmasted, as we have found by experience, for she has worked all the oakum out of her seams, and it's morally impossible to secure her masts in bad weather; her lower yards are much longer and squarer than any ships in the navy, and her topmasts are so taunt [ie high] that there is no securing them, for the angle the tops give are too acute.

It was tragic that this was the case, wrote Lloyd, for if these defects were remedied she would be 'full squarely rigged, and be one of the best ships belonging to His Majesty'.

It was equally clear that 650 men would not be enough to make her into a good fighting ship. Merchantmen could sail with much smaller crews because they did not need the men to handle the guns in action. A warship also had to sail well, and this meant carrying a large amount of sail which had to be taken in quickly if bad weather threatened. For this a large and skilled crew was needed.

In both men and masts, the Navy Board and the Admiralty had accepted the Portsmouth recommendations, although in the case of the Admiralty there are signs of doubt – at one point there had been an attempt to involve Admiral Warren in the decision about the masts, perhaps in an attempt to bypass the conservative Portsmouth officers. And the Admiralty had attempted, albeit half-heartedly, to increase the complement by giving Lloyd permission to carry more men if he could find them. But to regularise her complement at more than 650 would breach the rules of the establishment, and to do that an order in council, signed by the king himself, was necessary. In fact, Lloyd's complaints of early March had apparently had some effect for the Admiralty was given the

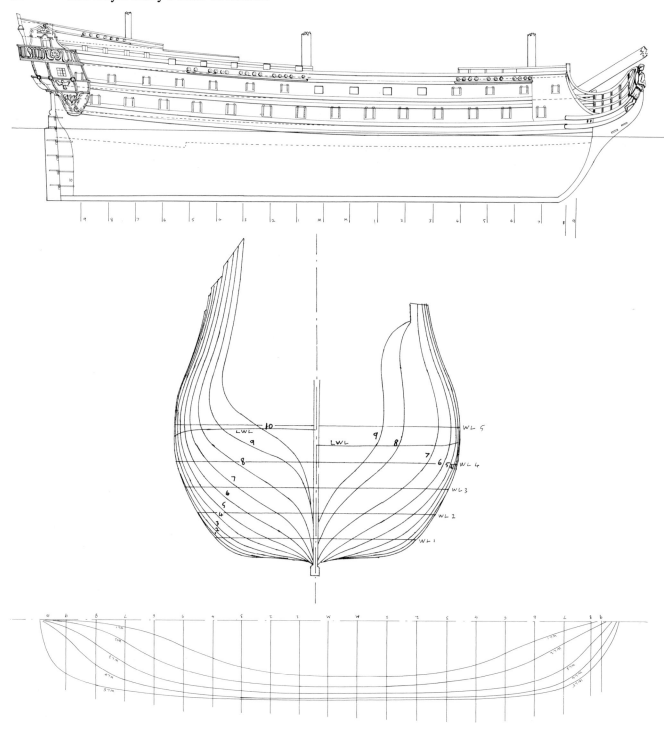

The reconstructed plans of the *Invincible*, based on the dimensions from the survey at Portsmouth, the Morineau plans, and the prints and paintings of the ship

council's permission for such a variation on 22nd March while the *Invincible* was still at sea on her first voyage. This was handed down by an Admiralty order of 1 April, by which she was to carry 700 men, with 5 lieutenants and 6 if serving as a flagship.

The Admiralty needed no convincing about the virtues of the *Invincible* and the 74-gun ship in general. The first attempt to introduce the class had been abandoned when the 1745 establishment was adopted, but the idea had been revived during 1747. None of the large ships of that establishment had yet been launched, but in August 1747 the Admiralty ordered the Navy Board to look again at the 74.

In the late establishment for building a ship of each class in the Royal Navy, there being no mention of a ship of two decks and a half to carry 74 guns, resolved that the Navy Board be directed to consider of proper dimensions for such a ship to carry that number of guns, and when they have so done, to propose a draught and solid [ie model] by which they propose to build her, taking good care to make good provision for bow and stern chase guns.[3]

There can be little doubt that the capture of the *Invincible* had done much to inspire this.

The Navy Board produced the draught and model in January 1748. In lay-out it was to be similar to the

Invincible, with 14 gun-ports on the lower deck and 15 on the upper. The other dimensions have not survived, except for those of the deck beams, so it is not possible to tell how large the ships were to be, but it is unlikely that they would be as big as the *Invincible*. The Admiralty ordered two such ships to be built, one at Woolwich when the *Lancaster* was launched in October and the other at Chatham on a slip which was already reserved. Neither of the ships was to materialise for no timber had been cut for either when the war ended, and both were cancelled owing to lack of funds.

Another feature of the *Invincible* was copied during 1748. When captured, she was fitted with a steering indicator, which showed the quartermaster or the officer of the watch the angle of the rudder at any given moment, thus making it easier to judge the trim of the sails and the efficiency of the helm. British ships had been using wheel steering for forty years, but since the replacement of the whipstaff by the wheel no one had any means of finding the precise position of the rudder, except perhaps by looking over the stern or going below to look at the tiller. The device in the *Invincible* was apparently built using a graduated scale placed above the wheel, on the foremost beam of the poop. This was fitted with a pointer, which was presumably linked to the wheel by ropes, and moved along with it. In March 1748 the Admiralty ordered a model of this device to be made, and later it was ordered to be copied for all ships. Such a mechanism can be seen on the model of the *Royal George* of 1756 and there are signs that it remained in use in the nineteenth century, although it is rarely mentioned or shown on models.

The *Invincible* was refitted at Portsmouth in the first week of April. There was no time to remast her totally, but a new foremast was taken from the second rate *Duke* and fitted. By the 5th it was in place and being rigged. The *Devonshire* arrived back at Spithead on the same day, with Warren and the rest of his squadron. On the 8th, he struck his flag aboard the *Devonshire* and at last hoisted it aboard the *Invincible*. This was to be her first service as a flagship, but not her last, and it is worth considering what advantages she had in that role. Some would hold that a flagship should be the slowest ship in the fleet so that the others would have no difficulty in keeping station with her. Clearly, the *Invincible* did not fit this demand. It was commonly assumed that three-deckers made the best flagships, partly because their sailing qualities were indeed poor, but also because they had an extra deck. This allowed two large cabins at the stern, with quarter and stern galleries. One, for the captain, was on the quarterdeck and the other, for the admiral, was below on the upper deck. But a three-decker tended to be rather unstable and this may have made her uncomfortable in a sea.

The new type of admiral, more daring and aggressive than his predecessors, was more inclined to lead his fleet into a mêlée battle, and a good sailing flagship would have helped him to get into action early and set an example. It is true that the two-decker was more cramped internally, but this did not affect the admiral himself for he merely took over the captain's cabin. On a ship like the *Invincible*, this cabin was as big as any on a three-decker and it had the advantage that, as a French-designed ship, it had no guns, thus creating extra space and ensuring that the admiral would not be disturbed during gunnery practice. Any overcrowding would be felt by the captain, who would be displaced to the wardroom, and by the junior officers, who would have to move into inferior cabins outside the wardroom. But a captain like Lloyd was lucky to be promoted instantly to the command of a third rate, and even his cabin in the wardroom would be more comfortable than what he had had aboard his sloop.

Admiral Warren, Commander-in-Chief of the Channel Fleet in 1748, who flew his flag in the *Invincible* for part of that time

The *Invincible* set sail again on 13 April as flagship of the Channel fleet. Since her capture a year before, the war situation had changed greatly. At sea, the British position had been much strengthened. Admiral Hawke had defeated another French fleet off Finisterre in October, in circumstances not unlike those of the previous battle. More of the French 74s, the *Monarque* and the *Terrible*, had been captured, along with another four ships. A fourth 74, the *Magnanime*, had been captured early in 1748, so most of the best ships in the French navy had been taken. French maritime commerce fared no better. Warships were not available to escort the merchantmen and insurance premiums were so high that few would dare to venture to sea. The French fortress at Louisbourg, at the mouth of the St Lawrence, had fallen to Warren in 1745, and the route to Quebec was open. Without ships, the French colonies in the West Indies and their settlements in India were indefensible. The homeward convoy from Martinique had lain loaded at anchor for months for want of an escort.

In Europe the situation was very different. Holland was threatened by the French armies, which had captured the great fortress at Bergen-op-Zoom. In the complicated strategy of the War of Austrian Succession, the campaigns in Italy and in Hungary were turning against Britain's allies and French power was triumphant. With one power victorious on sea and the other on land, the idea of a truce suggested itself. Already the negotiators, including Sandwich, the First Lord of the Admiralty, were meeting at Aix-la-Chapelle.

But the war still had to be carried on. Warren's position was now strong enough for him to divide his fleet, sending one section under Sir Edward Hawke to watch the Spanish in Cadiz, while he led the other in the Bay of Biscay, stopping commerce and watching the ports of Brest, Rochefort and Corunna. On the way down the Channel he stopped off at Plymouth to pick up a few more ships. By 17 April he was off Brest and he sent his frigates to look at the French preparations. Finding nothing of any danger, he proceeded south. He had received intelligence reports that the French and Spanish were planning to gather a fleet at Ferrol, ready to relieve the situation in Canada. He intended to concentrate his forces off Finisterre, not far from the scene of the *Invincible*'s capture. He reached his station early in May. On the 6th he was joined by six ships of Mostyn's squadron and on the 12th by the eight ships of Hawke's squadron, withdrawn from Cadiz to meet this new threat. The *Invincible* was now leading a fleet of twenty-four ships of the line. Believing that the French were calling on the resources of their more distant allies, including the Swedes, Warren had reason to believe that another great battle could be looming in which he might gain some of the glory won by Anson and Hawke in the previous year. But so far he had no luck in finding enemy commerce or warships; on the 16th he wrote: It gives me great concern to have had so little success since I have been out, which is likewise Sir Edward Hawke's case, and really think it owing to the enemy having very few ships on the sea.'[4]

It is not recorded whether his expectations were raised on the 19th, when a fleet of thirty sail was sighted. It was pursued, but found to be a British convoy for Newfoundland, under the escort of the *Panther*. Ambitious officers would have been further disappointed with the news the *Panther* carried, although the war-weary victims of the press gang would probably have welcomed it. Peace with France had been signed and hostilities were to cease within a few days. Captain Keppel wrote to Anson: 'We have heard of the cessation of arms, and you may imagine how disagreeable this news is to us, especially to me who has benefitted so little by this war.'[5]

Britain was still at war with Spain and Warren made his plans accordingly. His decisions were confirmed by new orders he received by the *Yarmouth* and *Defiance* a few days later. He sent groups of smaller ships to watch the Spanish ports, but took his main squadron to cruise off Palma where it would be in a good position to interrupt Spanish trade with Latin America and the West Indies. It arrived there on 5 June.

The *Invincible* herself was still manned largely as she had been at the beginning of March. She carried 60 officers and their servants, 243 petty officers and able seamen, and only 10 ordinary seamen. There were still 124 men of Richbell's regiment on board, forming part of the complement. Technically, she was 263 men short of her complement of 700, but the deficiency was made up by 202 'supernumeraries belonging to other ships', besides 22 'supernumeraries not borne as part of the complement of any ship', and two prisoners.

Despite the problems with the masts, the *Invincible*'s sailing qualities were beginning to attract attention. Warren had fallen in love with the ship on his first few days at sea, and on 16 April, while at Plymouth, he had written: 'The *Invincible* sails better than any of the ships that came with me from Portsmouth, and a charming ship.' A month later he wrote: 'The *Invincible* sails better in every way than any ship, and is in every shape a fine man-of-war.'[6] On the following day, Captain Keppel wrote: 'I must only say the *Invincible* outsails the whole navy of England. I cannot help saying what a shame I think it is to the English, who have always valued themselves upon their navy. I think the *Amazon* [a French frigate captured in 1745] would not hold way with her.'[7]

But it was now four months since she had been docked at Portsmouth and this was about as long as a ship was expected to go without losing her sailing qualities. There was no question of sending her back home, but the island of Madeira, belonging to Britain's ally Portugal, was nearby. The *Invincible* arrived there on 19 June, without Warren, who had temporarily transferred his flag. Madeira had no dockyard, so a more primitive and less effective method of cleaning the ship had to be used. This was known as 'hogging', and consisted of heeling the ship as far as possible to one side by moving the guns, suspending weights from the ends of the yards, and so on. Parties of seamen got into the ship's boats and burned off the weed, using brooms which were carried for this purpose. The process completed, the ship was heeled to the other side and the same thing was done. After her hogging, the *Invincible* took on stores, including Madeira wine, which the officers would have appreciated.

She sailed from Madeira on 28 June and had rejoined the fleet by 1 July. Warren rehoisted his flag and all captains were summoned aboard her for a council of war. On 23 June, during the *Invincible*'s absence at Madeira, the *Augusta* had captured the French frigate *La Fidelle*. It was maintained that this ship was legal prize, since hostilities with France had not formally ceased. The council of war backed this position, as did the Admiralty when it was informed of it.

This was virtually the last duty of the *Invincible* during the war of 1739–48. In the middle of July Warren received news that hostilities with Spain were to cease and he was to take his ships home. He was off Portland on the 23rd and at Spithead on the following day. The *Invincible*'s first service in the British fleet was over. Since her commissioning in January, she had spent 85 days in port and 119 days at sea – rather more than the average of 41 per cent of the time spent at sea for a ship of this size in the Seven Years War.[8] But her lack of contact with the enemy was something of an anticlimax; apart from gunnery practice, salutes and signals, she had only fired her weapons across the bows of an Irish brig.

5 Working the Ship

A ship of the line like the *Invincible* was a complex and subtle product of technology, as sophisticated as anything the human race had yet produced. It required about 60 acres of oak trees to build it. Its fire power was equal to that of an army and only the largest fortresses on land could match it in gun power. It ruled the seas as completely as any type of ship has ever done. Its predecessor the galley was a fair-weather vessel; its immediate successor, the steam battleship, was continually being overtaken by technological change, while the twentieth-century warship is constantly threatened by torpedoes, aircraft and guided missiles. But the ship of the line was expected to sail and fight in all weathers. It needed forty sails, including spares, 40 miles of rigging and nearly a thousand rigging blocks.

Clearly, to sail and fight such a vessel required an intense concentration of skill, expertise, organisation and discipline. The *Invincible* carried up to 720 men in wartime and nearly all of these had a role to play in sailing, cleaning, feeding, rigging, maintaining or fitting the ship; in battle, everyone found a role in serving the guns, handling the sails and steering, directing the ship and tending the wounded. Every man had many roles, according to the work being done at the moment.

At the head of this was, of course, the captain. When an admiral was on board he might pay considerable attention to the running of the ship, but the main responsibility remained with the captain. The Admiralty provided him with a set of commissioned and warrant officers, but the captain was largely responsible for finding the crew and for allotting their places aboard ship. He could order a seaman to be flogged with up to twelve strokes with the cat-of-nine-tails and could request a court martial for more serious offences. He was responsible for the ship and thousands of pounds' worth of stores aboard her. In action he was expected to walk the quarterdeck in full sight of the enemy snipers, looking unconcerned and setting an example. It is no surprise that casualties among captains were high, and some were tried by court martial for cowardice in failing to close with the enemy. In compensation, the captain was well paid and had up to three-eighths of the prize money from a captured ship; he had by far the largest cabin, unless displaced by an admiral, and he did not have to take any part in the details of the ship's work.

The first lieutenant, like the captain, did not stand watches. He was largely responsible for the routine running of the ship and usually organised the men into watches and divisions, and arranged the hammock lay-out. He was expected to take over the command of the ship in the absence or death of the captain. In battle he stood beside him on the quarterdeck, ready to advise, and take command if necessary. His pay was no more than that of the other lieutenants, but if the ship distinguished herself in action he was likely to be promoted commander or captain.

The other lieutenants, of which there were four or five in the *Invincible*, took turns to take charge of the watch on deck. This was their main duty, although the regulations still formally required the junior lieutenant to instruct the crew in small arms, and the divisional system, by which each lieutenant took responsibility for the welfare and health of a section of the crew, was beginning to come into use. When the ship was a flagship and had an extra lieutenant, it is likely that he served as flag lieutenant to the admiral. But it was not yet common for lieutenants to take responsibility for various aspects of the ship, such as gunnery, navigation, and so on, for these were left to specialist warrant officers.

Of these, the master was the most important. Although he was appointed by warrant of the Navy Board rather than the king's commission, he was higher paid than a lieutenant in a third rate and had a better cabin than any except the first lieutenant. According to Admiralty order, he was responsible for the navigation of the ship. This did not merely mean that he set courses and found the ship's position; the word is to be interpreted in a broader sense and the master often took charge of the ship when she was carrying out difficult manoeuvres, as Henry Adkins did in the *Invincible*'s last day afloat. It was said that

> The management and disposition of the sails, the working of the ship into her station in the order of battle, and the direction of her movements in time of action, and in the other circumstances of danger, are also more particularly under his inspection.[1]

He was responsible for the stowing of the hold, for this affected the trim of the ship and therefore her sailing qualities.

The master was a mature and experienced seaman. Often he had risen from the lower deck or had seen considerable service in merchant ships. He was not usually in the running for promotion to lieutenant or captain, and his only upward path was to be appointed to a larger rate of ship. Adkins, the *Invincible*'s last master, was able to produce 'a letter from William Townshend setting forth that he had been his master, and giving him a good character, also certificates from Captain Whitwell, Captain Suckling and others'. According to Captain Bentley, 'He was recommended to me as a very good man, and I thought myself lucky in getting him. The little time he was on board, he had taken great pains to inform himself of every circumstance relating to the ship.'[2]

Under the master were three mates. A master's mate had originally been an experienced seaman who might become a master himself one day. By this time it was becoming common for the 'young gentlemen'

Seamen raising the anchor of a British warship. Seventy-two men, apparently marines, are at the twelve bars of the main capstan. Six more men are at the 'swifters', ropes stretched between the ends of the capstan bars. In normal circumstances only the upper part of the capstan needs to be used, leaving the lower part free to wind the cable round. Forward of the capstan, men and boys operate the messenger. Below a large party stows the cable in the hold, while on the forecastle another gang operates the fish tackle which will finally haul the anchor out of the water

of the midshipmen's berth to spend some time as a master's mate before being commissioned. Unlike the master, they normally kept watches and so would be under the lieutenant of the watch. There were cases where lieutenants were promoted without the proper qualifications, and the master's mate of the older kind could serve as an expert seaman for the watch. Like the master, the mates needed a good standard of literacy and numeracy, and knowledge of navigation.

The other members of the master's small department were the quartermasters. These were petty officers who had been promoted from among the common seamen and could be disrated at the whim of the captain. The *Invincible* carried six of them, plus four quartermaster's mates. They stood watches with the seamen so that half of them were on duty at any given moment at sea. They carried out the more skilled and responsible tasks connected with the sailing of the ship. One supervised the men at the wheel and ensured the course was maintained. Another looked after the sand-glasses which recorded periods of half an hour and four hours, and they helped to mark up the log board which recorded the courses steered hour to hour. They also helped to find the speed of the ship. A piece of wood known as a log was thrown overboard, attached to a line with knots tied in it at fixed intervals. A sand-glass was turned over and the quartermaster stopped the line when the sand had run out, counting how many knots had run through his hand – hence the expression 'knots' as a

measure of speed. The *Invincible* was equipped with 14-second sand-glasses as well as the normal 28-second ones; because of her high speed, a different period of measurement was needed. Glasses of various kinds have been recovered from the wreck.

A third rate was allowed sixteen midshipmen. Most of these were young men, from 15 to 25 years of age, training to become commissioned officers. A typical example was Robert Keeler, who eventually became second lieutenant of the *Invincible*. It was necessary to serve three years at sea (but not necessarily in the Royal Navy) before becoming a midshipman, and he had done sixteen months in the *Berwick* as a 'captain's servant', and more than a year and a half as an able seaman on board the *Surprise* and the *Invincible*. In these ranks he had neither cleaned the captain's shoes nor lived among the common seamen, for he had almost certainly been taken on through family influence as one of the captain's followers with a view to eventual promotion. He would have lived with those in a similar condition, in the gunroom. After his three years, at the age of about 17, he had become a midshipman in the *Invincible* and moved to the cockpit. He had transferred to the *Monarch* and served a year as a master's mate, before being examined by three captains in 1756, at the age of 21. They were of the opinion that 'he can splice, knot, reef a sail, and co, and is qualified to do the duty of an able seaman and midshipman'. Being convinced of his 'diligence', they gave him his commission. His colleague Samuel Walton was slightly less successful. He spent nearly eight years as an able seaman and midshipman, including more than two years in the *Invincible*. He was 27 before he was commissioned.[3]

A midshipman might carry out many duties during his service. He would spend some in watches, learning to handle sails and rope. He might be put in charge of one of the ship's boats. He might take on the duty of signal officer, or as an aide to the captain. He had to be literate in order to keep his logs and numerate in order to learn navigation. In theory, each ship was supposed to have a schoolmaster to instruct him, but it was difficult to attract suitable candidates as the post had few privileges, and none was ever appointed to the *Invincible*.[4] However, a midshipman would certainly learn navigation under the eye of the master.

The greater part of the crew was made up of the seamen and their petty officers. They were divided into two watches, called port and starboard. This meant that half of them were on duty at any given moment. Furthermore, it meant that no seaman ever had a full night's sleep while the ship was at sea. For working purposes, they were also divided into six 'parts of the ship'. Three of these, one for each mast, were topmen – young, fit and experienced men who climbed up the rigging to bend, set, furl, reef and repair the sails. Each group of topmen had a 'captain' for each watch. He was not paid as a petty officer, nor did he have any share of the prize money more than the common seaman. His crew was mostly made up of able seamen, with a few ordinary seamen and landsmen attached for training. No detailed figures are available for the *Invincible*'s period, but in a 74 of around 1810, with a crew of about 600, there were 48 foretopmen in each watch, 50 main topmen, and 15 mizzen topmen.[5]

The other seamen worked mostly on deck, without going aloft. Either they were too unskilled or clumsy to climb about the yards, or they were older men, retained on deck for their experience, or because they were too aged to climb as smartly as the circumstances demanded. The forecastle men, who numbered twenty-five in each watch in 1810, included many skilled men, for their duties included much work with the anchors. The afterguard worked on the quarterdeck and poop and provided most of the men who actually handled the helm, under the instruction of the duty quartermaster. They were constantly under the eyes of the officers, so they tended to be smart young men, although not always skilled. They numbered twenty-two per watch in 1810, plus six for the poop afterguard. The 'waisters' were the least competent group of all, and included many raw landsmen. They simply hauled on ropes, with the aid of a few skilled seamen who directed their efforts. There were thirty of them on a ship of 1810. Thus a total of 244 men were placed in watches, and in parts of the ship. The figure was probably higher in the *Invincible* because there were more men in the crew and a higher proportion of them were likely to be seamen.

The rest of the crew were specialists in one sense or another and under the orders of their specialist officers. The chaplain was unique among officers in that he had no men under him, except his own servant. Although he was a member of the wardroom, his status was in many respects low; he was paid at the rate of an ordinary seaman, but was also given a groat, or 4d, per month from the pay of every seaman on board. His main duties were to bury the dead and to perform divine service before the assembled crew on Sunday mornings. Marriage and baptism were presumably rare aboard ship. The chaplain of the *Invincible* in her later years was Alexander Fordyce, who had served aboard several ships since 1750 and been transferred from the *Torbay* when Colby took command in 1756.[6]

The surgeon was also a wardroom warrant officer. He was the head of a small department and under him were three mates. These were also qualified surgeons, although they did not use the wardroom but slept in the cockpit. On the face of it this was very satisfactory, with a ratio of one medical practitioner to less than two hundred patients, but it must be remembered that surgeons had very low status in the eighteenth century. Before anaesthetics it was rare to perform any kind of delicate operation, and the surgeon was largely trained in bleeding and amputation. It was not so long since his profession had been separated from that of barber. Many considered naval surgeons to be particularly bad examples of the trade, drunken or incompetent. There was a high influx of Scottish surgeons in the war of 1739–48, including the novelist Tobias Smollett. Apart from his duties in action, the main work of the surgeon was in treating men for accidental injuries and in diseases, especially scurvy. The *Invincible*'s surgeon, Ramsay Karr, had some views on that. In 1755, while still in the *Torbay*, he had put forward a theory that wood smoke was useful in curing scurvy, and had earned the praise of James Lind, the pioneering naval surgeon.[7] However, Karr was aware of the real problem, for in 1756 he sent the *Invincible*'s patients ashore with the knowledge that fresh vegetables would cure them.

The sick berth was simply a row of hammocks reserved for those too ill to work. Smollett described it in one of his novels:

> Here I saw fifty miserable distempered wretches suspended in rows, so huddled one upon another, that not more than fourteen inches space was allotted for each with his bed and bedding; and deprived of the light of day, as well as of fresh air; breathing nothing but a noisome atmosphere of the morbid streams exhaling from their own excrements and diseased bodies.[8]

The surgeon's mates were aided by ratings with no medical training, known colloquially as 'loblolly boys'. The surgeon's store-room was next to his cabin on the orlop deck. It was small, but the surgeon was provided with a substantial quantity of drugs and implements. The quality of surgeons varied much, but naval medicine was beginning to develop as a real science under the inspiration of men like Lind.

The purser was responsible for the ship's supplies of food, clothes, candles, firewood and sundry other items. Like the chaplain, his basic pay was very low, but he was not guaranteed extra income; he expected to make a profit on some of his business, particularly on the sale of clothes and tobacco, and in saving provisions and returning them to store. His position was highly ambiguous, for he was both an officer under naval discipline and a business contractor. He was expected to find a bond of several hundred pounds to take up his post and most men wanted some return on that investment. The system virtually incited the purser to make a profit by swindling the men, by cheating them on quantity or quality.

The food, of course, was stowed in the hold, where it was kept in casks, with the meat cut into pieces of specific sizes. Each day's supply was brought up and distributed by the purser's steward in the steward's room, aft on the orlop deck.

The three standing officers were so called because they stayed with the ship even when she was out of commission. They were the boatswain, carpenter and gunner. All three were mainly responsible for maintenance, and the boatswain for the ropes and sails of the ship. The boatswain also had certain disciplinary duties, for he and his mates had to rouse and muster the crew, and wield the cat during floggings. All three had store-rooms on the orlop deck in the bows, tended by a petty officer known as a yeoman. The boatswain had two mates, plus four 'yeomen of the sheets' whose job was to 'see that the fore and main sheets are properly belayed on working the ship, and that they are kept clear for running'.[9] These men, obviously, kept watches. The sailmakers were also under the boatswain's direction. There were four of these on a ship like the *Invincible* and they did not stand watch.

The carpenter had one mate and eight 'crew', and they had the vital job of keeping all wooden parts, including boats and spars, in good condition. The gunner had a large team, with two mates and one 'quarter gunner' to every four guns – eighteen in the case of the *Invincible*. They had to keep the powder in good condition, which meant airing it occasionally and keeping it dry; to clean the insides of the guns and test the tackle attached to them; and to make sure that each gun was issued with the right equipment in case of battle. They made up cartridges by taking powder out of its barrels and putting appropriate quantities into paper or flannel cartridges. All this did not keep the gunners fully occupied and they also had duties in handling the sails. For this purpose they were often regarded as an élite group of seamen.

The captain's clerk was appointed at the instigation of the captain. He was often quite young, for regulations demanded that a man could not become a purser until he had served some time as captain's clerk. He was the only member of the clerical staff who was officially recognised by higher authority, but the paperwork aboard ship was quite extensive, with logs to be written, accounts to be kept, musters to be taken and letters to be sent. Other men seem to have been given some clerical duties, particularly to help the first lieutenant who had a large amount of administrative work but no regular assistant of his own.

The master-at-arms was, like the junior lieutenant, formally charged with training the crew in small arms. There were those who suggested that the post should go to a soldier rather than a sailor. His other duties were disciplinary, for, with the ship's corporals, he was expected to patrol the ship's decks to see that order was maintained and especially that no lights were kept burning in improper places.

The men who kept no watch were known as 'idlers'. They had the privilege of sleeping eight hours every night except when all hands were called for an emergency or a major manoeuvre. Apart from those already mentioned, they included the holders (who worked in the hold), the ship's cooper, butchers, barbers, tailors and the 'captain of the head' who was given the unpleasant task of cleaning the sanitary accommodation of the ship.

The marines, whether marines proper or soldiers sent on board by the army to form part of the complement, had their own organisation under their officers. In the normal working of the ship, about thirty were needed to give a rotation of sentries. These men were dressed in full uniform with red coats, pipe-clayed belts and military hats. They stood guard at the captain's cabin, the store-rooms below decks and especially the spirit-room, and in harbour at the gangway to check visitors to the ship and prevent desertion. The rest of the marines wore simpler dress and took part in the working of the ship. The marines were seen partly as a 'nursery for seamen'. They could not be ordered to go aloft, but were often encouraged to do so, and if they gained some experience they were to be re-rated as able seamen.

At sea, the ship's day began around 7am, as the men off watch and the idlers were roused from their hammocks by the boatswain's mates. The hammocks were taken down and stowed, and the decks were swept and usually washed. Some captains began to realise that too much water about the decks was causing rheumatism among the men and were tending to cut down on deck washing. After cleaning the decks, breakfast was served, probably to both watches at once, with only a few look-outs and helmsmen being left on duty above. At 8 o'clock the watches changed and a new set of hands took control of the ship.

In fair weather and steady winds, there was not much essential work that had to be done on deck. Four men and a quartermaster were allocated to the wheel, but only one would need to handle it in light winds. He was the helmsman proper and was an able seaman. At the other side of the wheel stood the 'lee helmsman', who was far less skilled and would assist if extra strength was needed. Some captains tried to ensure that all the seamen had a turn at the wheel from time to time, although this must have been difficult on a large ship like the *Invincible*. The wheel was double so that four men could operate it if needed in strong winds.

Look-outs were also necessary and usually one was placed at the head of each mast. They normally did a turn of half an hour, but the man who sighted something first would be relieved early, while if they failed to spot something and it was seen first from the deck, they were given extra duty.

John Bingeman stands beside a rack block from the *Invincible*. It has been placed alongside the bowsprit of *HMS Victory* to indicate the position it would have occupied in the *Invincible*, serving to lead several ropes from the bowsprit to the forecastle

The rest of the watch spent much of their time in maintenance duties. Out of the 40 miles of rigging and 1,000 blocks, there were always some parts which needed repair, and the boatswain and his mates had the job of identifying them and issuing replacements. Topmen were sent aloft to get at them, and if it was a small job it might be done in situ; topmen became used to spending their working lives hundreds of feet up a mast, swaying about with the sea. Larger repairs often involved sending items down and hoisting up their replacements; this made work for the less skilled men of the waist and afterguard. Otherwise, these men would carry out routine work on deck, cleaning and polishing, painting and paying, and moving heavy items. Hands were often needed for the pumps and most ships had to operate them for a few hours every day. After ventilators were fitted in 1756–7, regulations demanded that the bellows be manned for at least one hour in every watch.

Obviously, a ship was a very elaborate organisation and much depended on correct timing. The ship's bell was rung every half hour by the quartermaster of the glass. The men at various duties changed and the officer of the watch recorded on the log board. Various other operations were carried out according to the time of day; the hammocks were brought up, the holders began to get food up from the hold in preparation for the next meal, and the sentries changed. At noon every day the officers of the ship, down to the lowest midshipman, tried to calculate the ship's position from whatever means were available: visually, if an identifiable piece of land was in sight, or the sun was visible to allow a sextant angle to be taken; or by dead reckoning if nothing else was

possible. Each officer recorded this in his personal log and officially the ship's day at sea began at midday rather than midnight.

If the weather was rough, the winds variable, or the ship carrying out intricate manoeuvres in restricted waters, then there was much more work to be done and the ship's elaborate organisation came into play. Men were allocated stations for all kinds of manoeuvres – for hoisting sails and yards, reducing and reefing sail, altering the trim by means of the braces and sheets, setting the studding sails in very light winds, and a hundred other tasks which needed great skill and teamwork. Most of these operations could be carried out by one watch alone, but others required both watches, plus idlers, to be on deck. Tacking and wearing could probably be done with one watch in light winds, but in heavy weather a full crew was needed as it had to be done smartly. Raising the anchor needed all hands, and so did the heavy work of reducing sail and taking down yards and masts in very heavy weather. Often sail had to be reduced very quickly as a sudden squall threatened and the watch on deck had to cope with this.

To cover all this, the first lieutenant had to draw up a complicated set of duties for each man. In our sample ship of 1810, 'tacking ship with the watch' required the main brace to be handled by the marines; the main topsail brace by the main topmen; the main topgallant brace by the second captain of the poop afterguard. The main tack was operated by the waisters and fore topmen, the main sheet by men of the afterguard, while some of the quarter gunners were to 'attend on both gangways to see the fore and main tacks of the sheets clear', and the rest were to handle the main top bowline. The other two masts required yet more hands to operate them.

Tacking ship did not require anyone to go aloft, but reefing sail was very different. The topmen manned the appropriate yards, while some of the gunners assisted in reefing the main topsail. The fore topsail brace was manned by the forecastle man and waisters, the downhaul tackle fall by the idlers, the main topsail brace by the marines, afterguard and the rest of the gunners, and the mizzen-topsail brace by the poop afterguard and boys. Other men attended the halyards.

A watch lasted for four hours, except for the two dog watches between 4 and 8pm. These were intended to cause variety so that the same men would not have to do the same watches every day. Dinner came late in the afternoon and was the main meal of the day. Captains usually tried to give the hands quite a long time, about 1½ hours, and to ensure that the meal-time was uninterrupted as far as possible. After that, at about 8 o'clock, the hammocks were brought down again and those men who were not on watch bedded down for a few hours. If they were lucky, they might get about seven hours' sleep. They would be woken at midnight to go on watch again, but at 4am they would be able to return to their hammocks for about three more hours. The men of the other watch were not so lucky; they would only have four hours in

A selection of items related to gunnery which have been recovered from the wreck. They include a single and a double block, a fire bucket, tompions, heads for flexible rammers, and wads made from rope

their hammocks that night, even if they were not called on deck in an emergency. At night, the duties of the watch were comparatively light, and in wet weather they tended to huddle under the quarterdeck for shelter. They were not normally allowed to sleep and this would have been difficult in cold North European weather; but they were mostly on standby in case sudden danger threatened.

As well as sailing and maintaining the ship, the crew had to be ready to fight her. Opportunities for real action were rare and gun drill was rarely carried out. This was beginning to change under the influence of Anson who exercised his ships almost daily when weather and conditions permitted. This normally meant running the guns in and out without firing, but the crew of the *Invincible* sometimes practised firing at a target; in 1756, for example, the log recorded:

> exercised the great guns and small arms. Fired several volleys of small arms. Unlashed the lower deck guns and exercised them. Fired nine of the upper deck round shot, three double headed shot, and three grape at a mark.[10]

Such practice, carried out on ships actually at sea, was already beginning to give the British an edge over their opponents.

A 32-pounder gun had a crew of seven men, but the ship did not often have to fight both sides simultaneously, so it had an effective crew of fourteen in time of action. The gun captain directed the operation and carried out the actual firing. The second captain assisted him and took charge of the other gun if the ship was engaged on both sides. When loading, the gun was run back so that its muzzle was inside the ship and the gun-port could be closed. The first operation was to sponge out the inside so that any burning fragments from the last charge would be put out. A 'flexible rammer' was used for this. The sponge was attached to one end of a very thick rope so that it could be pushed in without the need for a stiff wooden rammer, as this would have involved opening the gun-ports and exposing at least one member of the gun crew to enemy fire.

After that the charge of powder was inserted. This was made up in a cartridge with a certain weight according to the type of action being engaged and to the type of shot in use. A wad was put in to separate the powder from the shot, and the shot itself was put in after that. Solid iron round shot was by far the most common as that was best for penetrating a ship's hull. Other possibilities included bar and chain shot for use against the rigging, and grape or case shot for use against personnel. A wad was put in after the shot. This was made of old rope and fitted tightly into the gun barrel, retaining the shot and charge in place against the movements of the ship. While loading was taking place the gun was held in position by a train tackle attached to its rear and to a ring bolt fixed in the deck. This prevented the gun from rolling about.

The whole charge, including the powder and wad, was rammed home using the other end of the flexible rammer, which was fitted with a cylinder of wood for that purpose. The charge was primed by pricking it through the touch hole, using a special instrument. The gun captain poured some of the contents of his powder horn down the touch hole so that it would be ready to ignite when the match was applied.

All that remained now was to open the gun-port and run the gun forward so that its muzzle protruded well beyond the side of the ship, thus reducing the danger of fire. Running the gun out was heavy work and involved the whole crew. A tackle was fixed on each side and about six men hauled on each. The work was especially hard if the ship was engaged on the weather side as the gun would have to be hauled up the deck.

Aiming of the gun was obviously inaccurate, but there are signs that some attempts were made to improve on this. In 1756 the captain of the *Invincible* asked for her gun-ports to be widened, and this can only mean that he wanted more room for traverse. And in 1756, as we have seen, there is specific reference in the ship's log to aiming at a mark. Elevating the gun was relatively easy. It pivoted about its trunnions, and a wedge under the breech could be pushed out or hammered in to alter its angle. However, this was less important than the movement of the ship itself. Probably the gun captain fired when the roll of the ship caused the target to come into view. Traversing was more difficult, for the wheels of the gun caused it to run fore and aft rather than sideways. Possibly something could be done when running the gun out by hauling more on one tackle than another. Failing that, it had to be done by means of a hand crow. This was a kind of wooden lever which was placed under one of the rear wheels and used to lift it round to a new position.

In the older method, the actual firing was done by applying a lighted match, fixed to a forked stick known as a linstock, to the touch hole of the gun. This had several disadvantages. In the first place, the match had to be kept lit even when the gun was loading, and this had obvious dangers. Furthermore, it obliged the gun captain to stand quite close to the gun when firing, putting him in danger from the

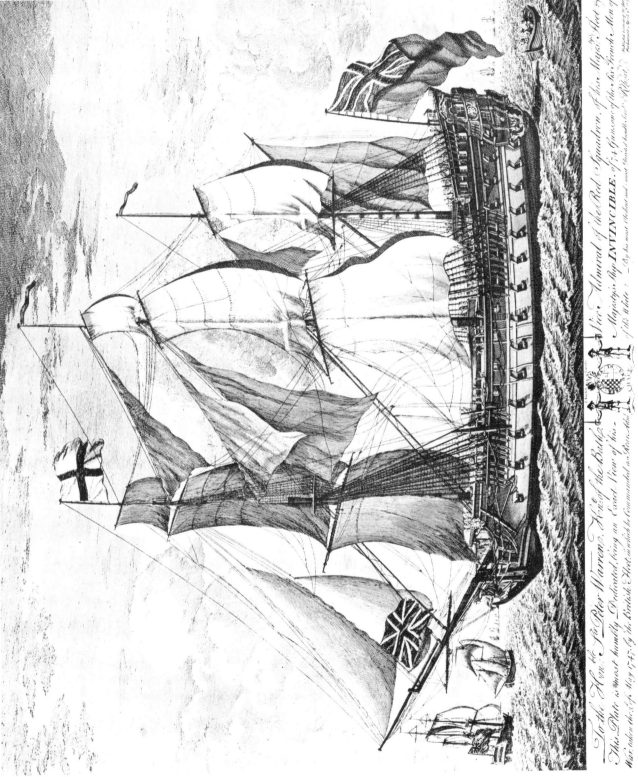

The *Invincible* going about, showing the use of many of her rigging lines. In this manoeuvre, it is intended to turn the bows of the ship towards the observer, by backing the fore sails in one direction, and the main and mizzen in the other. It was after such a manoeuvre that thё ship went aground in 1758

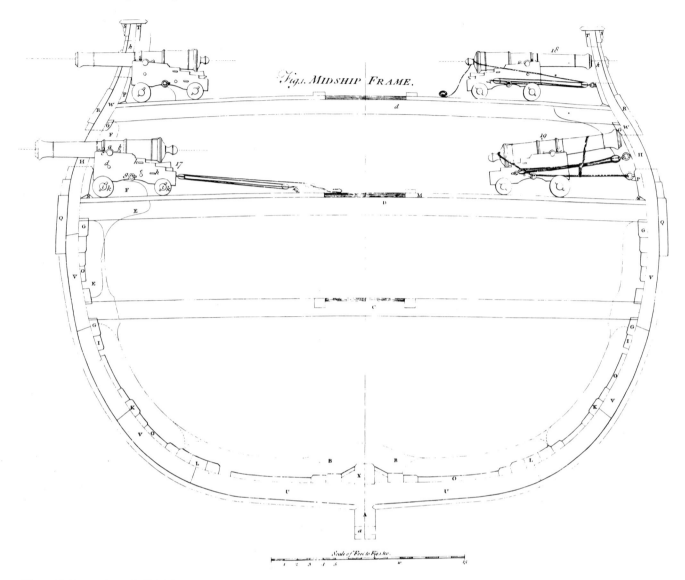

Fig. 1. MIDSHIP FRAME.

The midship section of a British 74-gun ship, c1765, from Falconers *Marine Dictionary*. It shows the guns in different positions. 17: run out, ready for firing, with the train tackle extending behind it, to take the strain after the gun is fired. 18: inboard, for loading. 19: stowed, with the muzzle raised above the level of the gunport, and the tackle 'frapped' to hold the gun tight in position

Simon Aked demonstrates the use of the 'hand crow levers' to traverse a gun in *HMS Victory*. He is using one of the blocks recovered from the wreck to give height to the lever. It is possible that two such levers were used at once, one on each side of the carriage.

recoil; and there was a short time-lag between applying the match and the actual ignition of the powder which cannot have aided accuracy. The

alternative method was to fit a flint-lock to the gun and fire it by means of a lanyard. There are references to this being tried aboard British ships as early as 1747,[11] and it was proposed for French ships twenty years earlier. In 1755 the *Invincible* was one of the thirteen ships chosen for tests with 'new invented locks and tubes for guns'.[12] The lock was a larger version of that used by contemporary muskets. The tube was tapering and made of tin. It was inserted through the touch hole to carry the spark down to the cartridge. The locks were expensive and were presumably taken off the ship when her stores were rescued. Many large flints have, however, been found aboard the wreck. In the short term the gun lock was a failure, as the tin tubes tended to fly out, causing injury to men and damage to the ship. The system was reintroduced with improvements in the 1770s and was much more successful.

The gun's recoil was restrained by the breech rope. This was thick, $7\frac{1}{2}$ in in circumference in the case of a 32 pounder. The middle of this rope was seized around the button at the rear of the gun and each end was fixed to a ring bolt at the side of the ship. The direction of the recoil was quite unpredictable, and the breech tackle tended to draw it up rather sharply. One seaman had to stand by the train tackle at the rear in order to take it in before the gun rolled itself out again. After that, the process of loading was ready to begin again.

Ammunition supply was crucial to rapid firing. Shot was kept stored in the shot lockers amidships in the hold, but a ready use supply was kept in racks along the side of the ship. Powder was more difficult for it was extremely dangerous to keep any excess on deck. Made-up cartridges were kept in the magazine forward and the after powder-room. Both these were below decks out of the way of gunfire. The gunner and members of his crew worked there, passing cartridges out and making up more if necessary. The powder-monkey boys carried the cartridges to the guns. Each had a round wooden box with a lid, which protected it from sparks on the way.

After firing had ceased, the gun was usually kept loaded against any sudden emergency. A round wooden tompion was placed in the muzzle to keep rainwater and spray out. These were turned in groups of six and cut apart as required. They had none of the decoration of modern tompions. A flat piece of lead known as an apron was bent over the touch hole and tied under the breech. It prevented any accidental sparks from reaching the powder. The muzzle of the gun was lashed to rings above the gun-port, and the tackle was drawn tight and bound up with the breech tackle.

In battle there were other tasks to be performed. Some men, especially on the upper-deck guns, were told to help trim the sails if this was necessary while in the presence of the enemy. Others, probably one for each gun crew, formed part of the fire party and

were called in the case of that emergency. Leather buckets hung from the break of the poop for their use. Other men were boarders and would arm themselves with pikes, cutlasses, hatchets and small arms for hand-to-hand combat with the enemy. The marines do not seem to have taken much part in working the main armament in this period, but were drawn up in ranks on the poop and forecastle with their muskets. Swivel guns had recently been reintroduced and six were mounted in the tops to fire down on the enemy's decks in close action.

The surgeon and his mates, along with the chaplain, the loblolly boys and some other assistants, were employed in the cockpit, deep in the orlop deck, to treat the seriously wounded. In view of the state of medicine at the time, it is not surprising to find that the work was horrific and distressing, even to hardened surgeons. It was described thus in 1755:

> At the very instant when I was amputating the limb of one of our wounded seamen, I met with almost continual interruption from the rest of his companions, who were in the most distressed circumstances; some pouring forth the most piercing cries to be taken care of, while others seized my arm in their earnestness of being relieved, even at the time when I was passing the needle for securing the divided blood vessels by a ligature. Surely, at the time when such operations are in contemplation, the operator's mind as well as body ought to be as little agitated as possible; and the very shaking of the lower gun deck, owing to the recoil of the large cannon which are placed just over his head, is of itself sufficient to incommode a surgeon.[13]

With this in mind, it is perhaps a relief to find that while in British service the *Invincible* never had to engage in serious action.

6 Peacetime Service and Repairs

In peacetime the active fleet was greatly reduced in strength. The seamen went back to the merchant navy and most of the officers went on half pay. Parliament reduced the active fleet from 40,000 to 8,000 men. It took two or three years to build a ship of the line, so there was no question of getting rid of many ships. Those that were already on the verge of falling apart were scrapped, but most were intended to be kept in good condition so that the fleet would be ready should war threaten again.

Ships in the peacetime fleet fell into three categories. A few were kept 'in sea pay'. They were almost fully manned and spent their time in patrols and kept up a certain minimum of naval training. Such ships were mostly small, of the fifth rate or less. At the other extreme, most ships were laid up 'in ordinary'. They were moored in sheltered waters near the main dockyards of Portsmouth, Plymouth, Chatham, Sheerness, Deptford and Woolwich. Their guns, sails, masts and stores were taken out and laid aside to be ready when the ship was needed again. The 'standing officers', the carpenter, boatswain, gunner and cook remained on board with a few assistants – four in the case of a third rate – to help them in the basic maintenance of the ship. They were visited by parties of dockyard labourers who pumped out the bilges occasionally, or by dockyard workmen who did the more extensive repairs.

Between these two categories was a third, the 'guardship'. Such a ship kept most of her guns, stores and masts and sails. Her complement of officers was only slightly less than on an active ship, but the total ships company was only about a fifth of normal. She was not expected to put to sea in this condition, but remained moored, ready to be manned quickly and to sail in any sudden emergency. Meanwhile, her crew were occupied by rowing guard around the ships in ordinary and by helping with their routine maintenance.

The first orders about the peacetime role of the *Invincible* were issued on 26 July 1748, two days after she arrived back at Spithead. She was to enter Portsmouth harbour to be paid off and laid up. Lloyd was

> to cause all possible dispatch to be used in clearing her of her sails, anchors and cables (except one large anchor and cable, and a stream anchor and cable) provisions and spare stores, but not to dismantle or unrig her; and having struck your yards and topmasts you are to leave the ship in this condition under the care of the officers of the yard.[1]

This was an unusual order, leaving the *Invincible* halfway between the ordinary and guardship status. Presumably, the Admiralty intended to fit her out, either as a guardship or for sea service, in the near future.

The crew was paid off on 12 August. By an order of 29 July, all the three hundred supernumeraries who had served as part of the complement were to be paid along with the regular crew. Large sums of money were brought down from the Navy Office in London, and the Clerk of the Cheque, one of the dockyard officials, went on board the different ships in turn. The whole procedure was a tense period for both civilian and naval officers. At Plymouth that year the seamen of the *Lion* rioted when they heard that *Salisbury* was to be paid before them.[2] The seamen, released suddenly from naval discipline, might threaten violence against any officer or petty officer they believed had been over-oppressive. When one ship was paid off a few years later:

> The first lieutenant, a severe disciplinarian, had been threatened, so he wisely set out for London two days before; but this did not avail, for a party of men, headed by the gunner's mate, hunted him in town, and meeting him at Cheapside gave him a severe drubbing.[3]

Each able seaman was paid at the rate of 24s per lunar month, from which was deducted 1s 6d for Greenwich Hospital, the Chatham Chest, the chaplain and the surgeon. There were also deductions for any goods the man had bought from the purser – clothes, bedding and tobacco. In all, the crew of the *Invincible* had earned £4,713, from which £690 was deducted for various reasons. The captain was paid £142 9s 1d. Thomas Osborne was the longest serving able seaman, having transferred out of the *Otter* with Captain Lloyd; his full wages were £8 9s 0d, from which were deducted 3s 4d for clothes bought on board, 7s for Greenwich Hospital, and 3s 6d for the Chatham Chest, a fund for the relief of distressed seamen. Twenty-eight men who had been treated for venereal diseases had £1 10s each deducted from their wages and 186 men who had received tobacco from the purser had up to 9s 6d deducted from their wages to pay for it. The best paid of the ABs was Daniel Duncan, who was owed from the beginning of 1747 for service in previous ships. He was given more than £21. John Thomson, who had deserted at Portsmouth while the ship was fitting out for her first voyage, forfeited all his wages.[4]

The ship was left in ordinary, but still with some rigging and stores on board, until the beginning of December, when the Admiralty decided that she should become a guardship. Again, this was something of an honour, for naturally the best ships tended to be chosen for this role as they would be the first line of defence in case of a surprise attack. Since the small ships of the fifth and sixth rates were at sea already, and since the three-deckers were expensive and unhandy, most of the guardships were large two-deckers, already becoming recognised as the most efficient fighting ships. The *Invincible* had seven companions at Portsmouth during 1749, and two of these, the *Monarque* 74 and the *Fougeaux* 64, had been captured from the French. There were also two relatively new 70-gun ships, the *Berwick* and *Kent*, and three smaller ships of 50 and 60 guns.

According to the order of 1 December, the *Invincible* was to have a total complement of 140. She was to have a captain and three lieutenants, instead of the five carried at sea. Other officers included a surgeon, master and purser, as well as the boatswain, carpenter, gunner and cook. They were allowed 14 servants between them. Intermediate ranks included a surgeon's and a master's mate, 4 midshipmen, and 12 other petty and warrant officers. This allowed for 96 able seamen, who would do all the manual work about the ship and on other ships of the ordinary.

According to the orders issued in November 1748, guardships were to keep their upper and quarterdeck guns only, and a third of their small arms. At 8 o'clock every evening a gun was fired from the flagship, and each ship was to set a watch of a quarter of her crew who were to stay on duty until 5am in the summer or daybreak in winter. Each ship was to be issued with a ten-oared boat, with a chest fitted to keep small arms and powder dry. Ships were to take turns to provide a boat every night, which was to be under the command of a lieutenant or master, and to be 'well manned and armed'. It was to be rowed around the harbour, and to 'pass at least twice every night by His Majesty's ships laid up in ordinary', and if it was not hailed from any ship, the officer was to go on board and find the reason why. It was to look into the creeks around the harbour, 'as well for preventing therein embezzlement, or the running of clandestine goods, as any attempt at surprise by an enemy'. The crew of each guardship was to be exercised frequently at great guns and small arms, and the men were to 'assist in carrying on the works of the dock, rope yard and moorings in Portsmouth Harbour'.[5]

The command of a guardship was eagerly sought for it allowed an officer to be paid as captain of a fairly large ship in peacetime, without involving him in any risks or long-term separation from friends and family. It is not surprising to find that John Bentley, who took command of the ship that December, was one of Anson's closest associates. Although he had not gained his entrance to the inner circle of Anson's friends by accompanying him on the great circumnavigation, there were few officers who enjoyed more favour from Anson over the years. Since Anson was a very perceptive judge of character and gave promotion and appointments only to those who had shown they deserved them, we can assume that Bentley was an estimable man. Over the next ten years he was to be associated with the *Invincible* more closely than any other officer, and it is worth looking at him in some detail.

Bentley had been born in the early years of the century, apparently to a family of humble tradesmen in Deal, Kent. He had entered the navy around 1720 and been promoted lieutenant in 1736. In February 1744 he was second lieutenant of Admiral Mathews' flagship, the *Namur*, at the Battle of Toulon. That battle brought credit to few people, but Bentley distinguished himself and was promoted to commander. By August of that year he had been raised to be captain of a 70-gun ship, the *Burford*, but meanwhile his patron was in trouble. A series of courts martial followed the Battle of Toulon and Bentley was called home to give evidence at them during 1745-6. Mathews was dismissed the service as the scapegoat for the failure at Toulon, but by this time Bentley had attracted Anson's attention and in 1747 he became his flag captain aboard the *Prince George*. He first saw the *Invincible* during the first Battle of Finisterre, when his ship prepared to fire a broadside into her stern, causing her surrender. He had served for a time as captain of the *Defiance* and after the war he had been appointed to the guardship *Barfleur*, before transferring to the *Invincible*.

The *Invincible* had some repairs in June 1749. She was docked for graving on the 20th and 21st, and £1,777 was spent on other repairs. Since over £1,000 of this went on the rigging and stores, it can be assumed that some work was done to her masts and yards, but we can be certain that her foremast was not replaced and the work was probably not very extensive.

Normally the life of a guardship was uneventful, if not downright boring. In the middle of 1749, however, the *Invincible* had some share of drama, of one kind at least. At the end of June Sir Edward Hawke, victor of the second Battle of Finisterre and now port admiral at Portsmouth, decided to use the *Invincible* as his flagship. Although she had been a guardship for six months, she had not yet received her guns and Hawke had a single 6 pounder transferred from his old ship, the *Fougeaux*, so that he could fire salutes and make signals when necessary.

The immediate task was to deal with the unpleasant aftermath of the war. There had been several mutinies in the later years and the time had come for the alleged offenders to be tried by court martial. At 7.30 on the morning of 26 June, the day after Hawke arrived on board, the *Invincible* hoisted the signal for a court martial and the first trial began.

The case involved a rather bizarre mutiny aboard the *Chesterfield* in October 1748, off the coast of Africa. While the captain and some of the other officers were ashore, the first lieutenant, Samuel Couchman, had seized the ship and taken her to sea. Over the next few days the loyalties of the crew were divided, but eventually they took control from Couchman and his friends and sailed the ship to the West Indies where it was handed over to the proper authorities. It had taken several months to gather the accused and the witnesses from the far-flung places where the events had taken place.

The first trial was of Captain Dudley, accused of neglect of duty in being ashore with most of his officers, thus allowing the mutiny to take place. He was acquitted by five votes to four. Couchman was not so lucky. Despite his unusual defence that he had been continuously drunk for several days, he was

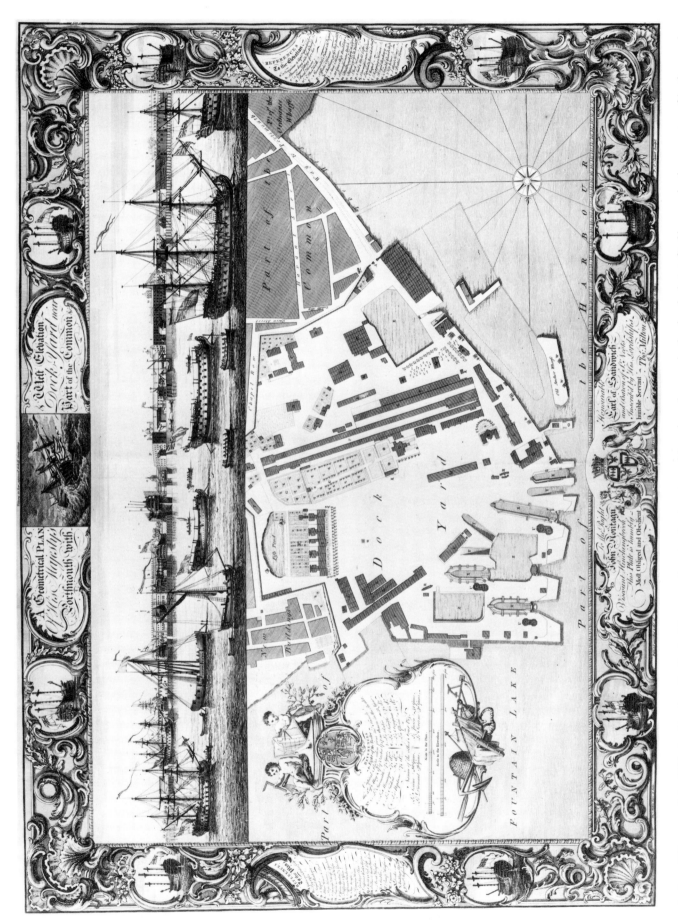

A plan of Portsmouth in 1752. At this time the *Invincible* was undergoing her 'great repair', and can be seen in the dry dock (no f). She can also be seen at no f in the margin

Edward Hawke, who used the *Invincible* as his flagship during the courts martial of 1749

pulled tight by a party of seamen and he was hauled up to the yardarm of the *Chesterfield* to suffer death by strangulation. In all, two officers were shot and three men, including the carpenter, were hanged during the month of July.

Perhaps it was a relief when Hawke hauled down his flag on the 27th and hoisted it aboard yet another French prize, the *Monarque*. The single 6 pounder was sent back to the *Fougeaux*, but three days later the *Invincible*'s own guns were brought alongside and by the end of the following day they had been installed. The *Invincible* shifted her mooring from the north end of Water Island to the north Jetty Head and at last she was equipped to carry on her duties as a guardship.

Almost immediately, routine was interrupted by a visit from the Board of Admiralty. The First Lord, the Earl of Sandwich, wanted to show their lordships something of the world outside their London offices and clubs, and at the same time to keep a check on incompetence and corruption in the yards. The Lords Commissioners arrived in Portsmouth by yacht on the 2nd, and on the 4th they found time to inspect four of the guardships, including the *Invincible*. They

viewed them all over, mustered their companies, found everything in order except the gentlemen on the quarterdeck not being dressed in the uniform, many of whom had blue trimmed with white, but almost everyone made in a different manner, and the Lords observing themselves that some of the officers on duty neglected to wear their proper clothing.[8]

found guilty and sentenced to suffer death by shooting. So, too, was Lieutenant Morgan of the marines. Men who did not hold the king's commission, including the carpenter and his mate, and three seamen, were also found guilty, but they did not have the privilege of being shot; they were sentenced to hang. In the following days, four seamen were tried for another mutiny aboard the *Richmond*. Two of them were also sentenced to hang. The *Invincible*'s service as a floating courtroom was over by the middle of July, but Hawke remained on board while the executions were carried out.[7]

By tradition, these took place aboard the malefactors' own ships, but only on the orders of the flagship, and after the sentences had been confirmed by the Admiralty. Despite appeals for clemency on behalf of Morgan, the two officers were shot aboard the *Chesterfield* on the 14th, after the *Invincible* had fired her 6 pounder and run a flag up to give the order. On the 26th, at 7am, the *Invincible* made the signal for each ship in the port to send a boat, manned and armed, 'to attend the execution of two prisoners late of the *Richmond*. At 10 the *Chesterfield* made the signal for the prisoners being ready. We made the signal for their execution, which was done to one, and one reprieved.' The Admiralty had decided to allow mercy to James Brown, but this was kept secret from him until the rope was actually around his neck. Thomas Ferryman had no such luck. The rope was

Naval uniform had first been introduced eighteen months before, for commissioned officers and midshipmen only. Although it was brought in at the request of the officers themselves, it was evidently not yet well established, if even an Admiralty inspection could not inspire officers to wear it properly.

At the end of the visit the Lords of the Admiralty were given a nineteen-gun salute from the *Invincible*'s newly installed guns and she was left in peace. The next eighteen months were uneventful and little occurred to disturb the routine of a guardship. In February 1750, the ship was put into dock for a routine graving, although this time she was not tallowed. Bentley did a brief turn as senior officer at Portsmouth in March 1751 and was ordered to carry out yet another court martial on the surgeon of the *Blandford* who, according to the charge, 'wrote several mutinous, insolent, threatening letters' to his captain. He was judged to have been under the influence of 'a violent nervous disorder', and was dismissed his ship.[9] In November of that year the *Invincible*'s foremast, the same one that had been installed in April 1748, was again found to be decayed and had to be replaced. According to Bentley, the decay was not sudden, nor caused by neglect. It had been surveyed twice already in the last two years and the main damage was 25ft above the forecastle. It was eventually replaced and the ship was virtually re-

A lieutenants uniform, of the pattern introduced in 1748 as the first uniform for naval officers. Such uniforms were worn during the Admiralty inspection of 1749, when it was complained that it was not worn properly

rigged early in 1752, at a cost of over £5,000 for work on the rigging and stores.

Few ships of the *Invincible*'s rate ventured out of harbour in peacetime, but in 1752 she was given the honour of a foreign voyage, albeit as a troopship rather than a fighting ship. The battalion of infantry guarding Gibraltar was due to be relieved and replaced by another, and the *Invincible* and another of the Portsmouth guardships, the *Tiger*, were to be given the job of ferrying troops there and back. Since Captain Steevens of the *Tiger* was senior to Bentley, he was to be in command, although his ship had only sixty guns. To make room for the troops, both ships were to sail without their lower-deck guns. The *Invincible* was to have a complement of only 240, of which 95 were actually mustered as members of the regular crew when she set sail, 24 officers and their servants, and 71 petty officers and able seamen; 140 supernumerary seamen were also borne. This is still a very small number, considering the difficulties Lloyd had with 625 men; but in peacetime men could be hand-picked, and perhaps the soldiers could help out with many tasks, such as hauling on ropes or pushing capstan bars. In any case, there was no need to fight the ship or maintain the guns, and in theory it was not necessary to carry large amounts of sail in dangerous circumstances.

The ships were cleaned during February and the

Invincible had repairs done at a cost of £1,374. The soldiers and their baggage had been received on board by 16 April, although the crew were still completing the rigging three days later. The *Invincible* took on 16 officers, including a colonel; 33 sergeants and corporals, 11 drummers and 398 privates. Also included were 72 'women and servants' and 18 recruits. The ship also carried 143 supernumeraries. Most of these seem to have been seamen lent from the other guardships, but two were shipwrights from the dockyard to help the ship's carpenter in his repairs about the ship. A total of 784 persons were on board.

A 5am on the 21st, the *Tiger* hoisted the signal for the ships to weigh from the anchorage at Spithead. The *Invincible*'s first anchor had been hauled in by 8.30am, and she was 'hove short peak' on the other – the cable had been taken in to such an extent that the anchor was only just holding and she was ready to sail. On a further signal from the *Tiger*, both ships weighed and set sail. By the afternoon of the following day, as the two ships approached Portland, the weather began to worsen, to 'fresh gales and squally'. A second, and then a third reef was taken in on the topsails, but early on the afternoon of the 22nd the fore topsail split. It had to be taken down and replaced with a spare one, not an easy task with a small crew in heavy weather. Sail was reduced to a minimum by taking all the reefs, but at 6pm the fore topmast staysail split. The wind was now west or north-west and the ships made slow progress around Portland. At midnight on the 24th the *Invincible* tacked and lost a main sliding boom for the studding sails. Bad weather continued on the 24th and the topgallant yards were taken down to reduce topweight. On the 25th the weather moderated for a time and more sail was set. Then,

at half past 10 the mainsail blew away from the rope. Not being able to keep company, fired two guns as signals to the *Tiger*. At 11 set main topsail. At 4 a.m. got in the mainsail, found part of the canvas blown away and split through a cloth in the middle of the sail. Lay to and bent another mainsail.

At 6am on the 26th the *Invincible* was ready to sail again. Steevens of the *Tiger* decided to head for the anchorage of Torbay to put his ships in order. His own ship had also suffered damage, having sprung the jib-boom. One seaman, John Ruby, had fallen off the main topsail yard and been lost.

The ships remained at anchor in Torbay for six days, while the crew of the *Invincible* got water from the shore and repaired the rigging. On 1 May Benjamin Whittaker was punished with twelve lashes for disobeying orders; flogging was a far less common event than it was to become forty years later, but it was not unknown aboard the *Invincible*, even in peacetime. On Sunday the 3rd the repair of the rigging was completed, the anchor was hove short again, the longboat hoisted in and at 9am both ships set sail again.

By the 5th the ships were well out to sea and the wind was north-westerly and still strong. Sails continued to suffer damage and on the 7th the foresail had to be taken down to be mended and the main topsail split. One seaman died on the 8th and two soldiers on the next day. But progress was good and on the 12th the ship was in sight of Cape St Vincent, the south-west corner of the Iberian Peninsula. On the morning of the 14th the ships entered Gibraltar Bay and anchored at 10am. The soldiers were disembarked the following morning and it is not difficult to imagine their relief at being on dry land again after such a voyage. Since leaving Torbay, the ships had been at sea for just twelve days.

The *Tiger* and *Invincible* remained at Gibraltar for nearly three weeks, repairing the rigging, taking on stores and water, and embarking the troops who were to be sent home. This time the *Invincible* was to carry a total of 588 passengers, including two officers' wives, 78 other women and an equal number of children. The ships set sail on 3 June. Some heavy weather was encountered on the 5th, but in general the voyage was much calmer than the previous one. The ships were almost becalmed for ten days until the 16th, although the *Invincible*'s sails continued to suffer; on the 8th, while the weather was 'light airs and fair', the fore topsail was found to be split in both clews. On the 17th, after the wind began to blow up again, to 'fresh gales and squally', the main topsail blew out. Another sail was put in its place, although the stock of spare sails must have been severely diminished by this time. The ships arrived back at Spithead on the 24th, after a voyage of three weeks.

Despite his difficulties Bentley was impressed, even ecstatic, with the performance of his ship. Later in the year he filled out the standard form for a sailing report, and could not praise her too highly. 60-gun ships like the *Tiger* were usually considered as fast as any in the line of battle, but the *Invincible* was much better and the need to keep station had in fact prevented her from showing her true qualities. 'Wrongs the *Tiger* very much, and weathers upon her in such a manner as when I tacked in her wake to get considerably to windward of her in two hours. Her leeway less than most ships I have been in.' Her speed was excellent – 'has gone 13 knots large and 8 by the wind, and would have went more could I have made a proper sail' – for Bentley had kept the mizzen-topsail aback for most of the voyage to slow her down to keep station with the *Tiger*.[10] Few British ships of the line had recorded speeds of more than 11 knots at this time.

Nevertheless, Bentley's report must be treated with some caution. First, like all captains he was proud of his ship and inclined to see her best features. He was not likely to lie, but one must be on guard against any tendency to exaggerate. Secondly, not many captains of ships of the line really tried to find the best sailing qualities of their ships. Most were confined to keeping company with a fleet and many were cautious, while the captains of 80-gun ships, for example, did not dare to carry too much sail in ships which were basically top-heavy. Bentley could not be accused of overcaution – his expenditure of sails alone is enough to clear him of that charge.

The third factor was the loading of the ship. Her lower-deck guns were taken out, and this must have helped her sailing. The basic problem for the designer of a sailing warship was to compensate for the great weight of the guns, which of course had to be carried well above the water-line and therefore tended to raise the centre of gravity and make the ship less stable. Without the lower-deck guns this problem was largely solved. Extra ballast would be added in the hold to bring the draught of water up to a suitable level, but this extra weight would be well below the centre of gravity, and so it would increase stability and allow the ship to carry more sail in given conditions.

For all that, there can be no doubt that the *Invincible* was a fast ship. Some of this speed was gained by good fairing of the hull, but not very much; less than a knot could be added in this way. She was better than other ships because of her greater length, her length to breadth ratio, and because she had less decks than British ships of a similar size, thus causing her hull to catch less wind and lowering her centre of gravity to allow her to carry more sail.

Often she was caught carrying too much sail, as the heavy loss of canvas in the outward voyage shows. She had only 240 professional sailors aboard, ready to take in sail in an emergency, and perhaps about 50 of these were officers, servants and artificers who would not be expected to indulge in this kind of work. The soldiers may or may not have been used in hauling ropes, but they would certainly not go aloft to furl or unbend sails, so the ship was left with a crew of about 190 effective able seamen. This compares with Lloyd's demands for a crew of 700, of whom about 500 would be seamen. A total of 190 men would be enough to sail the ship with great caution, setting a minimum of sail and taking it in well in advance of any bad weather; such sailing was evidently not in Bentley's nature.

After her return, the *Invincible* disembarked her troops. On 26 June there was an emergency when a fire started in the bread-room. Seamen's beds were used to smother it before it could take hold, thus saving the ship. The next day she sailed into Portsmouth harbour and dropped anchor near her intended mooring buoy. A line was led out to the buoy, the anchor cable was slipped and she was hauled up to the mooring buoy. The borrowed seamen were sent back to their own ships and she resumed her role as a guardship.

At the beginning of November the Admiralty decided to pay off all the guardships at Portsmouth and replace them with others. Again, the ships were not to be totally reduced, but the crews were

to put on shore their guns, powder and spare stores, but not to unrig them, or break up their ground tier; but to strike their yards and topmasts and deliver them in that condition into the care of the officers of the yard.

In January of 1753 the Admiralty changed its mind

OBSERVATIONS of the Qualities of His Majesty's Ship the *Invincible*

Her best sailing Draft of Water, when Victualled and Stored for Channel Service, {Afore 21 8} {Abaft 22 4}, or as much lighter (at the same Difference) as she is able to bear Sail.

being given this 15 Day of November 1752

Her lowest Gundeck-Port will then be above the Surface of the Water —— 6

1st. In a Top Gallant Gale. — *In one Tryal being in Company with the Tyger the Mizen Topsail constantly a back*

In a Topsail Gale. — *Do*

{ How she Steers, and how she Wears and Stays. } *Steers toward & stays Excceeding well*

Query the 3d. { How she behaves close haul'd, and how many Knots she runs. } *had no Tryal. Mizen Topsails constantly a back*

Under her { Reeft Topsails — *had no Tryal*

Courses — *had no Tryal*

And Query, Whether she will stay under her Courses. —

2d. { In each Circumstance above-mention'd (in sailing with other Ships) in what Proportion she gathers to Windward, and in what, the foreteaches, and in general her Proportion of Leeway.

3d. { How she proves in sailing thro' all the Variations of the Wind from its being a Point or two Abaft the Beam to its veering forward upon the Bow-line in every strength of Gale, especially in a stiff Sea; and a head Sea; and how many Knots she runs in each Circumstance; and how she carries her Helm

4th. The most Knots she runs before the Wind; and how she Rolls in the Trough of the Sea

5th. How she behaves in lying Too or a Try, under a Mainsail, and also under a Mizen ballanc'd. *had no Tryal*

6th. What for a Roader she is, and how she Careens? *Do*

Ft. In.

7th. { If upon Tryal the best sailing Draft of Water given as above should not prove to { be so, what is the best sailing Draft of Water? } Afore —— Abaft ——

8th. What is her Draft of Water when victualled to six Months, and stored for Foreign Service? Afore —— Abaft —— *had no Tryal*

9th. What Height is her lowest Gundeck-Port then above the Surface of the Water? ——

10th. The Trim of the Ship ——

J. Bentley

Bentley's sailing report for the *Invincible*

Two sandglasses recovered from the *Invincible*. The one on the left is a half-hour glass, used to time the ringing of the ships bell, the duties carried out during a watch. The other is a 28-second glass, used to time the log, and thus assess the speed of the ship. Between is a small barrel containing ink, and sand for blotting

about the *Invincible*. It appointed Captain Robert Pett to command her and ordered her to be fitted as a guardship with a hundred men. The dockyard was to carry out some repairs on her in preparation for that role.

Towards the end of January the shipwrights of the yard looked over the ship and were not pleased with what they found.

On carrying on the works necessary to be done to His Majesty's ship the *Invincible*, to fit her for a guardship pursuant to your order of the 10th inst, we found some pieces of spirketting on the starboard side of the gun-deck rotten, which required six breadth riders to be taken off to shift the said spirketting, and when they were overset we discovered all the clamps and thick stuff, from the gundeck down to the orlop beams in the wake thereof, between the bulkhead of the carpenter's store and the bread-room, also rotten; which defects, as several pieces of spirketting on the larboard side also appeared to be rotten, occasioned our examining the gun-deck clamps and riders to see the condition of them, and find many of the breadth and futtock riders and pieces of clamp rotten, and when all these riders shall be taken off, we expect to find her as bad on that side as on the other.

Furthermore, when the other riders were taken off, the dockyard officers were

apprehensive she will be found in bad condition; and as the said defects cannot be made good without her laying in a dock some time . . . we therefore forbear to carry on her works any further till we have your honours' directions thereon.[11]

The worst enemy of the wooden sailing ship was not storm, rocks or gunfire. It was decay of the timbers, which destroyed most ships after a few years. There is a common myth, based on the experience of ships such as the *Royal William*, which lasted from 1719 to 1813, and the *Victory*, which was forty years old at the time of Trafalgar, that wooden ships lasted for a long time. But such longevity was rare and expensive. The *Victory* was a much-loved ship and was kept afloat only by extensive repairs, amounting to several times the cost of her original construction. In the early years of the eighteenth century it had been reported that fourteen years was the average life of a ship, and things had not improved much by the middle of the century. A great deal depended on the construction of the ship and in particular on how well her timbers had been seasoned; but it is clear that the *Invincible*, after less than nine years in the water, was showing evidence of serious decay, and her future was in doubt.

Anson had now risen to be First Lord of the Admiralty and his power over the navy was increasing. He was undoubtedly the pre-eminent figure at the Admiralty, but the Navy Board was still dominated by an older generation which had no enthusiasm for the new type of ship. It was almost certainly at Anson's instigation that the *Invincible* was again singled out for special treatment. By an Admiralty order of 1 February, the dockyard was to put the *Invincible* into the first vacant dry dock, and 'carry on her repair in preference to any other works'.[12] Her place as a guardship was to be taken by the *Terrible*, the prototype of the French 74s, captured at the second Battle of Finisterre.

Work in the dockyard proceeded at a slow pace. By 16 May the guns and stores had not yet been taken out of the ship. She was put into dock on 30 August, and by 20 November the shipwrights had stripped off enough of her planks to be able to report on the condition of her timbers. It was even worse than expected. The frame was said to be entirely rotten from the mizzen-mast aft. The French type of construction was criticised: 'The shift of the timbers is very irregular, the double futtocks have in some places two timbers cut off between them.' It was pointed out that all her timbers had not yet been looked at and that more problems might be discovered. It was estimated that she would need two years to put right and that repairs would cost £26,000 – the same amount as the navy had bought her for in 1747. In effect, the dockyard officers were suggesting that it would be more economical to break her up and build a new ship.

Anson had no intention of letting his favourite ship be scrapped and making do with what the British dockyards could produce in her place. Her nearest equivalent would be a 70 on the 1745 establishment, but these ships, although almost as heavily gunned as the *Invincible*, were not doing well in service. It was complained that 'they do not steer so easy, nor sail so well, as was expected'. Because the 1745 establishment had been enforced by order in council, it was not easy to vary the design. Every year, as a new batch of ships was ordered, the Admiralty had to ask the council's permission to make small changes in the lines or dimensions.[13] In the circumstances, any ship built as a replacement for the *Invincible* would be greatly inferior.

In response to the second survey, the Admiralty sent the master shipwright at Deptford and the assistant surveyor of the navy to look at the ship and make recommendations. These men, Thomas Slade and William Bateley, were Anson's favourite shipwrights. Both had risen fast in the service since Anson had been at the Admiralty, and two years later, after a suitable vacancy had arisen, they would head the British shipbuilding effort as joint surveyors of the navy. Slade would go on to design Nelson's *Victory* and over forty of the new British 74-gun ships, which would eventually sweep away the outmoded vessels of the first half of the century. Slade was as taciturn as Anson and is little known, but he was easily the greatest British ship designer of the eighteenth century. In 1753 Slade and Bateley already represented the flower of British shipbuilding. They could be expected to look much more favourably at a ship like the *Invincible* than the old guard of the Navy Board and Portsmouth dockyard.

Yet they had to agree that the November survey had not been wildly exaggerated. They tried to take a more positive approach by pointing out that all but two of the floor timbers, a great part of the lower futtocks, the stem, keel, deadwood and two-thirds of the bottom were serviceable. It would be possible to remedy the bad shift of the toptimbers by 'running them down to make the futtocks and toptimbers in one, as the shape of her side will render their figure easy to obtain of proper length'. However, they had to agree with the dockyard's figure of £26,000 for the repairs, even if they believed that the work could be done in eighteen months rather than two years. The ship, they pointed out, had already had £5,952 spent on her hull and £16,748 on her rigging since her purchase in 1747.

But the Admiralty was not deterred. On 13 December it decided that it would be 'for the advantage of His Majesty's service to repair her instead of taking her to pieces'. She was to be 'repaired accordingly, taking care not to exceed the sum estimated'.

Thus began her 'great repair'. Unfortunately, the dockyard progress reports, which recorded the week-to-week work done to each ship, have not survived for this period, so it is not easy to tell exactly what was done to her. Certainly all her plank would have been stripped off, inside and outside. All the timbers mentioned in the surveys as being decayed would have been replaced. Probably the dockyard would have taken care to ensure that her hull form, highly regarded by those who knew her at sea, would be maintained as far as possible. We know that the double layer of planks put on just below her water-line was not restored, but since her breadth before the repair was registered in the Navy List as 48ft 11in and as 49ft 3in after, and the breadth was usually measured inside the plank, we can assume that the timbers were placed further out to give extra breadth, making the doubling unnecessary. Since her whole stern would have to be rebuilt, she would probably need new galleries and decorations. It is possible that the old French-style ones were kept and replaced later. It is more likely that she was fitted with new decorations in the British style – less angular and less 'artistic', executed by ordinary wood-carvers rather than sculptors. Unfortunately, none of the pictures show her after the repair, so it is not possible to be certain about this. Her keel was slightly reduced in length and this had an effect on her stated tonnage, although not on her actual displacement. After the rebuild she was registered as 1,793 tons instead of 1,826.[14] She kept her old rudder and she had no false

A painting from the British Library, apparently the original for part of the plan of Portsmouth. Again it shows the *Invincible* in dock (back, third from left) along with several ships in ordinary (without rigging), and some guardships (with rigging)

keel under the main keel, which was unusual as it exposed the main keel to damage.

Her repair took just as long as the Portsmouth officers had predicted. Early in 1755 the shipwrights expected that she would be ready to undock by the end of August. In June they reported that they might get her out soon, but only if they were allowed to take on extra men. August came and the Navy Board showed concern as a new war was threatening and docks were needed urgently to fit out the fleet. In September she was nearing completion and the dockyard asked whether to 'complete for the sea service, or to lie up in ordinary'. The Admiralty ordered that she be fitted for sea. In October she was still in the great dock, and it was estimated that she would not be ready until March and still needed £9,416 worth of labour and materials. The Admiralty ordered her to be fitted out as a flagship again, probably with Admiral Boscawen already in mind. Savage Mostyn, the port admiral, took a special interest in this aspect of the work at Boscawen's request.[15] New sails were made for her, not surprising in view of Bentley's heavy expenditure.

The most dramatic change was in her armament. Possibly she had been given stronger deck beams during the repair, or perhaps the authorities had gained confidence in her ability to carry a heavy armament. In any case, by an order of December 1755 she was to carry 24 pounders on the upper deck instead of 18 pounders. This made her a very powerful ship indeed, with 1,760lb of broadside, heavier than anything in the British fleet except a first rate.

On 17 January 1756 the *Invincible* was floated out of the great dock at Portsmouth, nearly two and half years after she had entered it. The repair of her hull cost £25,233, so the dockyard had obeyed their orders to keep it within £26,000. A further £4,559 was spent on her rigging and stores. She was needed urgently for the peace settlement of 1748 was rapidly breaking down and British forces were already in open conflict with the French in North America, India, the West Indies and in the Atlantic.

7 Flagship of the Western Squadron

There was no doubt that the Peace of Aix-la-Chappelle was a dead letter. Fighting between the rival East India companies had never really stopped. In North America the French had begun to build a line of forts in an attempt to stop the British spreading inland and this had caused Colonel George Washington to attack a small French force in 1754. The war had escalated from there. In 1755 Admiral Boscawen had been sent out to intercept the French reinforcements for America, with instructions to attack even though war had not been declared. In February of the following year the government had been warned that the French were about to make an attempt on the British-held island of Minorca. Britain and France were on the verge of a war which was to be fought on three continents and in as many oceans. This was a classic example of the type of colonial war for which the *Invincible* had been conceived and designed.

Admiral Boscawen had returned to England in November 1755 aboard his flagship the *Torbay* – another British 74, formerly the 90-gun *Neptune*, cut down in 1750. The *Torbay* needed a refit and the Admiralty ordered that the *Invincible* be fitted out in her place. The *Torbay*'s captain, Charles Colby, was transferred to the *Invincible* and took command on 11 January while she was still in dock. The crew of the *Torbay* were transferred with him and by 8 February Colby was able to muster 627 men. The complement of the *Invincible* had, however, been increased to 720 men, for the admiral was allowed a retine of 20, including his secretary and 19 servants and seamen.

It was not easy to find a good crew for her. At the end of the last war nearly all her men had been able seamen, but perhaps this was because they had been in the fleet long enough to gain experience. In February 1756, the standards were lower. On the 11th she was still 93 short of complement, and those on board included 99 ordinary seamen and 129 landsmen with no experience at all of the sea.[1]

On 13 February she was involved in an incident when strong winds caused the swivel of her mooring buoy to break and she was driven aground. Admiral Holbourne reported:

> She lies very easy aground fore and aft, and hope she will get no damage, as they say it is soft mud there. It being ebbing water there was no possibility of getting her off then. Everything is preparing for her safety. They are endeavouring to lash shores to prevent her heeling, anchor and cable carried out as soon as she is afloat to heave her off. All proper assistance is given her from the yard.[2]

At 9pm she was floated off, after about 12 hours aground.

The process of fitting out the ship had begun soon after her undocking. She was given a new iron fire-hearth instead of the old type of brick furnace. Most of her old masts, anchors, guns and stores were taken out of the dockyard warehouses, but there was a considerable confusion about her new upper-deck guns, the 24 pounders. In the first place, Portsmouth yard had misinformed the ordnance board about the number required and the latter had to query whether she needed twenty-eight or thirty, as she had carried in the past. It was decided to renew some of her quarterdeck 9 pounders, as they were 'old and defective', and the new ones were taken from the *Deptford* storeship. Thirty 24 pounders were shipped to Portsmouth from the ordnance depot at Woolwich aboard the sloop *Hyam* and arrived on 28 February.[3] Twenty-one of her new guns were brought alongside on 8 March and hoisted on board. It was soon realised that the new carriages were too high for the *Invincible*'s gun-ports, and everything, guns and carriages, had to be hoisted out again so that the carriages could be taken ashore to be altered. It was the 17 March before all her guns had been put on board.

Three days later the ship sailed out to Spithead to finish taking on her stores and await the assembly of the fleet. While she was anchored alongside the Buoy of the Spit, she witnessed the ill-fated Admiral Byng lead his squadron out to attempt to forestall the French in the Mediterranean. The discipline of the ship had to be attended to and on the 22nd Israel Blackman received twelve lashes for going ashore without leave. More severe punishments were given to men on other ships. On 1 April the *Invincible* was ordered to send an officer in a boat to attend the execution of a man aboard the *Stirling Castle*. Two days later, the ship's crew saw an even more gruesome punishment when Charles Bond, of the *Barfleur*, was flogged around the fleet. Triced up to a pair of capstan bars in one of the boats from this ship, he was rowed around six ships, including the *Invincible*, to receive part of his sentence of 150 lashes opposite each, while a medical officer stood by in case he fainted or died under the pain. The exercise was repeated on the 5th, when two men from the *Nassau* were brought alongside to receive ten lashes each.

On the 8th there was better news, as the commissioner of the yard came alongside in his yacht and supervised the distribution of two months' wages to the men. This was the normal preliminary to a foreign voyage and crews sometimes mutinied if they were ordered to hoist anchor without being paid. Work still had to be done and on the 19th the ship was heeled over and 'boot topped' by putting tallow along the starboard side under the water-line. More pressed men were received and the complement was nearly full.

The admiral came on board at 11am on 25 April. Edward Boscawen was one of the great sea comman-

The Hon.ᵇˡᵉ Edward Boscawen
One of the LORDS COMMISSIONERS of the ADMIRALTY and
Rear Admiral of the White Squadron of His Majesty's Fleet

Admiral Edward Boscawen

ders of the mid-eighteenth century, alongside Anson and Hawke. He had been born in 1711, the third son of Viscount Falmouth. He had been in the navy since 1726 and was promoted captain in 1737. He had served in several important expeditions – Hosier's disastrous voyage to the West Indies in the 1720s, when his crews were decimated by disease, and Vernon's capture of Portobello in 1740. In 1747 he had been in command of the *Namur* during Anson's victory. Like Bentley, he had first seen the *Invincible* as an enemy ship and he had exchanged several broadsides with her and been wounded during the battle. He was promoted rear admiral soon afterwards, even though several less distinguished captains above him in the navy list had to be promoted with him in order that the rules of seniority could be maintained. He had become one of the Lords of the Admiralty in 1751 at the same time as Anson became First Lord. In 1755 he had been entrusted with the delicate mission of stopping the French reinforcements for North America, even though war had not been declared. This was the one major failure of his life; he had captured two warships, enough to annoy the French, but not enough to damage them seriously.[4]

There were rumours of disagreements between Boscawen and Anson, and Horace Walpole claimed that 'when they came together after the victory off Cape Finisterre, [Boscawen] complained loudly of Anson's behaviour',[5] mostly in the allocation of

promotions and rewards. But Boscawen shared Anson's tactical skill and his desire to reform the navy. He was never really one of Anson's followers, but there is no doubt that the two men respected one another. He was much more socially confident than Anson and far less reluctant to put pen to paper. His wife was a noted intellectual, of whom James Boswell wrote, 'her manners are the most agreeable, and her conversation the best, of any lady whom I have ever had the happiness to be acquainted'.[6] Boscawen's letters to her give an intimate and charming picture of the life of a senior officer in the middle of the eighteenth century.

The political situation at sea was still unclear. France had not declared war following the seizure of her ships the previous year, but reports were already coming through of a threat to Minorca. Britain had not declared war either, but in February the commanders at sea had been given orders to seize French ships. For Britain, the war was essentially a colonial one, although the French navy might be used to divert attention from the colonies by threatening an invasion of England. Boscawen was to take his ships to join Admiral Hawke off Ushant where he could blockade the main French naval base at Brest.

The French fleet had been largely rebuilt since the last war, and 15 of the new 74s, 3 two-decker 80s and 11 of 64 guns had been launched since 1749. They now had about 60 ships of the line in the water, generally superior to British ships of the same type. British ship design was beginning to catch up with the French, for Slade and Bateley had taken over as joint Surveyors of the Navy in 1755. Almost immediately Slade began to design the first British 74s to be planned and built as such from the beginning. These ships, of the *Dublin* class, were still quite small, with a gun-deck length of only 165ft compared with the *Invincible*'s 171ft; but the dimensions were slowly increased in the vessels ordered over the next few years to reach 168ft in 1757. None of these ships would be ready for some years and the British still had to rely on captured ships, those reduced from other rates and obsolescent designs.

The Western Squadron off Brest served two main functions. Since the French had no large natural harbour on their Channel coast, Brest would serve as the base for any fleet which might cover an invasion of England, or an attempt to reinforce the colonies in India, the Caribbean or North America. The first job of the squadron was to keep the French fleet bottled up – not an easy task as the ships had to leave station by turns for cleaning and revictualling, while the whole force might be driven away by gales and storms. The second task was to patrol the entrance to the English Channel. Most of northern Europe's overseas trade – from Holland, Germany, Scandinavia and the Baltic as well as Britain and France – passed close to Ushant on its way in or out. It was the job of the Western Squadron to control this and prevent enemy action or communication. While the French fleet was undefeated, this was the most important command in the British navy.

John Terry's painting of The Battle of Cape Finisterre, commissioned by the *Invincible* Committee

A contemporary painting of The Battle of Cape Finisterre. It shows the British flagship the *Prince George* in the thick of the fighting, whereas it was hardly engaged at all

John Terry's painting of the surrender of St Georges, Captain of the *Invincible*. Recent research shows that it was the crew of the *Pembroke* who took charge of the *Invincible*, and it is quite possible that this incident never took place. Legend has it that St Georges said to Anson, 'Vous avez vaincu l'*Invincible* et La Gloire vous suit' (You have vanquished the *Invincible* and Glory follows you). There is no contemporary evidence for this, and it seems likely that the remark, if it was made at all, was made some time after the surrender

Items recovered from the wreck: a child's shoe, woollen sock, army and marine buttons. The leather shoe was for a child of 5–6, too young to be a member of the crew, so he was probably the son of an army staff officer travelling to North America on board the *Invincible*. The buttons are amongst the earliest examples of their type, pre-dating the official warrants for issue

Items recovered from the wreck: Ram-rod heads, a hand grenade and a cartridge holder with a leather cover. The hand grenade was a hollow cast-iron sphere filled with 3oz gunpowder and ignited by lighting powder packed into a wooden fuse; on exploding, fragments of hot sharp metal would fly in all directions, making a vicious anti-personnel weapon. The cartridge holder was for use with muskets, and bears the crest of George II (1726–60) – very useful for dating the wreck before its identity had been proved

Items recovered from the wreck: Bowl with spoon. This bowl is the only one found so far with the 'broad arrow' (Government issue) stamped on it. The bowl's crack pre-dates the wreck – an attempt to tie the bowl back together with string can be seen. The spoon was found actually inside the bowl as shown

Items recovered from the wreck: square plate, pewter and wooden spoons, brandy bottle, wooden beer or grog tankard. These plates were made of solid oak, 1ft square, and were issued to the crew for their 'three square meals a day' – hence the saying. The spoons and tankard would be some of the very few pieces of personal property allowed to crew members. The pewter spoon bears the initials 'TH', probably one Thomas Hilliard, a captain's servant on board at the time

John Terry's painting of the loss of the *Invincible*

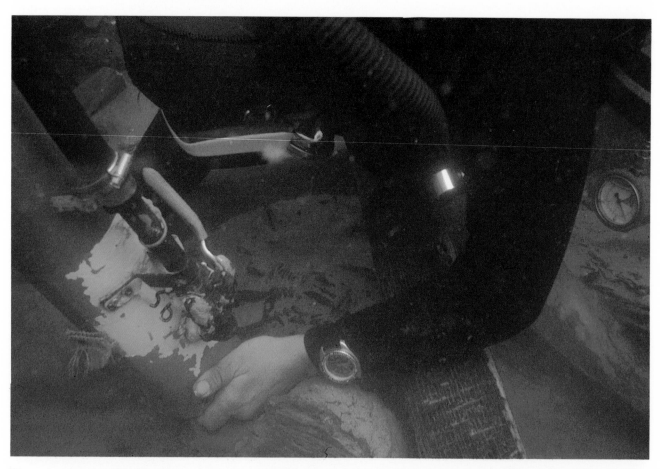

Diver operating an airlift. The divers disturb the sand which envelops the artefacts and then use the airlift to suck the sand away

Diver drawing features of the wreck as they become uncovered

Gunnery stores as found on the orlop deck. Once neatly stacked, the stores probably tumbled into this position as the ship rolled on to her side

A painting by Vernet of the dockyard at Rochefort during the eighteenth century. In the foreground, men are pushing a large coil of rope away from the ropeyard

Boscawen's ships set sail on 29 April. Besides the *Invincible*, he had six ships of the line and two 50-gun ships. Some merchant ships were stopped on the way out, including a French vessel loaded with salt. Four men were taken prisoner out of her and she was sunk, being too small to take home for prize money. Boscawen was pleased with his flagship. On his first night at sea he wrote to his wife: 'I should have told you the *Invincible* sails well, rather better than every [other] ship, nothing but the *Bedford* comes near us.'[7] The *Yarmouth*, a British-built 64-gun ship, was 'the worst of the nine sail now in company', while the *Cambridge*, a three-decker 80, was 'as solemn as the commander thereof'.

On 5 May the look-outs caught sight of the island of Ushant. Next day a fleet of thirteen sail was sighted and they were soon identified as men-of-war. At 2.30 the private signal, intended to identify ships of a friendly fleet, was made. There was no reply, but no one believed they were enemies and none of Boscawen's squadron cleared for action. The two fleets lost each other in a fog for a time, but it lifted and the other fleet made its private signal. It was Sir Edward Hawke's squadron, waiting for its relief after several months of blockade. The next day Hawke went home in his flagship *St George* and a few other ships, leaving Boscawen in command with eighteen ships.

Boscawen enjoyed the comforts of the *Invincible*'s great cabin. He found it was well fitted, better than her near-sister the *Magnanime*, though 'strong and plain like an old country hall'. He wrote to his wife: 'my cook pleases me very well and would please you more. He is quite a dab at pastry, and what I still more approve of him for is his economy.'[8] He sat at table every day with five of his officers, and 'my tables are so well made that we sit down without trouble and the table cloths fit exactly'. He lamented the lack of books to read, but he experimented with means of preventing illness among his crews. Unfortunately, his ships had had to leave before they could be fitted with Dr Hales' ventilators, intended to air the lower deck, but he had marmalade for breakfast, 'the best anti-scorbutic we know of'. He was pleased with the health of the *Invincible*'s crew. 'I continue well and the ship's company surprisingly well. None of the old men are ill, the new ones have their turn, but none are dangerous. Out of the whole 700, but 30 have the least complaint.'

Prizes were few. On 24 May there was considerable excitement when many sails were sighted to the south-east. According to the log of the *Invincible*, 'we saw them out of our tops, but could not get their number. At sunset saw them plainer but could not tell how many, the weather being hazy and they close together.' Next morning, Boscawen hoisted the signal for line of battle abreast, at 1 mile distance, but 'neither the rear admiral nor the *Bedford* took notice of the signal', and the *Invincible* had to fire several signal guns to attract their attention. The strange fleet was found again and the officers were 'big with hopes', believing them to be a French fleet of equal strength to their own, of eleven ships of the line and two frigates. On closer inspection, they were found to be a neutral Dutch convoy of 12 merchantmen and a 50-gun man-of-war. The British fleet was well off station by this time, and had to get back in the teeth of 'a wet, black, dirty easterly wind'.[9]

Early on the morning of 1 June, six sails were sighted to the north-east. Four ships of the line were sent to investigate and the private signals were exchanged. It was a small squadron led by the frigate *Unicorn*, whose captain came on board the *Invincible*. He 'brought with him the declaration of war against the French, which was read to the ship's company'. Boscawen ordered copies sent to the other ships to be read, and called his captains aboard the *Invincible* for dinner and tactical planning.

In mid-June Boscawen took part of his fleet south to seek out French commerce off the Spanish coast. A vessel was chased in the expectation that she was a French privateer, but she turned out to be a packet from Falmouth. From it came the erroneous information that Byng had destroyed the French Mediterranean squadron. On the 15th he turned back to Brest.

The fleet continued to grow in strength. Admiral Mostyn arrived on the 19th, with twenty-three more ships, and a few were sent home. There were more false alarms, as more Dutchmen were sighted. On 3 July

> the *Orford* made the signal of discovering a fleet in the north-west. Made the general signal to chase in that quarter, and made all the sail we could. We ran an hour and a half, but could see nothing but two small Dutch ships standing to the westward, and a small snow going to the eastward.

Boscawen had no love for the Dutch: 'These rogues carry on a swinging trade while the English and French languish in port, and laugh at us both.'

News of Byng's failure in the Mediterranean was coming through in bits and pieces, often via enemy sources. By 21 June 'Mahon and the misbehaviour of our fleet' were 'the constant topics of conversation', and Boscawen was so depressed that he was losing sleep. Minorca had been taken by the French, and Byng, after an indecisive battle, had taken his fleet back to Gibraltar, in the belief that this was what his instructions demanded in the circumstances. This was seen as a great defeat in Britain, hence Boscawen's depression.

He was weary of blockade service, and 'heartily tired of this prison kind of life'. By the beginning of July he was 'Tired with waiting so long off Brest'.[10] He decided to try something different. On 5 July, taking advantage of a westerly breeze, he led his squadron away from its station off Brest, on a cruise to the south-east. He was going to harass the men of war and merchantmen using the natural harbours of the west coast of France, in the same area where the *Invincible* had been battered by storms nine years before. He was 'in hopes of affronting them in some way or other'.

Next day his ships passed the small islands of

The Bay of Biscay and the English Channel, showing the importance of the Brest squadron, and the area where the *Invincible* sailed during 1756

Glénans, where they saw a French frigate at anchor among the rocks. On the 7th, the fleet was off Bellisle. Captain Keppel in the *Torbay* was sent to the south of the island to cut it off, while the rest of the fleet, headed by the *Invincible*, formed line and steered through the dangerous channel between the island and the mainland. Leadsmen constantly sounded the depth of water, which varied from 13 to 17 fathoms, but they found the channel successfully and came to no harm. According to Boscawen, 'We passed so near that isle that we put all in a hurry and many curses were sent after us, I suppose, as I could see all hands under arms marching, as I conclude, to their alarm posts.'[11] Unfortunately, he found neither man-of-war nor merchantman within the Channel,

but only fishing boats, from one of which he bought his catch, 'John Dories and soles, and paying for them twice as much as they could have got otherwise'.

By evening, the fleet was approaching the Ile d'Yeu, 50 miles to the south-east. That night eighteen or twenty small vessels were sighted inside the anchorage, protected by three frigates. It was too late in the day to attack, so Boscawen left three of his ships to lie off the harbour all night, but after dark the enemy vessels succeeded in getting past them and were seen taking flight to the south-east. Four ships of the line and a frigate were sent in pursuit, and by noon they had brought back eight prizes, small sloops, snows and brigantines, but the frigates escaped. More merchant vessels were brought in that afternoon as the main body of the fleet continued to the south-east. By nightfall, the fleet had eleven prizes in company. Not all of these were valuable. The *Invincible*'s longboat was sent aboard one which was carrying salt. Her crew was taken off and she was set on fire. Another 'had nothing in but ballast, sailed very leaky', and she, too, was disposed of. But the others were loaded with wine, bound for the French fleet at Brest; 6,690gal were taken on board the *Invincible* alone, and all the prizes but two were burnt. Boscawen had this distributed among the ships, being 'more wholesome drink than the brandy we give them instead of beer'.[12]

By now the fleet was off the Île d'Oléron, near the *Invincible*'s original home of Rochefort, but the wind did not permit an attack. The fleet continued south, approaching the Spanish coast and picking up a few more prizes on the way. By the 16th it was off Finisterre. Near the island of Sisargas, outside Corunna, the fleet was becalmed and found itself being driven on to the shore by the current. All the ships except the two furthest off anchored. The *Invincible* got out her longboat ready to tow if necessary, and re-erected her jeer capstan which had been taken down to make room to stow the boat. As the sun rose on 17 July, the *Invincible* was three-quarters of a mile from a rocky shore and there was doubt about whether the anchor would hold in deep water and a rocky bottom. At 5am a light breeze got up off the land. The ships weighed and hoisted their boats back in.

Soon after, Boscawen ended his voyage and headed back to Brest. He wrote to his wife:

The French will not be pleased with this cruise of mine. We have insulted his coasts, destroyed their home trade, and made some little impression on their foreign trade, while their squadron at Brest (though ready for sea) has not dared to stir out. By the letters I have seen their trading towns are in great distress, many of their merchants bankrupt, their manufacturers idle, and the wives and families of their seamen starving.[13]

Maybe so, but he had neither won a fleet battle, nor made much in prize money; moreover, the French were not in such 'great distress' that they were unable to support many more years of war. Perhaps the best result of the cruise was to restore morale in the fleet, after the boredom of the blockade.

On the evening of the 26th, Boscawen arrived back on station off Brest. There he found a squadron of ten ships sent out to reinforce him. They included the brand-new first rate, the *Royal George*, launched only five months before. She was the first 100-gun ship on the 1745 dimensions, and perhaps the most successful ship built to that establishment. She was a three-decker, 200 tons larger than the *Invincible*, and beautifully decorated and furnished. Boscawen made preparations to transfer his flag to her.

At 9am on the 29th, the *Invincible* hoisted out her longboat and began to transfer the admiral's goods, furniture and papers to the *Royal George*. This work took five hours, and then seventy-four men, includ-ing a lieutenant and twelve petty officers, were sent on board the new flagship, which was undermanned. At 6pm Boscawen left the *Invincible* and was rowed across to the *Royal George*. His flag was struck from one ship and hoisted on the other and a 13-gun salute was fired.

By this time the *Invincible* had been at sea for three months. Compared with other ships, she had remarkably little disease aboard, but her supplies were running out and her turn for replenishment had come. Boscawen ordered her to go to Plymouth to take on beer and water. She parted from the fleet on the 30th, and at the last meeting between Boscawen and Captain Colby, the latter had 'tears in his eyes and a heart full of gratitude'.[14]

Part of the cabins of the Royal George. This remarkable photograph was taken by fibre optic photography aboard the contemporary model of the ship. It is not clear why the modelmaker should have taken so much trouble with parts which would remain concealed

Boscawen had mixed feelings about his new flagship. He found her sailing qualities surprisingly good for a three-decker, and commented,

She is in many particulars as good a ship as ever I was at sea in, works as well as any frigate in the service, carries a very good sail and sails well; she falls too quick in a head sea, which makes her uneasy and stops her way.

Her cabins, however, were not so good. He wrote to his wife, 'I can tell you she is not so convenient in many particulars as the *Invincible*, though fitted for Lord Anson'.[15] To the Admiralty he wrote in more detail:

I think her very ill fitted (don't mistake me that I mean conveniency or neatness) for great expense has been laid out which must be thrown away if I ever engage. Upon my first coming on board I knocked [down] fourteen cabins. I have cleared ship [for action] twice since I have been on board; had these cabins been up, we should have been in great confusion. I hope your lordships will order that none for the future be put up, after being once knocked down.[16]

Cabins were an important issue with Boscawen.

The *Invincible* arrived in Plymouth Sound a day after leaving Boscawen and dropped anchor. The cruise, although not crowned with great victories, had been quite successful. Illness and accident had been kept to a minimum, there had been few floggings and a little prize money had been earned. Five seamen and 4 marines had died during the voyage, but this was quite a small figure, and the *Invincible* was to exceed it greatly in the following year. A total of 17 marines and 25 seamen were sent ashore sick, but this, too, was tolerable, and a few days later the surgeon hoped 'the men sent sick on shore in condition to be taken off, and those that are on board, by the benefit of fresh provisions and greens will be greatly refreshed'.[17]

Captain Colby had been made commissioner at Gibraltar and left the ship on 7 August. His successor was Matthew Buckle who was 38 years old and had been a captain for eleven years. He was another friend of Boscawen and he had gained considerable distinction in 1747 by capturing the Spanish 80-gun ship *Glorioso* in a noted single ship action. Previously he had been with Boscawen's fleet in the *Swiftsure*, but that ship had been damaged by a fire in the cook-room and sent to Plymouth for repairs.

On 8 August, immediately after taking command, Buckle reported to the Admiralty that three months of food was already on board and most of the beer and water. (Unlike most ships, the *Invincible* was no longer to take as much beer as she could hold. Boscawen had found that she could stow three months' supply of it, but that was longer than beer would keep.) Buckle reported that:

> The ship likewise wants her rigging to be set to rights, and put a little in order. But I hope to have her completely ready by this day sennight . . . by which time the surgeon acquaints me he hopes the men sick on shore will be in condition to be taken off.[18]

The *Invincible* set sail on the 16th. She was soon becalmed just outside the sound and obliged to anchor to await a favourable wind, which came a few hours later. For the moment Buckle's greatest problem was the shortage of men. He had only 631 on board, largely because of those lent to the *Royal George*. While still in the sound he had pressed five seamen from a brigantine from Milford, and on the way out he pressed one more from a brig bound from Guinea.

On the 21st, after a slow passage, he joined Boscawen off Brest. The *Invincible* assumed her old station, but with a slightly different role. She was no longer a flagship and as one of the faster ships she was often chosen to chase and inspect strange sails. By the end of the month she was chasing two Dutch galliots and fired a shot across the bows of one to cause her to stop. On 4 September she sent her boat manned and armed to witness punishment of a man aboard the *Eagle*. A court martial had given him only twelve lashes for desertion and he must have considered himself extremely lucky. On the 11th, she 'fired two shots at a snow to make her stop; brought to and sent an officer on board her. She came from Portsmouth bound for Montserrat, and gave us an account of Sir Edward Hawke having gained victory over the French'. But she was misinformed and no such victory had taken place. On the 21st, she fired a shot across the bows of another ship, which turned out to be Portuguese. Such were the frustrations of blockade service.

On 11 September, Boscawen had been optimistic about the health of the *Royal George*: 'We continue very healthy . . . This ship has been at sea now twelve weeks, which is longer than I ever knew a first rate at sea'. But two weeks later the situation had changed. There were '150 men far gone with the scurvy, and no more than 20 tons of water on board, and as ten or twelve complaints of that terrible disorder appears every day, I dread losing so many good men'. No one had died yet, but Boscawen decided to send the ship back to Portsmouth.[19]

On the 26th the *Invincible*'s longboat was hoisted out and began to transfer the admiral's belongings back on board. The men lent to the *Royal George* were returned and Boscawen hoisted the flag at 5pm. The *Invincible* settled into the routine of several months before. She no longer chased ships herself, but signalled other ships to do so. The health of the crew was not what it had been in the last cruise and several deaths were recorded in this period.

On 14 September, Boscawen had reported that smallpox was spreading on the ship and many on board had not had it. It seems to have caused a few fatalities. The food and drink left much to be desired. Boscawen had no faith in the Plymouth beer: 'There is much of it in the ships that came from thence sour, and will be condemned. The captains also say the brewer is very idle, and don't attend his business. Both the agent-victualler at that port and he are to blame.'[20] On 19 October, Buckle 'had a survey, and condemned 27 butts of beer, 300lbs of cheese and five firkins of butter, being all unfit for service'. On the 27th, several ships saw lights to the south-west and the *Invincible* made the signal for a general chase. It turned out to be a group of merchant ships under convoy of the *Berwick*.

It was still not normal to keep many ships of the line out through the winter, and at the beginning of November Boscawen sent the *Invincible* home again with five other ships. At 3pm on the 7th she anchored again at Spithead, her year's service over. In December Buckle was promoted to be captain of the *Royal George* and left the *Invincible*.

Despite her fine performance early in the year, there was now a question mark over the *Invincible*'s sailing qualities. Boscawen had been enthusiastic in his early letters to his wife, but in June she had cautioned him against taking too much of a leading role in any future battle. He replied:

> As to what you desire of the *Invincible* not performing in person, that will scarcely be in my power. Many of the ships here sail better, but it is the custom of the French to wait for the commanding officer, so that before they will submit I must come up and give the *coup de grace*.[21]

Boscawen was suggesting that in a general chase, as at Finisterre, the *Invincible* would be overtaken by other ships. But by this time the ship had been eight weeks at sea and fourteen in the water without cleaning; presumably the weed had begun to reduce her speed.

More serious was his criticism in an official letter to the Admiralty on 22 August:

> I can't help mentioning to your lordships that both the *Invincible* and the *Magnanime* had a doubling on their bottoms from the water's edge several feet downwards. It is to be presumed that the French put it there for some reason. They neither of them now sail well, work well, or carry sail, and as the *Invincible* was known to do these things well, I cannot see why these were not put on again. The doubling being of fir is but a small expense, and labour very little ... I could wish when these ships are refitted these alterations might be attempted.[22]

There is no sign that the Admiralty or the Navy Board replied to Boscawen's criticisms, but Savage Mostyn also complained about the *Magnanime*. Late in August the Admiralty ordered that she should be doubled and have her masts altered. This was carried out the following month, but it was not done to the *Invincible*.

Boscawen's comments contradict his early letters and he may simply have been reluctant to admit that anything good could come out of the British dockyards. Nevertheless, they deserve consideration. The reason for not restoring the doubling was simple enough – the timbers of the hull had been let out to give greater breadth, so it was no longer necessary. It is not likely that the lack of breadth was affecting the sailing qualities, although the altering of the timbers may have changed the lines of the ship to some extent. More likely, it was because she did not have a false keel, and this may have reduced her weatherliness. The new guns, 24 pounders instead of 18, would also have added several tons to her topweight.

Captain Stephen Colby took command of the ship in December while she was still at Spithead. He was a junior captain of only a few months' seniority, transferred out of a frigate. It is not clear whether he was related to the *Invincible*'s previous captain with the same surname. His command of the ship was to be short and not very glorious.

The ship was now under the orders of Admiral Temple West, a Lord of the Admiralty and a cousin of the Pitt family. He was to form a squadron of ten ships of the line for a 'particular service' – to patrol off Cape Finisterre in order to interrupt French movements. His ships were stored and ready by 17 January 1757, and he took them down to St Helens to await a favourable wind. On the 23rd he sailed, but encountered bad weather almost immediately and returned to the anchorage at St Helens. A few days later it was discovered that the *Invincible*'s rudder, the same one she had carried throughout her career in the French and British navies, was in a dangerous condition. A shipwright from the dockyard came on board on the 29th and condemned it. The rudder was unhung on the following day and taken ashore. Meanwhile, West was obliged to sail without the *Invincible*, although he left a rendezvous and instruc-

tions to join as soon as possible. The workmen of the yard 'were employed day and night' to make the new rudder, and it was ready by 2 February. Since 1754 it had been the custom to fit rudders with an extended head, which protruded through the upper deck and allowed the fitting of a spare tiller if the one below the upper deck was damaged. This had not been done to the *Invincible* during her great repair because the old rudder was retained. There was no time to do it now as it would involve alterations in the ship itself. Therefore, the old pattern rudder was made, and fitted to the ship on the 3rd. It was to cause much trouble later.

Meanwhile, further defects in the *Invincible* had been noticed and it was pointed out that 'His Majesty's ship the *Invincible* carries a slack helm, and in light winds a lee helm, and is not so weatherly and quick in staying as might be expected'. Perhaps in response to Boscawen's complaints of the previous year, it was decided to take her into dock for various repairs. She was taken in on 21 February and kept there for four weeks, during two spring tides. Her hull was shored up to lift the keel off the blocks on the bottom of the dock, and a new false keel, 5in deep, was fitted under the main keel.

It was probably at this time that the ship was chosen for an important and unrecorded experiment – her false keel was covered with copper. More than twenty years later, coppering of the underwater hull was to add greatly to the performance of British ships and to reduce their maintenance costs dramatically. It is no exaggeration to say that coppering did much to save the British fleet from major defeat in the War of American Independence. But its initial fitting was very expensive and it had to be tried for many years in service before the government could be persuaded that it was a worthwhile investment. It is commonly assumed that the first test was made on the frigate *Alarm* in 1761. But, as one historian has commented, 'one wonders about the circumstances which prompted the Admiralty to order the coppering of the *Alarm* in the first place. Surely there must have been some prior encouragement, based on earlier tests, on a smaller scale.'[23] Certainly, the *Alarm* was the first ship to be fully coppered, but records show that several ships had already had their keels coppered in 1758. No written record of the experiment on the *Invincible* has been discovered, but copper has been found on the false keel of the wreck off Portsmouth. This was almost certainly fitted in her spring refit of 1757, for the false keel was not easy to get at, unless the hull was shored up, as it was then. It seems that the *Invincible* was the pioneer of a very important change in ship fitting.

During the month of March the boats of the *Invincible* were again used to take men to witness an execution. But this was no ordinary punishment. The log for 14 March records: 'Moderate and cloudy weather. a.m. the boats attended the execution of Admiral Byng, who was shot on board the *Monarque*. Carpenters employed as before.' Thus Byng paid the supreme price for failure, even though a court martial

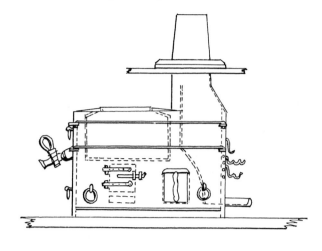

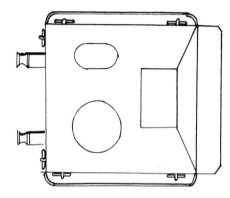

The new type of galley stove, as fitted to the *Invincible* in 1756. Records show that it was removed from the wreck during the salvage operation in 1758

had cleared him of cowardice and found him guilty only of 'failing to do his utmost' in the presence of the enemy. The Articles of War allowed no lesser sentence than death for this, and no politician was prepared to sacrifice his popularity by giving him a reprieve. In Voltaire's famous phrase, it was intended *'pour encourager les autres'*. In view of the success of

the British navy over the next fifty years, it is possible that this execution, barbaric though it was, might have succeeded in that.

Other work was done on the ship during her month in dock. The upper-deck and quarterdeck gun-ports were widened by taking some wood from the timbers which formed their sides. She was also fitted with the new type of iron fire-hearth for cooking, instead of the old brick hearth. The crew lived on board the *Exeter* hulk and was employed filling water casks for other ships. On 18 March, the ship was refloated and the crew began the tedious work of getting the stores and guns back in and re-rigging her. The mizzen yard was sent ashore to be shortened and the dockyard joiners came on board to fit a ventilator in the gunners' store-room, forward on the orlop deck. By the 28th, she was completed with twelve weeks provisions, and on 1 April 400 barrels of powder were taken on board, along with the rest of her sails, 164 tons of water and 140 tons of beer. She was now ready for sea, and the next day the pilot came on board, she slipped the bridles which attached her to a mooring buoy and sailed out to anchor at Spithead.

Meanwhile, the situation had changed again. Temple West, disgusted with the execution of Byng, had resigned his command and his seat on the Admiralty. The *Invincible* was placed under the command of Admiral Osborne, who was to sail out to the Mediterranean with a small squadron and take command of the ships already there. The ship also had another change of command. Her old friend John Bentley evidently wanted to return to his old ship of five years ago. He changed places with Stephen Colby so that the latter took command of the 90-gun *Barfleur*. Through no fault of his own, Colby's command had been undistinguished. Out of 130 days in the ship, he had spent one at sea. But on the whole, it had been quite a happy year for the *Invincible*.

8 Life on Board

Few subjects have more mythology and melodrama about them than life in the eighteenth-century navy. The *Invincible* can tell us much about this life, both from the written records of the ship and from the artefacts recovered from her. Although she was an exceptional ship in the sense that she had a greater historical influence than most, as far as the crew were concerned she was rather typical. The only difference in this respect was that her captains and admirals were often able and far-sighted men who can be assumed to have applied the latest ideas of crew organisation and hygiene. Boscawen, for example, experimented with ventilators and anti-scorbutics.

The most pervasive myth about the eighteenth-century navy is the press gang. Undoubtedly, impressment was a very unfair, inefficient and cruel system of conscription; but two points are worth bearing in mind. First, it applied only to seamen. Press gangs did not have the right to take up landsmen from the streets, and they had very little incentive for doing so for captains wanted trained seamen for their crews. Possibly there were cases where non-seamen were taken up by mistake and not released because they were too poor to use the legal system, or were eventually persuaded that they wanted to stay in the navy, but there is no real proof of this during the time when the *Invincible* was in service. Secondly, pressing took place as much at sea as on land. Buckle, for example, stopped several British merchant ships to take on men for the *Invincible*.

On arrival aboard his ship, the sailor, whether a pressed man or a volunteer, was given a rating by the first lieutenant on the authority of the captain. If he had little or no previous experience, he was rated landsman. If he had some experience, he was rated ordinary seaman. Typically, the holders of such low ratings were young men, often under 20 years, and hardly ever over 30. The able seaman was a fully experienced man, qualified to 'hand, reef and steer' – to bend the sails to the mast, to reef them to reduce sail area when necessary and to take his turn at the helm of the ship. He was paid £1 4s 0d per lunar month, compared with 19s for an ordinary seaman. For all of her career, more than half of the *Invincible*'s seamen were rated able or higher.

There was no naval uniform for common seamen, but aboard ship the men had to purchase their clothes from the purser and the choice of style would be very limited. After a time at sea, the crew would begin to take on a certain uniformity. Some captains tried to take this further and put pressure on men to buy clothes from the purser, while others fitted out the crews of the personal boats at their own expense. Captains sometimes tried to regulate a minimum amount of clothes for each man. A typical list of clothing was: 'Two blue outside jackets, two inside jackets, four shirts, one frock, two pairs of breeches and drawers, three pairs of white trousers, two pairs of shoes, three pairs of stockings, two hats or Dutch caps, one black silk handkerchief'.[1] But probably not all seamen were so well provided for. Apart from his clothes, the seaman had little property. He had a bag to store his clothes, and at sea his shore-going articles were put in a sea-chest and stowed below. Since there was only one chest for every eight men, he could not have taken very much with him. More valuable articles could be left with the first lieutenant for safe keeping.

The seaman also had his bedding. When he came on board he was issued with a hammock, which consisted of 'two breadths of duck, and is $2\frac{1}{4}$ yards long, and is tabled round with a small line, and has 12 holes in each end'.[2] This was provided at government expense, but his bedding he had to buy from the purser, unless he brought some with him. This usually consisted of a mattress, a blanket, a coverlet and a 'bolster' or pillow. Around this time it was becoming common to wash hammocks regularly. The government still only provided one per man, but some ships had a surplus of about 10 per cent so that these could be issued to some of the men while their own ones were wet. Another practice, introduced in the last few years, was to rig hammock nettings along the gunwales of the ship. The hammocks were taken down in daytime, rolled up and stowed in the nettings to give the ship extra protection against small arms fire in action.

If there is one aspect of eighteenth-century naval life which seems intolerable to the modern mind, it is the overcrowding below decks, especially at night. The great majority of the *Invincible*'s seven hundred men lived on the lower gun-deck, a space 167 × 44ft. Not all that space was available, for it was shared with twenty-eight guns and there were gratings, hatches, ladders, capstans, pumps, the tiller and the manger; all of these reduced the space available to the seaman to sling his hammock. The men slept in regular rows and the berthing plan was drawn up by the first lieutenant. Each had a space about 6ft long and 14in wide. This sounds impossible, but it is attested by many good authorities. It was mitigated by the fact that while the ship was at sea, about half the men would be on duty at any given time. In harbour, where most ships of the line spent more than half their time, the overcrowding was barely tolerable.

On the same deck with me, when the crew was complete, slept between five and six hundred men; and the ports being necessarily closed from evening to morning, the heat, in this cavern of only six feet high, and so entirely filled with human bodies, was overpowering.[3]

Some men were slightly more privileged. The petty

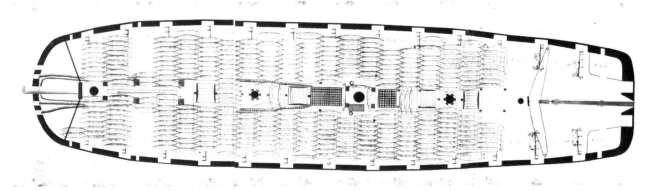

The hammock plan of a ship, c1755. It is possible that this ship is the Torbay, whose crew was transferred to the *Invincible* in 1756, which means that many of the men whose names are written on the hammocks later served in the *Invincible*. In particular, Mr Fordyce, in one of the stern cabins in this picture, may be the man who later served as chaplain of the *Invincible*

officers were allowed 28in and had their berths around the sides of the ship, although they must have been restricted by the guns and the knees which supported the deck. Sometimes they were allowed to hang canvas curtains to give an element of privacy, but it is not likely that Boscawen, for example, would have encouraged that. The most senior petty officers, the armourer and the master at arms, had cots rather than hammocks, although they still hung them on the gun-deck. Some of the seamen and most of the ship's boys were berthed one deck below, in the cable tier. This was apparently regarded as a privilege, perhaps because there was less disturbance during the day.

At sea in home waters, the sailor's diet was carefully regulated. Each day he was allowed 1lb of ship's biscuit. On Tuesdays and Saturdays he had 2lb of salt beef, on Sundays and Thursdays, 1lb of salt pork. On the remaining three days he had 4oz of cheese. He had $\frac{1}{2}$pt of peas for four days a week, 1pt of oatmeal on three days and 2oz of butter on four days. There was a distinct shortage of fresh vegetables and this was the main cause of scurvy. In port the ship was 'in petty warrant' and fresh provisions were supplied from the shore, often including some fresh vegetables, but only if the purser found them cheaply enough or the captain insisted on improving the health of his crew. On foreign stations, local items were often substituted. If food was short and the crew could not be issued full rations, they were given money in compensation.

The food was prepared by the ship's cook. He was technically a warrant officer, which merely meant that he was appointed by Navy Board warrant rather than at the whim of the captain. He was invariably a disabled seaman who had lost a limb in the service of the crown and been given 'an easy berth and sure bread for life' in compensation.[4] His culinary abilities were very slight for he had no training of any kind, and his equipment was little better. The galley stove was situated forward on the upper deck, under the forecastle. Until the late 1750s it usually consisted of a pair of round copper containers built into a brick hearth. The *Invincible* was given her iron firehearth in 1756, slightly earlier than the majority of ships. It was rescued from the ship soon after she was wrecked

in 1758. It contained a copper 'double kettle', with two cuboid compartments. It also included an oven, grill and a spit, but these were reserved for the officers' cooks who had no connection with the ship's cook. The latter used only the kettles and the meat was invariably boiled.

There were numerous complaints about the quality of the provisions and the corruption in the yards which caused it. In 1761 a former employee of the victualling board wrote of

the bread so full of large black-headed maggots that the men have so nauseated the thoughts of it as to be obliged to shut their eyes to confine that sense from being offended before they could bring their minds into the resolution of consuming it.

He also claimed that the men sometimes made trouser buttons out of the cheese issued to them, it being too hard for anything else.[5] Undoubtedly some of this was exaggerated, but no one ever praised naval food.

Simon Aked, Arthur Mack and John Bingeman demonstrate the use of some of the artefacts associated with eating and drinking, at one of the mess tables in the *Victory*

For eating, the seamen divided themselves into messes of about eight. Although a seaman did not have the right to choose whether he was in the navy or not, or to select his working companions aboard ship, he did at least have the right to choose his mess mates, subject to certain rules. The core of a mess was the table, usually slung between two guns on the lower deck. Benches were provided on each side of it for the men to sit on. Simple mathematics will show that not all the men could be accommodated at the tables between the lower-deck guns; at most, 26 such places were available, and this would allow for only 208 men. Perhaps the men ate by watch, but it is more likely that extra tables were erected inboard of the guns.

Cutlery and plates were kept in a rack against the side of the ship. Much of that recovered from the *Invincible* was government property and was marked with the broad arrow. Others had men's initials carved on them and were private property. The mess was the centre of the social life of the crew, and to have a congenial set of mess mates was the aim of every normal seaman. One man was appointed cook of the mess. Each morning he had to go below to the orlop to get the food for his mess, issued by the purser's steward. The cook of the mess took it up to the ship's cook who marked it and put it into his kettle for boiling. When mealtime came, the cook of each mess collected the food and the ship's cook marked off each mess with a pin as the food was issued.

For drink, the seaman relied almost entirely on alcoholic beverages. Tea was still a luxury in the mid-eighteenth century and plain water, after many weeks in the cask, was likely to be unpleasant. Rum was still largely confined to the West Indies during the *Invincible*'s career and there is no sign that it was ever issued to her. The staple drink of seamen in home waters was beer, at the rate of a gallon a day. That issued at Plymouth was notoriously bad, as Boscawen and other officers often remarked. The *Invincible* got most of hers from Portsmouth and there seem to have been no complaints about it. When the beer ran out, the men were issued with wine or brandy diluted with water.

At sea the work was hard and the hours were long, but some time was found for recreation, at sea and in harbour. A checker board has been found aboard the wreck, so it is quite likely that the men amused themselves with games of draughts. Dancing to the ship's fiddler was popular and in the *Torbay* the year before he hoisted his flag in the *Invincible*, Boscawen wrote to his wife:

Our men are very merry, we have most excellent dancers, but alas the fiddler was in a scrape and was whipped. But he has since played; they sometimes dance to the fife and drum and fiddle together, so well that you and I could dance country dances.[6]

But of course seamen liked the company of women, and officially this was not available at sea. According to the Admiralty regulations, the captain was 'not to carry any women to sea . . . without orders from the Admiralty'. No such orders were ever issued for the *Invincible*, except when she served as a troop ship, and there is no mention of women in logs or letters. However, women's shoes have been found aboard the wreck. Possibly a few women, perhaps

officers' or warrant officers' wives, were being carried unofficially; or perhaps the ship was merely carrying supplies for the families of some of the military officers going to North America.

In port it was a different story. Shore leave was rare and women were allowed to come to the ship. The regulations demanded

That no women be ever permitted to be on board, but such as are really the wives of the men they come to; and the ship be not too much pestered even with them. But this indulgence is only tolerated when the ship is in port, and not under sailing orders.

There is no doubt that this rule was often broken and only the strictest moralists even tried to apply it. The surgeon of the *Magnanime* reported that at one stage in 1756 there were 492 women on board for 750 men, and

A seamen of the 1740s says goodbye to his girl-friend aboard ship. Note the hammock and gun in the background

all declared themselves married women, and were acknowledged by the sailors as their wives, where or when they were married was never enquired, the simple declaration was considered sufficient to constitute a nautical and temporary union, and which was authorised by long established custom as practised time immemorial in His Majesty's Navy.[7]

The high rates of venereal disease, even when the

seamen had been aboard for some considerable time, suggest that not all of them conformed to the rules of marital fidelity.

The sanitary and hygienic arrangements of an eighteenth-century warship appear revolting to the modern mind, and they contributed much to the high death rate from disease. Washing of clothes and person was probably not common among the seamen, whether on board ship or on land. Some of the more far-sighted officers, and this must include most of the *Invincible*'s captains, were beginning to change this and ensure that the men kept themselves clean. In 1755 Admiral Smith had issued orders 'For the more effectual keeping clean the men belonging to His Majesty's ship under your command.'[8] Under Anson the Admiralty was beginning to take notice, and an amendment to the Admiralty instructions, issued in 1747, referred to 'Cleanliness being of great consequence to the health of the men'. 'All men on board', were to 'constantly keep themselves as clean in every respect as possible.'[9] But as yet ships had no real provision for washing, except that water could be pumped aboard and put in tubs, while on certain days of the week clothes and hammocks could be hung from the rigging to dry. There are signs that captains who tried to make seamen wash themselves encountered resentment from the crew who regarded it as an infringement of their liberty.

In theory, the disposal of waste was quite easy at sea for it could simply be dropped over the side. 'Seats of easement' were provided in the heads of the ship, and these overhung the water so that human waste could fall straight down. Judging by the fittings on contemporary ship models, there never seem to have been enough of these for a crew of seven hundred men. Seamen could urinate into a lead cistern fixed to the side of the ship on the upper deck, with a pipe leading out through the side. One of these has been recovered from the wreck. Possibly buckets were provided about the decks for immediate use. But another of the regulations of 1747 suggests that this was still not enough. Captains were ordered 'that all necessary precautions be used, by placing proper sentinels or otherwise, to prevent people easing themselves in the hold or throwing anything that may occasion nastiness'.

The ship's soldiers, whether marines proper or merely ordinary soldiers sent aboard from the army, shared much of the life of the seamen, slinging hammocks and eating at mess tables. Since part of their function was to operate as a force which could be used against a mutiny, steps were taken to keep them socially separate from the seamen. They slung their hammocks aft on the lower deck, traditionally so that they would be between the seamen and the officers in case of trouble. They were not allowed to sit at the same mess tables as seamen.

Marines did not always wear uniform, for only a small number, about thirty, were required to carry out sentry duties in rotation. The rest carried out routine duties aboard ship, such as hauling on ropes and maintenance, although they could not be forced to go aloft. Full military uniform was too expensive and restrictive for this, so most of the red jackets and grenadier caps were locked up in the marines' clothing room on the orlop deck, in bundles marked with the name of the wearer. The men were given a much simpler dress for working wear.

The life of the ordinary seaman was as basic and as rough as we can imagine. Above him stretched a hierarchy of different grades of officers and petty officers who enjoyed more privileges according to rank. The petty officers, as we have seen, were not far separated from the common seamen, and enjoyed only higher pay and slightly more space to sling their hammocks. 'Servants' were an amorphous group, reflecting the ambiguity of the term in the eighteenth century – it could mean a domestic servant, or an apprentice, or merely an employee, and all these groups were represented on board. Each warrant and junior commissioned officer had his own servant, and these were usually boys who carried out domestic duties. The captain of a third rate was allowed four servants for every hundred men in the complement, which meant that the captain of the *Invincible* was entitled to twenty-eight servants. Obviously, he did not need all these men and boys to clean his cabin, cook his food and prepare his clothes. Most of his servants were, in fact, young trainee officers, serving the three years they had to do at sea before being rated as midshipmen.

Previously, flagships had been clogged up with servants' cabins, but these were largely abolished under the influence of Anson and Boscawen. No special arrangements were made for accommodation of domestics, although it is possible that the captain could have found space for his own steward and cook in his cabin. The ship's boys who made up the rest of the officers' servants were usually put in the cable tier, and thus separated from the mass of seamen. Those among the captain's servants who were really trainee officers, lived in the gunroom, aft on the gun-deck, and again they were separated from the rest of the crew.

The cockpit, aft on the orlop deck and well below the water-line, was the berth for the midshipmen, master's mates and surgeon's mates. These men, mostly quite young, were the most junior warrant officers, but they were generally expected to rise in the service, and they had one important social privilege – they were allowed to take their recreation on the quarterdeck where only those who were socially acceptable were allowed to promenade. Their berth in the cockpit was less desirable. It was, according to a surgeon's mate of the period, 'a dungeon ... where the sun never shines', and where he 'almost desired the windows to be opened for daylight and fresh air'.[10] The area used by the midshipmen and their associates was a space in the middle of the deck, between the various cabins and store-rooms situated there. It had no particular amenities, and its denizens merely slung their hammocks and erected a table for their meals.

The standing officers were socially inferior to the

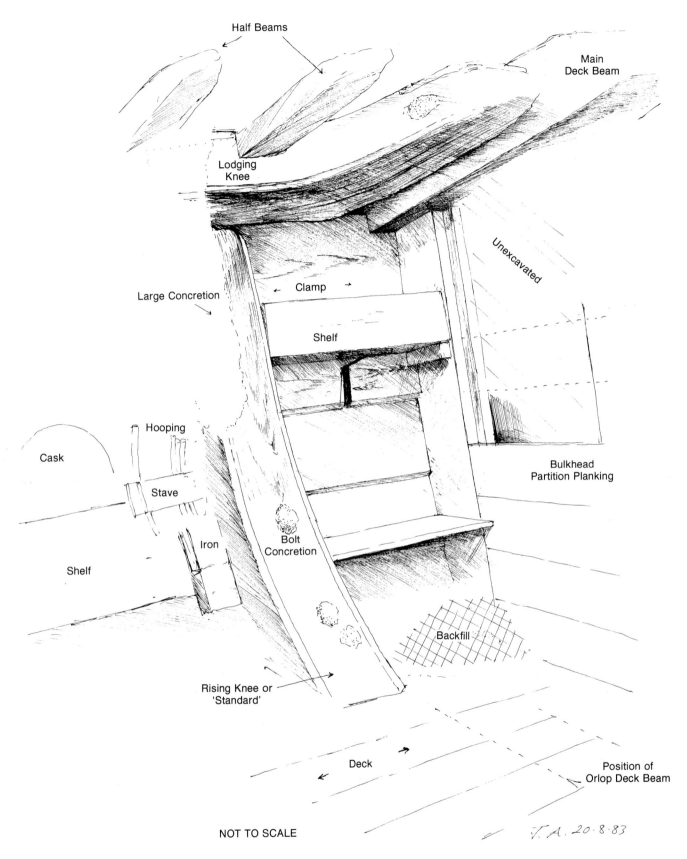

A drawing of the orlop deck of the *Invincible*, made in situ by Jon Adams. It was later found that some of the knees were iron, covered with a wood casing

occupants of the cockpit, but they were older, more experienced and had much greater responsibility. Each had a cabin of his own. The boatswain and carpenter were quite privileged in that they had semi-permanent cabins, 'put up with deal panels to slide in grooves, with battens on the deck instead of cants, to be taken down in a moment'.[11] These were placed under the forecastle. The gunner had one in the gunroom, aft on the gun-deck. It is not clear what eating arrangements they had. Presumably they ate the same food as the seamen and messed in their separate cabins. The ship's cook, although considerably junior to the other three standing officers in both pay and responsibility, also had his own cabin, near the cook-room.

Above them was a group of officers who had both social status and real responsibility. It included the naval lieutenants, the commissioned marine officers and the heads of certain specialised departments, the surgeon, purser, chaplain and master. Only the naval lieutenants and the marine officers actually held the king's commission, and the others were warrant officers in that they held their rank by virtue of a warrant from the Navy Board. There was no great gulf between the two groups in the eighteenth century, and surgeons, chaplains and pursers were able to live and eat with commissioned officers. On a third rate like the *Invincible*, the master, although junior in formal rank, actually had more pay than any of the lieutenants and more responsibility than any but the first.

This group of officers eventually got together and organised themselves into the wardroom. The origins of the term are obscure and contradictory, some holding that it was a room for storing valuable articles taken from prizes, others that it was used by the watch officers. It had appeared on three-deckers by the 1690s, as a room for the 'volunteers and land officers' who were numerous on a flagship of those days. Its use on a two-decker was quite recent, but it is mentioned in orders of 1745. The wardroom took up all of the upper deck from the mizzen-mast aft. It had a row of stern windows, but unlike the captain's cabin above, it had no open gallery. It had a quarter gallery on each side, used as toilet facilities for the officers. It was furnished with a table and enough chairs for its occupants and an enclosed pantry for the wardroom steward.

It is not likely that the wardroom was subdivided into separate cabins for the officers. The orders of 1745 allowed no permanent cabins above the gun-deck except for the boatswain, carpenter and captain. The other officers were permitted 'double hammocks and canvas curtains properly contrived to fall before them in the wardroom'. We can be certain that Boscawen would have enforced this. Of his previous ship the *Torbay* he had written:

All the officers swung in hanging cots and were stowed with conveniency. After I left the ship Captain Keppel permitted canvas cabins to be built, which I suppose remain, and prevent the stowing of the officers as well as if there were none . . . I never permit . . . standing cabins. In the *Dreadnought* in 1744, cruising to the westward in thick weather, I fell in with 13 sail of the enemy's ships, and taking down the officers' cabins to clear ship and bring the stern chase to bear upon the enemy, I found much bottled liquor, which being directed to be thrown overboard, much of it was drunk by the seamen, that when I was engaged soon after were so drunk as not to be able to do their duty.[12]

The rules were reinforced by orders of 1757, in which the wardroom was to be

parted off by a bulkhead across the ship, either just before or just abaft the mizzen mast as the ports will best admit, and from thence to the stern on each side (for three or four berths) by canvas hanging loosely before it like a curtain, or laced above and below with a parting in the middle of each berth to go in and out, and to roll up in the daytime when not wanted.[13]

Obviously there was not enough room for all the wardroom officers to sleep there and cabins were provided elsewhere in the ship. The surgeon and the purser lived on the orlop deck, near their respective stores. Four other cabins were provided aft on the gun-deck in the limited space left by the movement of the tiller. One of these was taken by the gunner himself and the other three by the junior wardroom officers. Such a cabin is described by a marine officer in 1755 as 'a place between two guns, about seven feet long and four feet wide, and divided only from some hundred hammocks, by a little canvas or an old sail, where there is no light, nor no air but what is unavoidably very foul'.[14] This cabin differed from those in the wardroom in that it was placed between two guns. Those above would be slightly larger, but the gun would actually be enclosed in the cabin, except for the two aftermost cabins which were reserved for the first lieutenant and the master.

The officers' furniture was sparse. The double hammock, as described in the regulations, was slightly wider than that issued to the men, and it had two clews at each end so that it was tied to four hooks and was spread rather more than the common hammock. Many officers used cots instead. These were made of canvas stretched on a wooden frame and were hung from the deckhead. Probably officers found room for a tiny table, a chest of drawers or a sea-chest. The first lieutenant was given more space than the others and his cabin opened directly on to the quarter, unless the ship was serving as a flagship, in which case the captain would take over that cabin and perhaps the one next to it.

The officers were entitled to the same food as the men, but it is not likely that they ate it. In general they would club together to buy a stock of fresh food which might well include live animals. Sheep, pigs and even cows were usually accommodated under the forecastle in ships of this period, while the Admiralty allowed hen coops to be placed on the quarterdeck so that a supply of fresh eggs was available. Other items were stored in the pantry which was separated from the wardroom, or in the lieutenants' store-room on the orlop deck. Much of the equipment and food had to be thrown over the side in time of battle. The *Bristol*, which was one of the last ships in the British line at Finisterre, 'sailed through vast quantities of chests, hen coops, sheep pens and lumber of all kinds from both fleets'.[15]

The wardroom food was prepared by the wardroom steward who used the more sophisticated part of the fire-hearth, equipped with an oven, a grill and a spit. Each wardroom officer had his own servant who would clean his room and his clothes and wait at

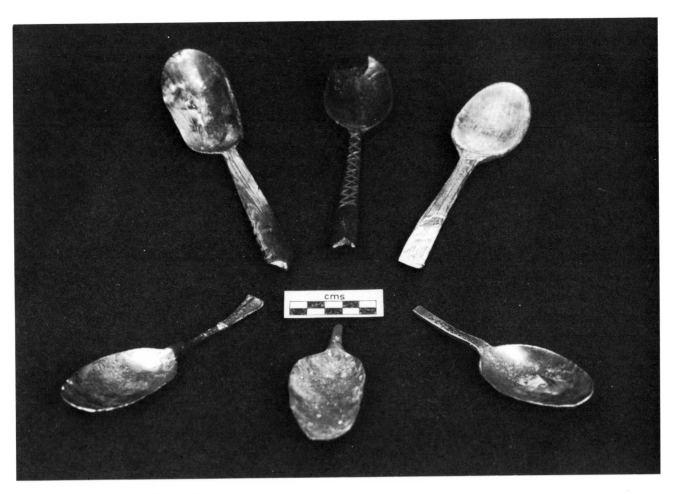

A selection of spoons from the wreck

table. Most of them were boys, but some, like Captain Bentley, rose eventually to high rank.

The wardroom was the centre of the officers' social life. They sometimes had the opportunity of good wine, as when the *Invincible* visited Madeira or when the fleet captured the French wine ships in 1756. They played games and backgammon seems to have been popular at this time. Lasting friendships could often be struck up between wardroom officers, but a dozen men of different backgrounds and experiences were cooped up together for months at a time and almost every account of wardroom life records tension between the occupants. A lieutenant commented:

> The master, though only a warrant officer, from his sometimes being allowed to take a watch, and put the ship about, is apt to give himself airs of consequence, and frequently has the astonishing impudence to consider himself your equal.[16]

A chaplain wrote:

> as yet designedly omitted to mention our second lieutenant of the ship; we disliked each other, I believe, mutually; at least I greatly disliked him, and those feelings are generally reciprocal.[17]

A surgeon commented:

> I have often compared the many feuds and jealousies which occur in many ships as a good picture in miniature of what is experienced on a larger scale in the courts and palaces of princes.[18]

Unlike the seamen, the wardroom officers did not have the opportunity to change mess if they did not get on with their companions.

The great cabin was on the quarterdeck, roofed over by the poop deck. It had a stern gallery, so the occupant could walk or sit in privacy in the open air. On a French ship it had no guns, although there is inconclusive evidence that gun-ports were fitted to the *Invincible*'s great cabin during her great repair. That of the *Invincible* seems to have had no quarter galleries, unless they were fitted during the great repair. The great cabin was about as long as the wardroom, but only about two-thirds of the width because of the tumble home of the hull. But, unlike the wardroom, it only had a single occupant with perhaps some of his servants and staff. It was reserved for the use of the captain or for the admiral when the ship was serving as a flagship.

The great cabin was partitioned off from the rest of the ship by 'frames of deal with slit deal panels, wrought strong, light and plain', and 'fitted in such a manner that they may be be taken down or disposed of out of the way of fighting the guns'.[19] The captain's privacy and security was maintained by

Part of a gaming board from the wreck

placing a marine sentry at the door. Because it was on the quarterdeck, the captain could be called quickly to the steering position when necessary and he had some view of what was going on through the glass in the bulkhead. Forward of the captain's cabin were placed two small cabins which were used as offices rather than for living in. On one side was the captain's clerk and on the other was the master. Since the latter already had a cabin in the wardroom, it was presumably used as a chart-room.

The great cabin was divided internally. The aftermost partition separated the cabin from the stern gallery, and was known as the screen bulkhead. The open gallery was about 6ft wide, about half of that width being under the taffrail and therefore somewhat sheltered. Within the enclosed part of the cabin, a bulkhead ran athwartships about two-thirds of the way forward. This created the great cabin proper, where the captain conducted most of his business and took his recreation. It would be used for conferences with his subordinates, for office work and possibly for trying minor offenders, so in a sense it was not the captain's exclusive preserve. He would certainly use it for dining, especially on the occasions when he invited his officers to his table. It would be furnished according to his pocket and his taste. Boscawen believed in the spartan life for others, but it took five hours to transfer his goods and papers from the *Invincible* to the *Royal George*, so it is not unlikely that he had a substantial amount of furniture.

The other part of the captain's accommodation was traditionally called the steerage and was forward of the great cabin. Usually it was divided by a fore and aft partition, with the captain's bedplace on one side.

The other formed a lobby and allowed visitors to enter the great cabin without passing through the bedplace. It is possible that visitors who did not merit the courtesy of the great cabin were received there. The captain was issued with a 'standing bed', which seems to have been similar to a normal bedstead; but at sea he may well have found a hammock or swinging cot more comfortable.

The captain or admiral had a large personal staff. Not all the twenty-eight servants allowed to the captain of the *Invincible* would really be domestics, but undoubtedly some were. A well-established officer would have a considerable following, which would include a cook and a valet, and he would also have a coxswain and crew for his barge; these would often follow him from one ship to another. A more junior captain like Lloyd could take only eight men with him to his new ship, so he would have had to find his personal servants among the crew allocated to him.

The social divisions aboard ship were immense, but they reflected naval rank as much as social class. In the allocation of living space, the gulf between a lieutenant and a captain was as wide as that between the lieutenant and a common seaman; but the lieutenant was often of quite high social rank. Other officers, such as the surgeon and chaplain, were undoubtedly of middle-class status, while some, like the master, had often begun as common seamen. On the other hand, many men of quite humble background rose to become captains and admirals. Bentley of the *Invincible* was such a case. The navy of the mid-eighteenth century was a 'career open to the talents' as much as anything in contemporary Europe.

Within this, the captain was well provided for aboard ship and took up as much space as about 130 seamen. But he had immense responsibilities, and an admiral like Boscawen, in command of the Western Squadron, had perhaps the most important job in the country.

9 The Voyage to Louisbourg

The *Invincible* did not go to the Mediterranean in 1757 as originally planned. On 29 April, as Captain Bentley was reading his commission to the crew, the Admiralty decided that it was more urgent to reinforce Admiral Holbourne's squadron which had been sent to North America. The *Trident* and *Revenge* were to take the place of the *Invincible* and *Nassau*, and the latter ships were to join with the *Defiance* and sail to find Holbourne. Captain Hervey of the *Hampton Court* considered this an

Admiral Holbourne, who had the *Invincible* under his command several times during her career

absurdity in the Admiralty proceedings. No sooner was Holbourne gone with ten sail than they order away the *Invincible, Nassau* and *Defiance* to sail immediately after him, which were only three or four days before us and much too late to overtake him, so that they risked these three ships falling into enemy hands.[1]

Hervey was wrong. Holbourne had put into Cork to pick up seven regiments for the expedition and had been informed that the three ships were on the way. They had sailed on 3 May and arrived at Cork on the 7th. On the way into Cork Harbour the *Invincible* was run aground 'by the ignorance of the pilot'. This happened at half-past noon and several boats came

out to the ship, one bearing the admiral himself. Topmasts were got down and anchors were laid out ready to haul her off as soon as the tide rose. She was floated off by 3.30 pm and, according to Holbourne, 'The water being very smooth, we think she has received no damage, and is now in a good berth.'[2] She joined Holbourne's fleet, which now consisted of fourteen men-of-war and nearly eighty transports.

During her brief stay at Cork four men deserted the ship by jumping over the side and swimming for the shore. Bentley sent out detailed descriptions of them in the forlorn hope that they might be apprehended later. They included William Halthorn, 26 years old, 5ft 5in tall, of fair complexion, of King Edwards Stairs, Wapping, London, who had a 'Smooth face with a small scar on the right side of the forehead; wears a wig.' Patrick Collins of Dublin was a year older and also wore a wig (as did six of the seven seamen who deserted the ship that year). He was 'marked with the smallpox', and was 5ft 4in tall. Joseph O'Brien was also from Dublin, the same age, 5ft 7in tall, and had a 'pale face slightly marked with the smallpox'. Samuel Allcock of Ipswich was 26, with a 'thin smooth face'.[3]

Holbourne's force was intended to recapture the French fortress of Louisbourg. According to his orders,

Wheras we are determined, with the assistance of divine providence, to attempt the reduction of Louisbourg in the Island of Cape Breton, and, with the blessing of God upon our arms, to proceed from thence to the attack on Quebec, the capital of Canada, you are, as far as you shall be able with the fleet under your command, to be aiding and assisting the Earl of Loudon in the performance of the service aforesaid.[4]

Louisbourg had already been captured by Admiral Warren in 1745, but handed back at the subsequent peace treaty. It was situated on Cape Breton Island and dominated the Cabot Strait, between Nova Scotia and Newfoundland. Thus it controlled the main entrance to the St Lawrence river. The fortress was placed at the mouth of a large and deep natural harbour, which was known to contain French ships of the line. While they held Louisbourg, the French could prevent any attack up the St Lawrence towards Quebec, the capital of French Canada. Holbourne was to carry eight thousand troops with him, and these were to join with others under the Earl of Loudon, the army commander.

Holbourne was already behind schedule. The French bases could not be used in winter because they iced up. The ideal time to begin a campaign would be in the early spring, before the French had time to send out their fleet and British troops who had wintered in the area could have been used. British ships could use their bases at Halifax or Boston

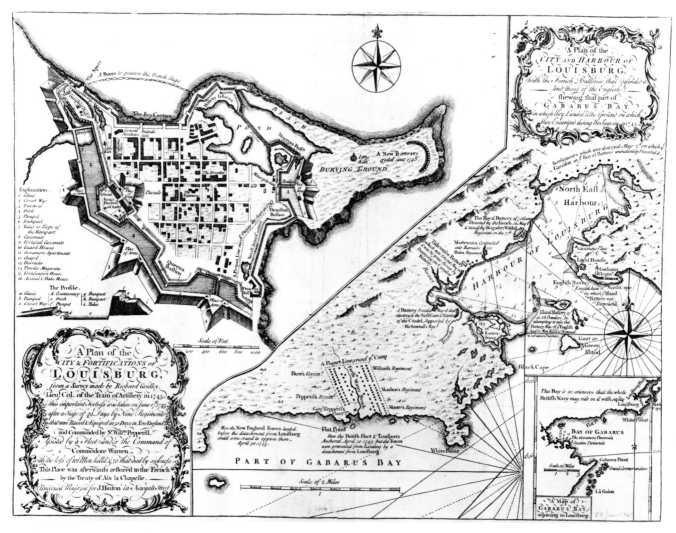

The French fortress of Louisbourg

throughout the winter and thus get into action much quicker than the French. Furthermore, hurricanes were not unknown in the Louisbourg area and tended to reach their maximum frequency around September. It was important that the operation be completed before then. Problems had begun months before, when his vast fleet was assembling off Portsmouth. Numerous minor items – medical supplies and tents, for example – had been delayed and some army officers were late in joining their regiments. The scale of the operation was beyond Holbourne for in early March he found 'the ships lying so thick at Spithead and Mother Bank, East and West India convoy and ours mixed together, being I believe above 200 sail, besides men-of-war'.[5] Such a quantity of ships made him cautious, for 'there is no turning such a convoy loose without a fair wind. It's inclining northerly won't let us get hold of the coast of Ireland.' He had arrived at Cork on 25 April and spent two weeks there, partly to wait for the *Invincible* and her consorts. As he left Cork on 8 May, he was already losing confidence in the success of his mission.

As the *Invincible* sailed out of European waters for the first time under the union flag, she was leaving a country in political turmoil. The shock-waves of the loss of Minorca were still being felt and they had brought down the government in November. It is impossible to sort out exactly who was responsible for the débâcle, but in the recriminations Anson, too, had lost his place at the Admiralty, and perhaps for once he was at fault. If he had a weakness, it was political rather than naval. In running his own department he was possibly the best First Lord of the Admiralty the country had ever had, but his scope did not extend beyond that. He is not known to have spoken in parliament, and his role in cabinet was purely departmental. He was not good at fighting his case for more money for the navy, and during his peacetime administration the fleet had fallen to the very low level of eight thousand men. In strategy, too, he was often overruled. If he had persuaded the cabinet to send a stronger fleet to Minorca, or at least to appoint a more efficient admiral and given him a clearer set of instructions, defeat might have been avoided. But the job of the Admiralty was to provide the ships and men. Decisions on higher strategy were taken by the cabinet as a whole. Anson had no great voice there and the Prime Minister, the Duke of Newcastle, was too concerned with petty economies and with the distribution of political favours to see any broader picture. Thus the government had blundered and fallen.

Their successors were not significantly better. They included the great William Pitt as Secretary of

State, and he was one man who had the strategical vision to win the war, but he was in a weak position. The First Lord of the Treasury, the Duke of Devonshire, was not a man of any distinction. The Admiralty was headed in succession by Earl Temple and the Earl of Nottingham, but neither had stayed long enough to settle in to the department. Boscawen was retained on the board, but he was not the senior naval lord and he was at sea for much of the time. There was much confusion in the department, as is shown by the succession of orders to the *Invincible* and by the inefficiencies in organising Holbourne's fleet. The government as a whole was politically weak, having the full support of neither the king nor the House of Commons. A victory was desperately needed, but already the attack on Louisbourg was looking unlikely to succeed.

The fleet inched its way towards North America. On 25 May it was becalmed north-east of the Azores and the *Invincible* had to hoist out her boats to tow clear some transports which were in danger of drifting into her. On 3 June the *Invincible*'s tiller broke. She had to heave to for a time, while the remnants of the old one were taken out of the tenon in the rudder and a spare one put in. On the 6th Holbourne wrote:

> We are so far in our way, having been very unlucky in winds for a long time, now 15 days, since we came the length of the western islands, very thick hazy blowing weather, which I have endeavoured to get to the southward and out of, but we have never been able to get more than 43 degrees north.[6]

On the 28th the *Bedford* was in even worse trouble when her mainmast was carried away. By that time the fleet was encountering the fogs of the Newfoundland Banks and getting close to its destination. On 5 July, the Halifax pilots carried aboard the flagship were distributed to the major ships, but it was the 9th before they anchored outside Halifax Harbour. Two days later the wind carried them into the harbour itself, after a voyage of more than two months.

The fleet remained there for five weeks, taking on stores, exercising the troops and repairing the ships. It joined with Sir Charles Hardy's squadron and he hoisted his flag on board the *Invincible* as second in command of the fleet. By this time Holbourne had so lost confidence that he wrote to the Admiralty expressing his fears that the French were too strong and the season too late for him to succeed. Nevertheless, having come all this way he had to make some attempt and on 1 August the fleet was ready to sail. Then he received news which discouraged him further. The French at Louisbourg were considerably stronger than supposed. They had 6,000 European troops, 3,000 colonials and 300 Indians. Their storehouses and armouries were well stocked. Even worse, from Holbourne's point of view, their fleet was far stronger than the seven ships he had expected. At Louisbourg the French had 17 ships of the line, including 5 new 74s, and 6 frigates. This compared

with Holbourne's own force of 16 ships of the line, 5 frigates and 6 sloops.

A British admiral was expected to face such odds in a fleet battle, but not while tied down by the need to protect a helpless convoy of 100 ships and 11,000 men. He anchored at St George's Island and called the senior army and navy officers to a council of war. Like all such councils, they decided on caution. The transports were to be sent back, but the fleet was to continue on station in order to blockade Louisbourg and prevent the ships there from damaging British interests in North America. On the afternoon of the 16th the two forces parted company. Most of the frigates were sent away with the transports, while the sloops continued with the ships of the line and the main fleet.

On the afternoon of 19 August, the fleet sighted Louisbourg through gaps in the fog. The following day it formed a line of battle and stood in closer. From 5 miles out they could see the enemy clearly and confirmed the reports of his strength. They 'saw in harbour a vice admiral and a rear ditto. In all 21 sail, 17 of which we take to be line of battle ships. The French admiral made several signals.'[7] This was taken by some as a sign that the French were getting ready to unmoor. Holbourne called the other two flag officers on board his ship, and 'they agreed with me that it was not advisable to continue cruising off the port of Louisbourg, as the squadron would be thereby exposed to the risk of separation in the fogs so frequent on this coast'. He led the fleet away to the eastward.

He tried to find an anchorage near to Louisbourg which could serve as a base for his blockade. On the 24th the squadron arrived at Chedabucta Bay, near the Island of Torbay. But again caution prevailed. Pilots were sent in to survey the bay, and it 'was found to be very rocky, and open to southerly winds, which made it unsafe for the ships to ride in; beside that whilst we are embayed there, the enemy might pass us to the westward. For these reasons the rendezvous was changed to Halifax.'[8] The fleet went to that port immediately, but once there the onshore wind prevented the ships from leaving and they were obliged to stay. The squadron remained for more than a fortnight, completing its water and carrying out minor repairs. Holbourne had asked for the co-operation of the colonial authorities in finding men, but it was not forthcoming. He made himself unpopular by pressing local seamen. Sixty-eight pressed men were put aboard the *Invincible* on the 7th for she was now short of crew. Her men were not healthy, and twenty-one had been put ashore sick on arrival at Halifax. Deaths from disease were quite common on this cruise and, during the two weeks in port, two men died. Morale seems have been suffering and floggings became more regular. On 31 August, for example, a seaman and a marine were flogged for mutiny.

Holbourne sailed again on 9 September and the squadron soon ran into difficulties. The faint land breeze failed and the ships had to anchor again. He

The mouth of the St Lawrence river, showing the importance of Louisbourg, and the *Invincible*'s area of operations

tried again on the 10th, but the breeze did not last long enough to get the ships out of harbour. They had to anchor to prevent being driven on to rocks. At last, on the morning of the 11th, the *Invincible* 'Weighed per order and came to sail, as did the fleet, consisting of 18 sail of the line, three frigates and a fireship.'[9] For once Holbourne took the daring approach and set sail against the advice of the pilots. By the 16th the fleet was off Louisbourg again and the look-outs counted twenty-three ships in the harbour. There it remained for eight days, mostly in fog and light winds.

Sunday, 24 September began as an ordinary day on blockade service. The ships spent much of their time hove to, with their sails arranged so that some were filling and some backing so that they cancelled each other out, and the ship was almost stationary in the water. After daybreak the admiral ordered the ships to fill their sails, and they carried out a few manoeuvres, apparently to counteract any tendency to drift away from the station. They hove to again and, late in the morning, the admiral signalled the *Invincible* to come alongside and a boat was sent to the flagship to receive some routine message. By this time the weather was 'fresh gales and squally', but the term 'gale' was used rather liberally in those days and it was not strong enough to prevent boats being used. In the afternoon the fleet sailed again for a short time and fog fell around 2pm, so again the ships hove to.

By 5pm the wind was beginning to increase, but it was westerly and likely to drive the ships along the shore rather than into it, so there was no immediate cause for concern. The ships began their usual preparations for heavy weather. At 5.30pm, the

Invincible took down her topgallant masts and took in her topsails. The lower sails, the courses, were reefed to reduce sail area and she lay to in order to ride out the storm, as did the rest of the squadron.

By 8pm it 'came to blow very hard' and by midnight there were 'very hard gales and a large sea'. By 2am it 'blowed excessive hard, lost sight of the admiral'.[10] The squadron was separated in the storm and each ship had to look after itself. The crew of the *Invincible* took in the rest of their canvas – the courses were brailed up to the yard. It was still not enough and the wind pushed the ship over on her side so that she was 'on her beam ends'. The guns and every other movable object had already been lashed down. A gun breaking loose in these conditions would have allowed 3 tons of wood and metal to crash about the decks, destroying everything in its path – but fortunately everything held. In the hold all was not so well and several casks broke loose, smashing themselves against the ship's timbers and often damaging the structure in the process. Water was coming in on the lee side, through the gun-ports and perhaps even over the top of the gunwales. The seamen struggled to lower the main yard down to the deck, to reduce topweight and wind resistance, giving the ship a chance to right itself. But it was too late for that. The mainmast itself, 3ft in diameter, broke under the strain, 20ft above the deck. Its shrouds were ripped out and the mast fell over the side. The mizzen-mast, which was attached to it by means of forestays, went with it. Two seamen, John Guttridge and Samuel Kivby, were lost in the fall. By now the wind was southerly, blowing the ship directly on to the shore.

The only hope was to keep the foresail, allowing the ship some means of sailing when the wind moderated; but it would not hold for long with its topmast up. There was no time to begin the careful procedure of unrigging the topmast and lowering it carefully to deck – its shrouds were cut and it was probably struck a few times with an axe. In any case, it was cut away and allowed to fall over the side, thus saving the foremast. Other seamen hacked at the remaining shrouds, forestays and running rigging which still caused the broken main and mizzen to be dragged along behind the ship. By 7am it had been cut away.

Then came the next crisis: the tiller broke again, so the ship was out of control in the hurricane. Because there was no spare socket at the head of the rudder, the carpenter and his crew had to pull the remains of the old tiller from the tenon in the rudder head and put a new one in. This they did quite quickly, but it soon broke again and this time it took part of the rudder head with it. The carpenters improvised desperately, while the ship wallowed in the trough of the sea, shipping much water and straining her timbers. Hands worked continuously at the pumps and were replaced by others when totally exhausted – turning the handle on a chain pump was one of the most gruelling tasks a seaman had to perform and in normal times it was often used as a punishment. Others were employed on deck, and they cut away the

jib-boom and cast the foreyard overboard to reduce windage yet more.

At 11am the visibility began to clear, but it brought no comfort. Some of the other ships could be seen, with their masts standing, riding out the storm. By 11.30 the land was in sight, still some miles away, but the *Invincible* was being driven closer and could do little to stop herself. Close inshore were five more of the squadron, one completely dismasted, three with only their foremasts and one with her mainmast. They had dropped their anchors and were desperately hoping that they would hold; otherwise, they would be driven into the rocky coast of Cape Breton Island and destroyed. Four more ships could be seen further offshore with some control over their movements, but none had all her masts standing. The wind continued to blow towards the shore and Holbourne's squadron, including the *Invincible*, was in imminent danger of total destruction.

Just before midday, the wind changed. It moved from south-west to west and began to moderate slightly. The ships were no longer being driven ashore and there was some hope. It was time to set some sails and bring the ship under control. Improvising with what remnants of spars and canvas were left on board, a very strange jury-rig was put together. Having lost all the larger sails and yards, smaller ones were put in their places. A spare topgallant was used as a foresail, and a tarpaulin was hung from the shrouds to extend it. The longboat's mast was lashed to the stump of the mizzen-mast and the tiny sail from the boat was hung from it. The longboat itself was dropped over the side, having first been stove in to prevent it falling into enemy hands. The ship was still labouring much and taking in water. There was up to $4\frac{1}{2}$ft in the hold and the hands still had to man the pumps continually while the carpenters were attempting to repair the tiller. The other ships of the squadron were still in peril themselves and no help could be expected from them. But with some kind of sails rigged and a wind which was blowing her away from the shore, the greatest danger had passed by the afternoon of Sunday the 25th.

By 4pm the tiller had been repaired, mostly by lashing and nailing together the parts of the old one, for the spare ones had been used up already. The jury-rig was improved by setting a spare main topsail yard across the foremast and bending a fore topsail to it. A spare jib-boom was raised vertically and lashed to the stump of the mizzen to form a jury mizzen-mast. A mizzen-topsail was used as a sail. The spritsail yard was got in from its position out on the bowsprit and crossed on the stump of the mainmast, still 24ft above the deck; this served as a jury main yard. A reefed main topsail was hung from it. The longboat's sail was taken to the ensign staff at the extreme stern and rigged there. This work took all night and most of the next morning.

The admiral and the rest of the fleet was sighted about mid-morning. The *Invincible* made the signal of distress and fired a gun to draw attention to

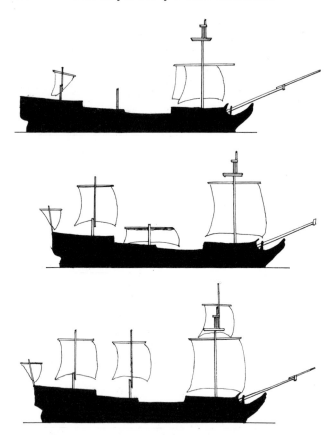

Jury rigs fitted to the *Invincible* after the hurricane

herself. At noon, the *Windsor*, one of the ships with all her masts standing, came up to her and took her in tow. By this time the wind was moderate.

It was now time to take stock of the damage. Nineteen masts and spars had been lost. The bowsprit was intact and the foremast was still standing, although it had been sprung and it had to be lashed and nailed up to keep it in place. Eleven sails had been lost over the side or blown out, and only the stock of spare sails was keeping the ship moving. The starboard main chains, which provided the anchorage for the shrouds which supported the mainmast, had been damaged when the mast fell, and several of the chain plates which were bolted to the side of the hull had been torn out. The fall of the mast had also damaged the side of the hull where it fell, on the starboard quarterdeck rail. Apart from the damage to the tiller and the head of the rudder, one of the pintles which formed part of its hinge was broken and another seriously damaged. The hull itself had been racked by the sea, and 'The gun-deck standards lifted in the toes near two inches, and [I] am of the opinion the bolts are broke. The upper deck worked much in the same manner'.[11]

The water had penetrated the magazine, leaving the ground tier of powder barrels underwater, although it did not enter the barrels themselves. The made-up cartridges, however, were ruined. Forty-one muskets, which had been kept ready in the tops, were washed away. 230 cartouche boxes and their ammunition had been kept ready on the poop for the use of the marines, and these had been lost, along with various small arms and edged weapons. The stores in

the hold had also been damaged. Various casks had been tossed about by the movement of the ship and had been destroyed, allowing the salt water to get at their contents. The food already in the galley, consisting of 268 pieces of pork and 146 pieces of beef, were lost, for the water had run clean through the galley. The plank of the platform in the bread-room, where a ready-use supply was kept, had collapsed, causing the loss of 396lb of biscuit and various other items. In the spirit-room in the hold, two casks of rum were lost by 'the perpetual rolling of the ship stoving in the heads, by which the stanchions were unshipped, and stove in the heads of the casks'.

The *Invincible* was towed back to the rest of the fleet at 8am on the 27th. She found that the other ships had suffered, too. Nine of them still had all their masts standing, although the flagship, the *Newark*, had cast some of her guns overboard to save herself and all had lost stores, sails, and in some cases men. Eight ships, including the *Invincible*, had some masts standing, but were seriously damaged. The *Grafton* and *Nassau* had lost all their masts. The *Cruizer* sloop 'was very near foundering, having been under water several times with the loss of his boats, guns and mizzen mast and everything above deck – and three men'.[12] And the *Tilbury* of 58 guns had been wrecked near Louisbourg, although some of her crew had been rescued by the garrison.

Clearly, there was no prospect of an attack on Louisbourg that year, and even a blockade was now impossible. Holbourne decided to send home his most damaged ships, including the *Invincible*. She was to go with the *Captain* and *Sunderland*, escorted by the *Windsor*, one of the least damaged ships. A few days were spent putting the jury-rigs in better order. The crew of the *Invincible* fitted a studding sail-boom as a jib-boom, and another to the stump of the mainmast so that a topgallant could be set on it to serve as a mainsail. A spare topmast was received from the *Lightning* and used for a fore-topmast. Its yard was a mizzen-topsail yard borrowed from the *Newark*. Yet another spare topmast was taken on board from the *Terrible*, and was eventually set up above the stump of the main to make a more solid jury-mainmast. Hardy transferred his flag to the *Windsor* and on the last day of September, according to the log, 'Half-past noon, bore away for England with the *Windsor*, Sir Charles Hardy, *Captain* and *Sunderland*, leaving behind Admiral Holbourne.'[13]

The voyage home was not without incident. On 18 October, 1,200 miles from Louisbourg, the ships became separated in a gale and the *Invincible* was alone for a fortnight. On the 28th she sighted a large ship ahead, coming towards her. The *Invincible* was cleared for action and the guns were got ready. The strange ship carried no colours, so as she came within about three-quarters of a mile of the *Invincible*, the latter ship hoisted her own colours and fired a shot at the stranger, which caused her to bear away. A few more shots were fired, but at such range they had little chance of hitting a mark. It was assumed that she was a French man-of-war and, if so, this was the

His MAJESTY'S SHIP *the* GRAFTON, Commodore CHARLES HOLMES, Commander, as she Sail'd to England with a Machine Constructed instead of her Rudder, which she lost in the late Storm off Louisbourgh. Drawn by an Officer on Board.

The *Grafton* under jury rig

Invincible's closest encounter with the enemy since she had been taken into the British navy. In her battered condition there was no chance of pursuing and the Frenchman showed no inclination for battle. Presumably, he had approached sufficiently close to see if it was one of his own ships in need of assistance, but did not attempt to engage his crippled enemy because he had orders to complete a more important mission.

Three days later, two more large ships were sighted, but they were correctly assumed to be the *Windsor* and *Sunderland*. On 3 November the look-outs at the mastheads could see the Scilly Isles. On the 4th several out-bound men-of-war were spoken to, and the ships witnessed a distant sea fight when three British frigates chased a French privateer, fired into her and captured her. The same afternoon, the English mainland was sighted. On the afternoon of 5 November, the *Windsor, Sunderland* and *Invincible* anchored at Spithead.

The *Invincible* was in a sad condition when she re-entered Portsmouth Harbour on the 9th. Apart from damage to her rigging and stores, her hull was now believed to be damaged, and Bentley had reported

'that his ship laboured so much in the last gale of wind in our passage that in our opinion has weakened her so much as to make it necessary to have her well examined by the shipwrights'.[14]

Her crew had also suffered. Only seven had deserted during the voyage, partly because opportunities had been few; but no less than forty-one had died from accident or disease. Two had been lost with the fall of the mast in the hurricane, but the rest had apparently perished from disease. The marines seem to have suffered the most, with 13 deaths, and only 62 of them were left, including officers. Despite the draft of pressed men in Halifax, the ship was 73 men short of her complement. She had only two weeks' supply of some provisions left on board, with 8 days' beer and 2 days' wine and brandy. She was, as the port admiral recorded in his returns to the Admiralty: 'Not fit for sea'.[15]

While she was away, the Admiralty had paid the *Invincible* her greatest compliment yet. It described her as 'in every respect the best ship of her class and answers all purposes that can be desired of a ship of war'. On 21 May it was ordered that two ships, to be called *Triumph* and *Valiant*, were to be built to her

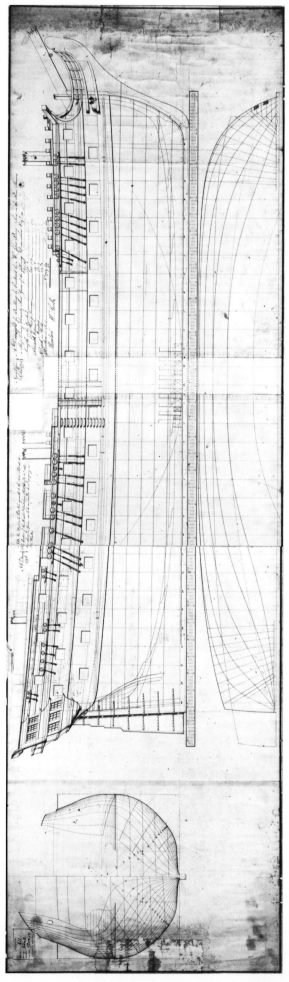

The draught for the *Kent* and the *Ajax*. These ships were built to the lines of the *Invincible* in the 1790s, but were lengthened by 11ft, as can be seen by the section drawn on lighter paper on the draught design.[16] This was done while Anson was not on the Admiralty board, but the order was signed by another admiral who knew the ship even better – Edward Boscawen. The new ships were considered a great success by some, and in 1801 John Charnock called the *Triumph* 'a ship which, for the space of more than twenty years, was considered the finest of her class then existing'.[17]

The *Invincible* was got ready for sea again, as quickly as circumstances permitted, for the government had resolved to renew the attack on Louisbourg as soon as possible, and to arrange for a fleet to get there early in the season. On 11 November, six days after their arrival, the Admiralty ordered that the ships of Holbourne's squadron be cleaned, graved, tallowed and stored 'with the utmost expedition'. Most of the repairs to her hull were carried out afloat and she was only docked for the minimum time, overnight on 27–28 November, to be graved and tallowed. Several specific points had to be dealt with, of which the most important was the rudder. With a certain amount of time in hand, it was decided to enlarge its head so that it could carry a larger tiller below the upper deck and to lengthen it so that it would protrude through the upper deck, where an iron tiller could be fitted in an emergency. This involved cutting a hole in the upper deck to allow the head of the rudder through. Since the rudder was constructed from several pieces of timber coaked together, it was decided to pull them apart and replace the central section, the 'main piece', which ran all the way from the foot to the head of the rudder. Thus some time and timber could be saved, but the rudder head could be both widened and lengthened.

Bentley wanted other changes. He asked for

preventer bolts to all the ports on the upper deck for the better security of the guns; the sweep of the tiller to be plated with iron; the mizzen topmast to be made 6 feet longer in the hoist; the yard to be 4 feet longer (the ship always requiring after sail); the jib and topmast staysails to be three cloths larger.[18]

All this was approved by the Admiralty and done. The ship sailed out of Portsmouth Harbour to Spithead on 24 December and began to take on stores. Manning was still a problem and on the first day of 1758 she was 94 men short. This was made good on the 10th when she received a draft of 50 seamen from the *Barfleur* and 2 officers, a sergeant, a corporal and 42 privates of General Cornwallis's regiment from the *Royal Anne*. These were not passengers, but were ordered to be borne as part of the complement to supplement the ship's marines. Since 1755 the marine regiments had been taken under Admiralty control, but evidently they had not yet raised enough men to supply all the needs.

The defects in fitting the *Invincible* had largely been remedied over the years. Rigging, rudders and hull fittings were now more suitable than they had ever been and she carried a very powerful armament, with 24 pounders on the upper deck. She was under the command of a very distinguished captain who loved and understood her. Her crew, though not all that might have been desired, was gaining in experience, and now carried a lower proportion of landsmen. In many respects she was in better shape than she had ever been, in French or British service.

Above her stretched a chain of command which would win the war against France. Holbourne had returned home and been appointed port admiral at Portsmouth. His place in command of the Louisbourg expedition was taken by one of the *Invincible*'s greatest supporters, Boscawen, with his flag in the *Namur*. Her most important supporter of all, Anson, was back at the head of the Admiralty, and now he was helped by a Navy Board which supported him in his efforts at reform rather than obstructing them. The war effort was directed by William Pitt the Elder, the greatest British war minister in all the long series of wars with France. He was in coalition with the Duke of Newcastle, who willingly undertook the detailed business of government and allowed Pitt to concentrate on wider matters.

Boscawen's squadron would go to capture Louisbourg without any difficulty. The way would be opened up for the fleet to go to Quebec and take it in 1759, destroying the French position in Canada. In the same year, the 'Year of Victories', the navy would win a battle at Lagos under Boscawen, and a greater one at Quiberon Bay under Hawke. The British would be left in control of the seas as much as they ever were under Nelson or anyone else. But the *Invincible* would play no part in any of this.

10 The Loss of the Invincible

The crew of the *Invincible* were roused early from their hammocks on the morning of Sunday 19 February, for the signal for the fleet to weigh anchor was hoisted from Boscawen's flagship, the *Namur*, at 2.30 am. Part of the work of raising anchor had already been done, for the night before, the crew had 'unmoored', i.e. they had taken up one of the anchors so that the ship was now riding at single anchor. Only half a cable, or 360ft, had been let out on that anchor so that there was relatively little to haul in and the ships could get the anchors up and sail without wasting too much time. There was now an easterly wind, suitable to carry the squadron down the Channel, and Boscawen was anxious to get away.

The crew took up their positions for raising anchor. Some men, about a hundred in normal circumstances, pushed at the capstan bars to provide the power that actually raised the anchor. Since the cable itself was too thick to wind around the capstan, an endless rope known as a viol was used. This was temporarily attached to part of the cable as it entered the ship through the hawse holes, by light ropes known as nippers. It was led aft through a block tied to the mainmast, and then forward to the ship's fore-capstan, and turned around it a few times. The viol was then led back to the cable, where the process was continually repeated as the cable was hauled in. Other men stood by on the forecastle, ready to 'cat' and 'fish' the anchor as soon as it broke surface, while the most agile of the seamen would be aloft, ready to unfurl the sails as soon as the anchor was up.

At first all went well. Within half an hour the *Invincible*'s anchor was hove short peak, almost ready, in theory to be lifted off the ground and hauled up into the ship. The topsails and the fore-topgallant staysail were set, and the ship should have been ready to sail.

But the anchor was stuck fast in the mud and refused to move. Henry Adkins, the *Invincible*'s new master, was a very experienced seaman and tried all the tricks he knew. He used the fish tackle, intended to lift the crown of the anchor after it had broken the surface of the water, to get extra purchase on the cable. He led another viol rope to the main capstan so that both could be used in tandem. If both heads of both capstans were used, nearly four hundred men could haul at once. But the crew 'hove till we broke many of the bars at both capstans'. In another attempt, they 'made a fresh purchase with a large treble block lashed on the cable and another to the mainmast, and reeved an 8 inch hawser'. At last, two hours after the signal, the anchor came off the ground and the ship was under way.

The main and mizzen-topsails were filled and the fore-topsail was backed to hold the ship hove to while the operation of raising the anchor was completed. It should have been hauled up until its ring was out of the water; the cat tackle, suspended from a kind of crane called the 'cat-head' in the bows of the ship, would be attached to the ring, and the anchor would be hoisted by the cat tackle, keeping it clear of the side of the ship. The other end of the anchor, the crown, would then be lifted so that the shank was horizontal and the anchor would be stowed in that position until needed again.

Again, there was a problem. The anchor was under the bow of the ship, but no amount of force would cause it to come up to the surface. It was believed that it had caught itself around the underwater hull. In an attempt to clear it, all the sails were backed and the ship began to make stern way, but to no avail. Yet another tackle was rigged and brute force was used to haul the anchor up some more. It broke surface, but still could not be catted. The master, in consultation with the captain, decided to proceed with the voyage, as the main fleet was already some way ahead.

Since the wind was from the east-south-east, the *Invincible* sailed to the north-east. This was as close to the wind as a square-rigged ship would sail. Her yards were braced round as far as they would go, with the starboard edge of the sail forward and the port edge aft so that it would catch the wind. This course would eventually bring the ship to the Dean Sand on the other side of the Solent, where she would go about through the wind and set course to the south, taking her out to sea. The wind was moderate, and with only her topsails set, the ship would have made about 5 knots in such conditions.

All the officers and crew were on deck except for the fifth lieutenant, who was about to take over the watch and had been allowed to rest by order of the captain. Although Bentley was on deck, he left the conning of the ship to the master, Henry Adkins. Although the master was new to the ship, Bentley seems to have had complete confidence in him and considered himself lucky to get a man with such a good reputation in the fleet.

As the ship made its way across the Solent, two experienced and reliable seamen, Thomas Francis and Thomas Gray, were stationed in the chains to heave the lead, one on each side of the ship. They called out the depth of water continuously to let the master know as the ship approached the Dean Sand. The depth reached 12 fathoms in the middle of the Solent and then began to shallow – 11, 10, 9, 8 and $7\frac{1}{2}$. At this stage there was still more than 20ft of water under the keel, but when the depth of $7\frac{1}{4}$ fathoms was called, Adkins decided to put the ship about by tacking through the wind. The fore-topmast staysail, which would contribute nothing to the operation, was hauled down. The helmsman put the wheel over to turn the ship into the wind. As she came head to wind

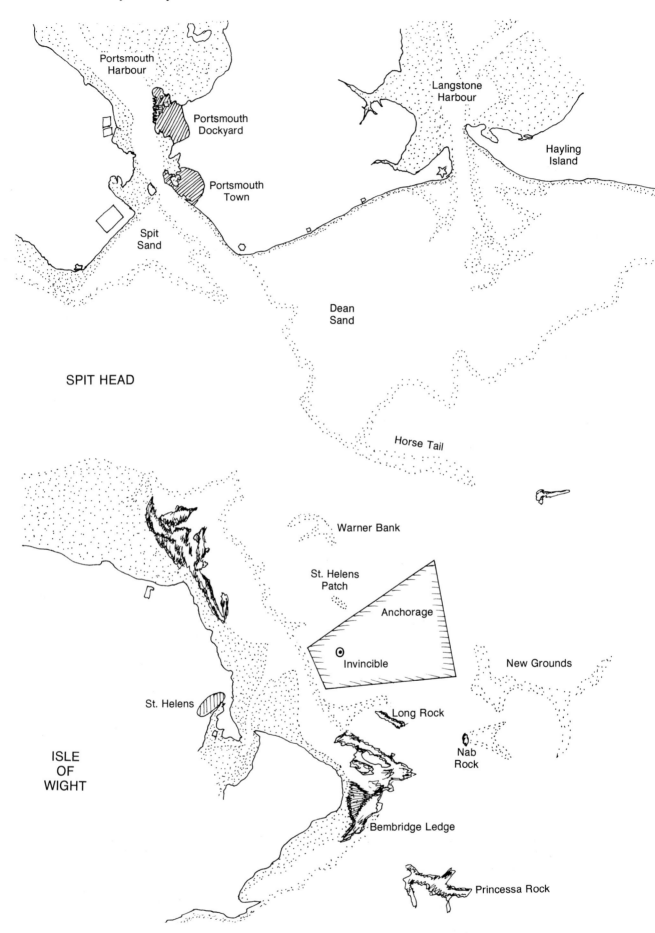

The Eastern Solent, showing Portsmouth, Spithead, St Helens, and the *Invincible*'s position at anchor

the seamen manned the braces of the main and mizzen sails. They hauled the sails on to the opposite tack so that their port edges were now forward. The sails were backing and tending to push the stern of

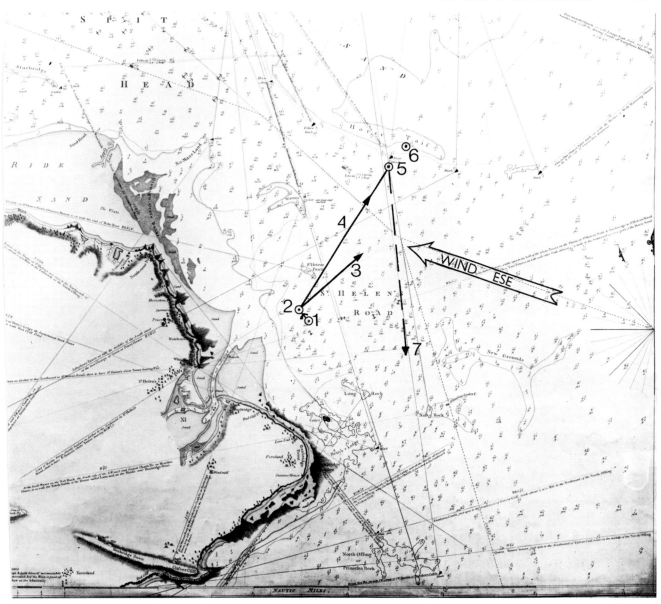

The *Invincible*'s movements on 19 February: 1) the position at anchor; 2) The estimated position after drifting while trying to raise the anchor; 3) The course steered; 4) The probable course made good, allowing for tide and leeway; 5) Point where the ship went about for the first time; 6) Where the ship went aground on the Dean Sand; 7) Intended track out into the English Channel

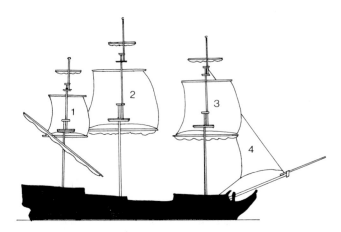

The sails carried by the *Invincible* on her last voyage: 1) Mizzen topsail; 2) Main topsail; 3) Fore topsail; 4) Fore staysail

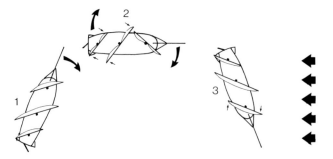

Tacking a square rigged ship: 1) The helm is put over to turn the ship into the wind; 2) The main and mizzen yards are braced round, so that they are pushing the stern to port, while the fore remains in its original position, to push the bows to starboard; 3) After the ship has turned enough to bring the wind on her other side, the fore yards are braced and all the sails are filled on the other tack

the ship round to port. The sail on the foremast was also backing, but it had not yet been hauled round, so it was pushing the bow to starboard and thus aiding the turning motion of the ship. The operation was completed successfully, the foresail was braced round and the sails began to fill on the other tack.

The helmsman had allowed the ship to fall off the wind to some extent in order to get the sails filled. He now began to correct for this by turning the ship back into the wind in the hope of getting her to sail as close to the wind as possible without backing any of the sails. It was then, as the rudder was tending to turn the ship to port and into the wind, that the crisis happened. The helm jammed.

Because of the geometry of the system, it was necessary to leave some slack in the tiller ropes. Thirteen years later one of the shipwrights of Portsmouth dockyard would invent a new system of leading the ropes in order to prevent the 'many inconveniences and fatal accidents that have happened and are generally known to have been by the unavoidable slack rope when the tiller is near its greatest angle'.[1] But in 1758 no such system was in use and the tiller rope had either got tangled around something below or had twisted and would not go through its block.

Adkins reacted swiftly to the crisis. Already the quartermaster and four seamen were hauling at the wheel. The master himself and a spare quartermaster also pushed at it, so there were now seven men trying to move it. Adkins sent one seaman, and then another, down below to see what was wrong. On the way down they met the gunner coming up and he reported that the fault had cleared itself. But meanwhile the ship had gone back through the eye of the wind. Adkins had ordered the foresail to be sheeted out to port to try to prevent this, but the *Invincible* had tacked against the effect of the sails. That she could do so says much for her sailing qualities, but the consequences were very unfortunate; she was now heading straight for the Dean Sand and there was very little room left for manoeuvre.

Captain Bentley intervened to suggest that the ship be made to wear round. This meant that she should be put about by turning her stern, rather than her bows, to the wind. This had the advantage that it could be done while the ship was only moving slowly; presumably she had lost much way during the accidental tack. It had the severe disadvantage that it required much more room than tacking and there was very little of that available between the ship and the shallow water of the Dean Sand. Adkins, inexperienced in the ship, told Bentley that they had room to wear 'if the ship would wear quick'. It was decided to go ahead.

The after sails were shivered, i.e. they were braced round so that the yards pointed into the wind and the wind passed on both sides of the sail, causing it to have minimum effect. The foresail, which did most of the work, was filled and used to help pull the ship's head around to port. But the operation had not gone very far before one of the seamen in the chains reported a depth of only $6\frac{1}{2}$ fathoms. Adkins 'told Captain Bentley we must not run the risk of wearing, but begged we might clap the helm hard a lea'. The helm was turned in the opposite direction in an attempt to put the ship into the wind in order to stop its movement. At the same time the small bower anchor was got ready to drop (the best bower was stuck under the bows and was not available). The

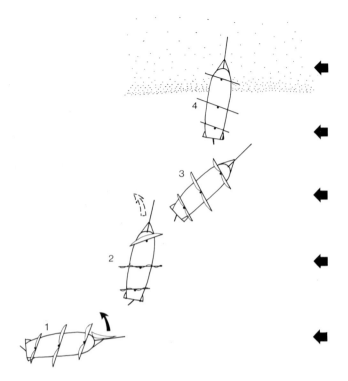

The *Invincible*'s manoeuvres before going aground:
1) The helm jams, and the ship turns back through the wind, despite the effect of the sails
2) The attempt to wear. The foresail is kept filled to bring the head round, while the main and mizzen are 'shivered' – the yards are kept pointing towards the wind, so that the sails have minimum effect
3) The attempt to wear is abandoned, in view of the shallowness of the water. The ship is turned into the wind in an attempt to stop her movement, and an anchor is prepared.
4) The ship goes aground on the Dean Sand. The sails are quickly taken in

order to let go the anchor was repeated several times, but it was never complied with, and in any case it was too late. The ship almost came head to wind, but then she fell off again and immediately she went aground on the Dean Sand.

The situation was serious, but not desperate. The *Invincible* had been aground twice before and had lifted off without any perceptible damage. It was two hours before high water and the tide would rise several feet to lift the ship off. The first task was to prevent her driving in any further. The sails were braced round so that they were taken aback and the topsails were taken in. The signal of distress was made by firing a gun and hoisting two lights in the mizzen-shrouds. Boscawen saw the signal, but he was not expected to react; in view of the disasters caused by the delays of last year, he was not likely to stop his fleet for the sake of a single ship. Portsmouth was expected to help, but the wind was still blowing straight up the Solent and it would not be easy to get anything out to the *Invincible*.

The yards and topmasts were got down to reduce topweight and windage. The obvious way to get the *Invincible* afloat again was to lay anchors out astern so that she could be hauled up to them as soon as the tide rose. The ship's second smallest anchor, the stream anchor, was slung under the longboat and

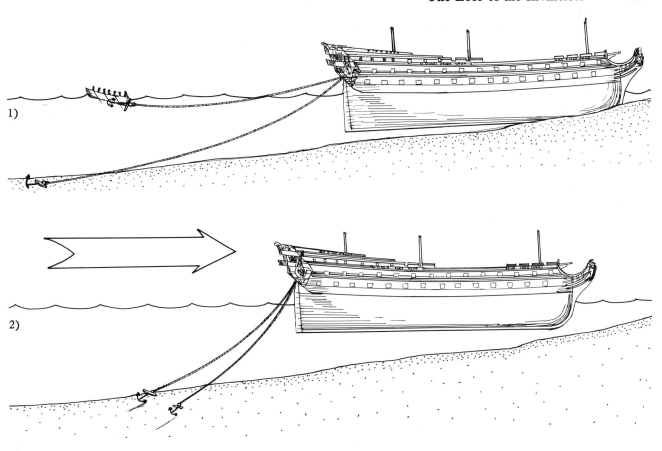

The attempt to kedge the ship off:
1) One anchor has already been laid out, and another is slung under the longboat, which is rowed into position and the anchor dropped
2) The anchors are hauled in by means of the capstan, and the ship is hauled off the bank, but as the anchor cable becomes shorter the pull becomes more vertical, and the anchors lose their grip. The wind shifts and freshens, and drives the ship back onto the sand

rowed several hundred feet astern. Its cable was led through one of the stern gun-ports to the main capstan. The smallest anchor, the kedge, was also slung under a boat and it was being put in position by 6.30am. Half an hour before high water, the ship floated again. The men at the capstan took up the strain on the anchor cable and the ship moved slowly astern, into the deeper water.

But as the cable was shortened, the pull on it became less horizontal and the anchor's hold gradually loosened. The kedge was dropped some way aft of the stream anchor and the two might have been used in turn to haul the ship some way, but the kedge was a very small anchor, only 8cwt compared with about 18cwt of a stream and 60cwt of a bower. Furthermore, the wind was increasing, and it changed direction. At 7.30am 'the wind blowing very fresh at south-east and having no assistance, the stream and kedge anchors coming home, the wind being right aft, the ship forged ahead and went aground again'.

The best chance of saving the ship had gone, for it was now past high water. At 8 o'clock Bentley ordered his first lieutenant, John Bucknall, into one of the ship's cutters, 'to go on shore and acquaint Rear Admiral Brodrick . . . that unless speedy assistance was sent to the *Invincible*, as anchors, cables, gun-hoys and co, it was to be feared she would be lost'. The firing of guns as a distress signal continued

and as it was now daylight the ensign was hoisted upside down.

Because of unfavourable winds, it was midday before any help came. The longboats belonging to the *Prince George* and *Royal Sovereign* arrived, but carried 'neither anchor but cable', and were of little use. Bentley decided to lighten the ship in order to float her off at the next high tide, even at the cost of expending some of His Majesty's stores and equipment. Six of the after upper-deck guns were jettisoned, while many water and beer casks were emptied over the side. Three of the quarterdeck guns, relatively light, were put into the boats and taken ashore.

At about 7pm Mr Gastrin, the Master Attendant of the dockyard, and Mr Locket, the pilot, came on board to attempt another way of getting the ship off. In a total reversal of earlier practices, they had the yards hoisted again, set the sails and around the time of high tide attempted to drive the ship forward over the top of the bank. This had no effect and the ship was now making much water. The pounding against the bank had caused some of the timbers to work loose and there was the possibility that the anchor, which had been left over the side, had penetrated the hull. The hands were put to the pumps and others bailed with buckets, but between 10 and 11pm, two of the four chain pumps broke. The water began to gain fast and it was not possible to repair the pumps because they were largely underwater. The wind was still unfavourable and Brodrick wrote to the Admiralty that he was 'very much afraid of the consequences'.

At 6 o'clock the next morning several vessels began to arrive from the dockyard. They included two 20-gun ships, the *Rye* and *Penguin*, some tenders, two busses (fishing boats) and other small craft. The soldiers, most of whom were presumably unused to the sea, were of little use in the crisis and were sent ashore. Shipwrights from the yard came on board, bringing hand-pumps, which they fitted to supplement the ship's chain-pumps. The ship was no longer pounding against the bank; she had dug a bed for herself in the sand and was afloat except at low water, although she was trapped within a hole.

The main task now was to get out all her stores and equipment, either to lighten the ship with a view to floating her off eventually, or simply to save as many valuable goods as possible. The upper-deck guns were lifted out on the afternoon of the 20th, and at 5 o'clock next morning work began on the heavier guns of the lower deck. Bentley was still optimistic: 'If the weather prove moderate, I have great hopes that we shall yet be able to save her.' Brodrick believed the opposite: 'I am in hopes a great part of her stores will be got out, but there is very little probability of saving the ship.' Hughes the dockyard Commissioner was of similar opinion. He had been informed that 'The water is got up quite to the orlop beams, and that there is reason to fear, from the ship's striking so hard and so long together, she is not in a condition to be got off again.'[2] On the spot, the captain of the *Rye* wrote: 'The *Invincible* so much a wreck, no hopes of getting her off.'[3]

By the afternoon of the 21st, after the *Invincible* had been aground for two and a half days, all the guns and carriages had been got out, along with 'a hoy load of shot and gunners stores, with a great deal of lumber'. But the weather worsened. At 7pm 'the wind shifted to the south-south-west and began to blow very hard, which continued to increase to a most violent storm.' At 9 o'clock as the tide rose, the stern began to rise with it, but the bows were largely underwater and the sea 'made free passage over the fore part of the ship'. The wind, coming from astern of the ship, was causing her to bear hard against the sides of the hole she had dug for herself. The ship had moved position within the hole and, as the tide fell again, she was balanced precariously. At 1.30 on the morning of the 22nd, she fell over violently on her port side, breaking many timbers.

This was enough for most of the crew. They had been aground for nearly three days, toiling ceaselessly at ropes and capstans to get the guns out. They had worked the pumps continuously and hopelessly, and they had felt the tremors as the ship battered herself against the sand. If any of them had slept during the last days, it must have been uncomfortable and interrupted. Only Bentley's optimism and determination had kept them going this far. But no longer.

Despite the efforts of their officers to stop them, forty-four seamen piled into two longboats belonging to the *Royal Anne* and *Barfleur*, taking a midshipman with them. They were next heard of, 'terrified and fatigued', in Portsmouth. Bentley was furious and regarded it as plain desertion. The rest of the crew were, according to the first lieutenant, 'very uneasy on board'.

By now even Bentley had to admit that the ship was lost. At 4am a rope was passed to the commissioner's yacht which was anchored nearby, and the crew got into the remaining longboats, using the rope to haul themselves over to the yacht. Still they were not lucky for the rope got foul of the yacht's anchor, which cut it. The boats went back to the *Invincible* and the whole process had to start again. At 6 o'clock, as the weather began to moderate, the first men were taken on board the yacht, while others went to the busses and a tender which were standing by.

Bentley decided to stay on board, along with his officers and a boat's crew, to save what stores they could. They remained until 5pm, and then transferred to a buoy boat anchored nearby. They spent the night there in slightly more comfortable conditions and went back to the wreck next morning. They continued taking out rigging and stores, with the help of men sent from the dockyard. Bentley went ashore on the afternoon of the 23rd to confer with the port admiral, but after that he came on board every day until 6 March, supervising the removal of stores and rigging.

As custom demanded, a court martial was held to enquire into the loss of the ship. It was held on board the *Royal George* in Portsmouth Harbour on 6 March, presided over by Thomas Brodrick, the port admiral, and composed of eleven captains. Admiral Holbourne, about to take over as port admiral, was also present. Enquiries were concentrated on the events leading up to the grounding of the ship and paid little attention to the attempts to save her after that. Bentley, Adkins, and the Second and Third lieutenants were called to give evidence, along with the boatswain and gunner, the two men who had been sounding depths, and the quartermaster who had gone below to find out why the tiller was jammed. The Portsmouth pilot, William Locket, testified that the master had not been at fault in waiting until $7\frac{1}{4}$ fathoms before going about. 'I would if I had the charge of a ship of that draught have stood in to the same depth of water.' He had been a pilot for thirty-six years and his evidence carried much weight. Furthermore, 'the sand has increased more than I have ever heard, or could imagine, and I should not have known there was so little water now, had I not gone out to the assistance of the *Invincible* when she was ashore'. Until shortly before the loss of the *Invincible*, it would have been possible to sail the ship over the bank at high water, and indeed Locket had tried this. The officers and crew were acquitted of all blame for the loss of the ship.

The next day another court martial was held to try the forty-four seamen who had taken to the longboats when the ship had fallen over. They were accused of 'mutiny and desertion in cutting adrift a longboat and leaving the ship when she was ashore and in distress, notwithstanding the captain and officer's endeavours to prevent them'. The court was sympathetic to their position, and concluded

> that they did not cut the boat adrift, but intended going on board the yacht or the nearest tender, which they were prevented doing by wind and sea, and in consideration of their good behaviour from the first [moments] of the ship going on shore, and their conduct afterwards in obeying the orders of the midshipman who was accidentally with them in the boat, and their going to the commissioner and Rear Admiral Brodrick for their orders, and it fully appearing that they had not any intention to desert His Majesty's service, but went voluntarily on board His Majesty's ships in this port, the court acquits them of the charge.

The Admiralty was not entirely satisfied with the result of the first court martial, and wrote to Holbourne, 'although it appears none of the officers were to blame for the loss of the ship, yet she being lost, and you directed to enquire into the occasion thereof, neither the public nor their lordships have received any satisfaction of the occasion of the loss by the result of your enquiry'.[4] Holbourne replied that part of the cause was the rise in the level of the Dean Sand; he was having that area surveyed. He appeared to attribute the accident to that, and to the tide forcing the ship back through the wind. He had apparently not paid much attention during the court martial for he made no mention of the helm jamming.[5]

No lives had been lost as a result of the wreck and there is no sign of any serious injuries, except that one newspaper reported, 'The master in his hurry, when the ship struck, jumped from a considerable height upon the head of a cask, which broke with him, and he fell astride the edge of the cask, which wounded him so terribly in his fork that his life is despaired of.'[6] This seems unlikely, as there is no mention of it in any official sources and the master seemed quite fit at the court martial a fortnight later. Nor was anyone's career seriously damaged. Bentley went on to command the *Warspite*, a new British 74, at Boscawen's victory at Lagos in 1759. He was knighted after that battle, became a commissioner of the Navy in 1761 and died with the rank of vice admiral in 1772. Henry Adkins continued as a master and was appointed to another new 74, the *Lennox*. But none of the lieutenants went on to gain high rank. Only the sixth, William Browne, made commander, in 1779. The *Invincible*'s place in the Louisbourg expedition was taken by the *Dublin*, the first of the new British 74s, under Captain Rodney.

Thus the loss of the *Invincible* was not such a grievous blow as it might have been five years before; British ship design had much improved since then, especially under the influence of Slade. The new ships of the *Bellona* class and her near sisters were already on the stocks. These were only 3ft shorter

than the *Invincible* and they became the staple British design for more than thirty years. About forty were built and the design was used for some time after Slade's death in 1771. In 1761 the *Bellona* captured another French 74, the *Courageaux*, and this ship took the place of the *Invincible* as the British navy's best loved French prize. Forty-five years later she was still 'the favourite ship of the navy'.[7] More than forty ships were built on variations of her lines and the last one was not completed until 1822. The *Invincible* was not forgotten, and two ships, the *Ajax* and *Kent*, were built to her design in the 1790s. Ships had increased in length since 1741 and an extra section was added amidships to make them 11ft longer. They probably exceeded the safe limits for a wooden ship of this construction, and after that there was a tendency to build rather shorter ships, not much longer than the *Invincible* herself.

Although the *Courageaux* was copied more, this is partly due to the fact that she served for much longer than the *Invincible*, being wrecked in 1796. The *Courageaux* was captured at a time when British ship design was already set on the course which Anson and Slade had planned for it, but the *Invincible* came when British ship design was at its lowest point; there is no doubt which ship had the greatest historical importance, and it is not difficult to argue that the *Invincible* had more effect on the British navy than any other captured ship. It was not copied as much as the *Courageaux*, but only because the British navy had a designer as good as Slade; foreign ships were mostly copied when the designers were running out of ideas.

Naval architecture reached a plateau around 1740, as ships, especially two-deckers, expanded to the limits set by the system of construction. Within these limits, the *Invincible* was almost as good as any ship could be. Longer ships would tend to 'hog', or sag, at the ends, as the British were to find in the 1790s. This was less of a problem for French ships, which spent less time at sea, but the British eventually found that a length of about 175ft was as much as a two-decker could bear in service, until Sir Robert Seppings changed the whole picture by inventing a new system of construction in 1811. But until then it was difficult to make any serious improvement on the design of the *Invincible*. French design reached its peak in the 1730s and '40s, when excellent naval architects, such as Morineau, Coulomb and Blaise Olivier, were given a relatively free hand. It became rather sterile in the 1780s, when Sané imposed standard designs on the fleet. It is significant that the British continued to rely on the older French prizes to copy and only three of the thirty-seven ships of the line taken in the war of 1793–1801 were copied.

The 74 was a success in the British navy because she was the smallest ship to carry a full battery of 32 pounders, and at the same time have good sailing qualities. Within that class, the *Invincible* herself was a success because she was the right size, had the right proportions and had a well-faired hull. Perhaps she would have been less outstanding in the navy of 1800, but she could easily have held her own in such a fleet, and this is a tribute to the far-sightedness of her design as much as to the static situation in naval architecture. After all, the *Invincible* was only the second of the 'true' 74s to be built. The *Triumph*, directly copied from her, was still a first-line ship until 1813.

But the main historical role of the *Invincible* was to show the British how ships should be designed. The praise of those who sailed in her or saw her – Anson, Boscawen, Warren, Keppel and Bentley – served to reinforce Anson in his belief that ship design needed to be drastically improved. The *Invincible*, more than any other ship, pulled the British navy out of its rut of the first half of the eighteenth century.

Her operational career in the British navy was less significant, although this was not the fault of the ship herself. She had the misfortune to serve in the last few months of the war of 1739–48, when the enemy had been almost driven from the seas; and in the first stages of the Seven Years War, when the British navy was at its least glorious. This is not to say she had no effect. Every armchair strategist knows that a fleet can change history merely by its presence, just as a piece on a chess-board can alter the nature of the game without actually moving. Her service in the British navy was frustrating and in some senses disappointing, but this does not mean that it was futile. She might have achieved undying glory in the battles of 1759, had not ·a series of accidents destroyed her within sight of her home port.

The name, of course, survived, although it never seems to have carried much luck with it. The *Invincible* of 1744 belied her name by being captured in 1747 and then wrecked eleven years later. Her successor, another 74-gun ship of Slade design launched in 1765, was wrecked off Yarmouth in 1801. The third was another 74, which was launched in 1808 and survived to become a coal hulk in 1857, before being broken up four years later. The fourth *Invincible* was an iron-clad built in 1869. She became a training ship in 1904, and under the name of *Fisgard II* she was lost off Portland in the early weeks of World War I.

Her successor had already been launched in 1907. She was the mighty battlecruiser, the first ship of that type, 550ft long and armed with eight 12in guns. She was one of the most glamorous ships in the navy, but she was blown up with the loss of nearly all her crew at Jutland in 1916. Thus, only one of the first five *Invincibles* died a natural death. Perhaps the spell has been broken with the sixth, the aircraft carrier of nearly 20,000 tons. She has already survived action in the Falklands War and avoided being sold to Australia.

The wreck of the first *Invincible* was abandoned in March 1758, but work on her did not cease then. On 8 May the Portsmouth officers went out to the wreck to conduct a survey into her 'condition and situation'. They reported that she was lying in a hole which was up to 22ft deep, while the water around her was only 12ft deep. She was lying on her port side, with the lowest sill of her upper-deck gun-ports about 1ft out of the water at low tide. The main wale on the other side was about 3ft out of the water, so she was lying at an angle of about 30 degrees, with almost all of her gun-deck underwater. The water had 'a clear passage through her'. She was 'greatly twisted, waving and cambered'. The officers concluded that she was 'bilged, and from her situation know not any method of lifting her, and we are fully of the opinion that it would not be to the advantage of His Majesty's service to undertake it'.[8]

However, work continued on taking out stores and on 21 June a list of those rescued was sent to the Admiralty. On the 19th of that month the dockyard advertised for anyone prepared to attempt the salvage of the ship and attracted a reply from one Joseph Mason, a painter at the gunwharf. He proposed to

lash the ship's sides taut with 3 inch hawsers, one forward and one in the waist, and one abaft through the upper and lower deck ports, hove taut with capstans, and one hawser through the quarterdeck and upper deck ports, to keep her sides together. To float her, nail cleats on the lee side at low water, and on the weather side opposite, and have twenty butts ready slung to lash down close to both sides. Then another row of cleats for two tiers of butts, well lashed and slung. Then nail another row of cleats four feet below the bend, and lash three tier of butts with a rope fast to every butt, fore and aft, and a thwart nailed to the outer butt and the side of the ship to keep them together.[9]

The Portsmouth officers were not impressed, and the Navy Board was told that in response to the advertisement they had been offered nothing 'in consequence thereof that carries any probability of success'. It was decided to abandon all hope of salvage, but continue getting stores out instead.

Evidently the mainmast had been lost soon after the accident, for on 5 March part of it, 'very much shivered', was washed up at Hayling Island. It was decided that, rather than attempt to salvage it from a difficult position in the sand, it would be sold where it lay.[10] The main, mizzen and bowsprit were still in place and attempts were made to save them. By 3 September both the bowsprit and the mizzen had been taken out, but the foremast was somewhat larger and more difficult to move without a sheer hulk. The Portsmouth officers proposed to fit out the *Firedrake* bomb vessel with sheer-legs and a derrick, and with a large capstan. It would be towed out to the wreck and if its draught was kept low it would be able to float alongside the *Invincible* and take the mast out. The yard officers believed that they could fit her and carry out the operation at a cost of £100, while the mast was probably worth £360.[11] The Navy Board agreed to this, but urged the dockyard to hurry as the bomb vessel would be needed for active service soon. The mast was got out and the *Firedrake* was in commission as a fighting ship by 26 September.

Work on the wreck seems to have stopped soon afterwards. Large quantities of stores were left behind, largely because the bow of the ship, where the magazines and most of the store-rooms were sited, was deep underwater. The hull slowly disappeared from sight over the years as it sank into the sand. The sand itself gradually moved south and covered it so that it was forgotten. But after yet more time the sands moved further south and began to uncover the wreck again. When Arthur Mack eventually found it in 1979, it was still in the position noted in 1758, but on the north side of the sand.

11 Excavating the Wreck

Underwater archaeology is a science which has made enormous strides in the last thirty years, but its origins are a little earlier than many people realise. In a sense it can be said to have begun in the Solent, only a few miles from the *Invincible* wreck. In the 1820s John and Charles Deane, in partnership with Siebe, developed a successful form of diving suit, and in 1834 they began to salvage items from the wreck of the *Royal George*, the same ship which had succeeded the *Invincible* as Boscawen's flagship in 1756. Their main aim was to clear the fairway into Portsmouth Harbour, but they also recovered several cannon, including twenty-one bronze ones. More to the point, they dived on the much older wreck of the *Mary Rose*, not far away. Like the *Invincible*, it had been discovered by fishermen snagging their nets. The Deanes brought up several ancient cannon and took careful steps to record and preserve their finds; in that sense they can be seen as the fathers of underwater archaeology and the birth took place very close to where the *Invincible* now lies.

In the popular mind, nautical archaeology had a double image – either divers discovering vast hordes of pirate treasure and Spanish gold, or else the raising of the complete, intact hull of an ancient vessel. But, like the great majority of sites, the *Invincible* never really offered either of these prospects. There is no direct evidence that the ship was carrying any items which were seen as particularly valuable at the time (although even the ordinary stores cost a good deal of money and considerable efforts were made to rescue them). To recover and preserve the hull of a wooden ship costs a vast amount of money and can only be done in very rare cases. The hull of the *Invincible* is much larger than that of the *Mary Rose*, and much less intact than the *Vasa*, so it would cost considerably more than either of these ships.

Instead, the work on the *Invincible* is a careful and painstaking investigation, with slow progress in uncovering the hull and raising the thousands of items which were left on board when she was finally abandoned. From the beginning, the *Invincible* project has been aimed at recovering the past, preserving it and understanding it as far as possible. Many different skills have been employed towards this end, at sea and ashore, in workshops, offices, museums and libraries.

Historic wrecks in British waters are controlled by the Protection of Wrecks Act, 1973. According to this, a site can be protected by an order from the Secretary of State if it is found to be of archaeological interest. After that a licence is necessary to work on a wreck and to obtain this the applicants must prove themselves 'to be competent and properly equipped, to carry out salvage operations in a manner appropriate to the historical, archaeological or artistic importance of any wreck which may be lying in the area and

of any objects contained or formerly contained therein'. Arthur Mack and John Broomhead first considered such a licence in 1979. According to advice from the National Maritime Museum:

> If the wreck is to be scheduled, it will first be necessary to prove it to be of national importance ... If the wreck is scheduled you would have to obtain a licence to work on it, for which your team would have to prove themselves competent archaeologically ... Work on a scheduled site would have to be supervised or directed by an experienced archaeologist.

All this seemed to be beyond the resources of the small team then working on the wreck and, despite the growing problem of intrusion by other divers, no application was made at that stage. However, they did put in a salvage claim by reporting their finds to the Receiver of Wrecks, at the local offices of the Customs and Excise.

In 1980, after John Bingeman had joined with his considerable diving and archaeological experience, it was decided to apply. The wreck had not yet been firmly identified, so it was known simply as the 'Horse Sand Spit wreck site'. A pre-disturbance survey of the site was made during the spring and summer of that year. A grid pattern was laid out over the area using 3ft metal stakes driven into the sand and linked with nylon rope jackstays. This divided the site into approximate squares, the length and compass-bearing of each rope was logged, and this gave a basis for mapping the site. A detailed plan of the wreck was drawn, showing the location of all visible objects. Portsmouth City Museum conservation department agreed to provide facilities to preserve artefacts; Margaret Rule of the Mary Rose Trust agreed to serve as Archaeological Director.

The aim for the 1980 diving season was 'to dig an exploratory trench 2 metres [$6\frac{1}{2}$ft] wide, two metres [$6\frac{1}{2}$ft] deep, in an east/west direction ... This should prove the coherency of the structure and provide a vertical profile of the hull.' Work had begun in April, but it reached its peak in August when, in addition to weekends, two continuous weeks were worked, with some breaks owing to bad weather. Altogether, 408 hours were spent underwater. Diving was usually done from *MFV 119*, a $61\frac{1}{2}$ft motor fishing vessel specially converted for diving, with accommodation for 14. Arthur Mack's boat *Wishbone* was used for smaller-scale dives and to assist the *MFV*. Many divers from the Portsmouth Command Sub-Aqua Club and from other clubs gave their support to the original team.

In some respects the site is not a particularly difficult one to work. It is in shallow water, only 18ft deep at low-water springs. It is not far from the shore and close to the facilities of Portsmouth, where there are many trained divers, both amateur and profes-

MFV 119

sional, and all the material resources that anyone could need to carry out diving. The site is some distance from the main fairway, so there is no danger from large ships (although yachts and dinghies sometimes come too close, and sailing clubs have been known to use the wreck buoy as a racing mark). It is in sheltered water within the Solent, although that did not always guarantee good conditions. Sometimes fog reduced visibility to a few yards and it became difficult to find the wreck buoy. Sometimes conditions could become rough, as in May 1981: 'The crew on board the *MFV*, with the exception of John Bingeman and Peter Hales, were all seasick and therefore did not dive. The fact that there was a strong smell of stew coming from the galley did not help.'

Underwater conditions can vary from time to time. At the beginning of each season it is often found that the winter gales have moved some of the sand and left parts of the structure clear. In April 1981, the divers found 'structure standing three feet from the sea bed, which until now had been buried'. But levels changed during the season and much became covered again. This pattern was to be repeated from year to year as the scour of the tides cleared the site in the winter. Trenches which were dug one year filled in during the close season. A constant difficulty was seaweed: 'The amount of kelp on site is still presenting the biggest problem, and a lot of time is always spent in clearing this before excavation can commence.'

Sometimes visibility can be much better. In June 1981, 'the visibility was exceptionally good today, with Arthur being able to see me working on the site from *Wishbone* on high water'. At other times it could be as little as 12in after gales had churned up the sand or another diver had disturbed the water.

The 1980 trench, like all the others, was dug using an airlift to suck sand away from the site. It revealed two decks, supported by the normal structure of beams and carlings. Part of the keel of the ship was also found, and it was established that she was lying on one side at an angle of about 45 degrees. Most of the excavation was $1\frac{1}{2}$–3ft deep, except for an area known as the 'main pit', which was 5ft deep. In mid-October there was some rough weather, and on return to the site on the 18th, it was found that the trench had been filled in again – actually quite useful, because it helped conserve the timbers through the winter.

A protection order on the wreck was granted on 30 September 1980, so it was now possible to make the details public for the first time. John Bingeman told the press: 'Various divers have been pirating the site, and we have lost exciting bits of artefacts which should have been preserved for posterity. Anyone else who dives on the site will be committing an offence and can be taken to court.' It was reported in several newspapers, both local and national. Television interest was beginning, with short programmes made by local stations. John Bingeman wrote an article for *Diver* magazine and another for the *International Journal of Nautical Archaeology*. David Houghton began a booklet on the ship, to be sold at exhibitions.

1980 produced an interesting crop of artefacts. Tiny barrels, a few inches long, caused some puzzlement at first. Leather and wooden buckets were found, along with rigging tools such as fids, serving mallets and belaying pins. Several rigging blocks were recovered and some of these were quite large. There was an immediate problem over conservation, as the City Museum did not have the facilities to store so many objects in suitable conditions. David Houghton offered the use of the salt-water tanks at the Exposure Laboratory at Eastney, where the objects could await conservation. By now there was enough material to organise exhibitions of artefacts. The City Museum expressed interest in opening a standing display at Southsea Castle Museum, overlooking the wreck site. Plans were made to open another display at the Royal Naval Museum in Portsmouth dockyard. The marine artist, John Terry, was commissioned to do several paintings of the ship, and one of these, showing her aground on the Dean Sand with cannon being lifted out, was to form the background of a window display at the museum.

On 31 March, early in the 1981 season, the official wreck buoy, marking the *Invincible* as a protected wreck, was placed on the site by the Ministry of Defence Salvage and Mooring Department. The regular divers also went out

> To locate the wreck for dockyard boat in order that they may place the wreck buoy in the correct place. After grappling the wreck I dived down, to the northernmost tip of the wreck. The grapple had in fact gone into a rib not 6ft from the northern end. Having buoyed the correct end, the dockyard boat let down the historic wreck buoy 20 metres north of this point.

It was only the second such buoy to be used in British waters, the other being for the *Mary Rose*. In 1985 it was replaced with a new buoy, but owing to a mistake it was labelled '1785' instead of '1758'.

The aim for 1981 was to dig another trench, approximately westward of the 'main pit' of 1980. This would carry it across the whole width of the site and further prove the coherence of the hull. However, there was not enough time to do this, and instead the area of the 1980 excavation was widened and deepened. From this a partial cross-section of the ship was drawn, showing the positions of the decks and the keel of the ship. A total of 461 hours were spent underwater and this remains the highest figure for a single year. The sail tally, which finally established the identity of the ship, was found, along with many other artefacts.

'Piracy' is a problem on any wreck site, especially one close to the shore and near a major city. During 1980 divers often found that the site had been disturbed, objects removed and damage done. On 10 April, for example, it was recorded: 'It seems obvious to me that many other divers have been looting the wreck site, as much of the lead shot that was there last year is now missing.' There was evidence that even air-lifts had been used to work the site and in the early years there was a constant battle to patrol the site and protect it. One or two of the intruders have been conscientious and returned artefacts to the *Invincible* committee. Although pilaging the wreck became illegal after the designation of 1980, it is very difficult to stop. However, in June 1981 John Broomhead had a good try:

> When I drove along the seafront at lunchtime, I noted a small craft moored above our wreck. Noting that Arthur Mack and John Bingeman were in Alderney for the weekend, it was obvious that whoever was on the site was not supposed to be there. I therefore decided to take Arthur's boat and challenge whoever was out there. The only way I could get out to *Wishbone* was to swim as there was no one at ferry point to take me out.

However, the intruding vessel had gone by the time he reached there and there was no sign of any damage to the site.

Around this time, Arthur Mack made his first dive on the ship he had discovered. According to the log of 15 June:

> Work – primarily to get Arthur into the water and give him his first look at the wreck site. Arthur used about 55cu ft of air in 30 minutes at 25ft. This was only to be expected on his first-ever dive. He did very well and gave all the correct signals during the time in the water.

The project began to take on a more formal structure during 1981. The *Invincible* (1758) Committee was formed to work the site. John Bingeman was chairman, and the other members were Arthur Mack, John Broomhead and David Houghton. Jim Boyle had moved away from the area, but John Saulet, a solicitor, was approached for legal advice during the year. At that stage the committee had no money to pay his fees, but he accepted a partnership instead, and became the fifth member of the committee. Later he learned to dive and has spent much time on the site.

Little was done on the site in 1982. There was a disagreement with the City Museum and conservation facilities were withdrawn, so it was not possible to make an application to the Department of Trade and the licence was not renewed for that year. The naval divers were too involved in the Falklands conflict to make much contribution, while some of the most experienced civilians, including Margaret Rule, the Archaeological Director, were busy with the raising of the *Mary Rose*, which was brought to the surface in September of that year.

The *Invincible*'s successor, the aircraft carrier of nearly 20,000 tons, was perhaps the best known British ship in the Falklands conflict, and the *Invincible* (1758) Committee made links with her. Some members of the committee had met her then commanding officer, Captain Michael Livesay, socially in 1981, and he had been present at the opening of the *Invincible* exhibition in the Royal Naval Museum in April of that year. In November 1981 the

The opening of the *Invincible* Exhibition at the Royal Naval Museum, Portsmouth, April 1981. From left to right: Captain Livesay, of the *Invincible*; John Terry, who painted the pictures of the *Invincible*; Arthur Mack; The Flag Officer Portsmouth, Rear Admiral Tippet; John Broomhead; John Bingeman

Invincible (1758) Committee gave the ship a wooden bucket, which it carried all the way through the Falklands war, under the command of Captain Jeremy Black. One result of the Falklands War was to cause the *Invincible* of 1980 to be kept in the Royal Navy instead of being sold to Australia; Captain Black wrote to the *Invincible* (1758) Committee:

> We leave the Falklands with a real sense of achievement and a quiet satisfaction with the performance of the ship and her systems. If the standards of the first two years are anything to go by *Invincible VI* is set for an eventful and hectic career. Perhaps our greatest reward, however, was the news that *Invincible* will remain with the Royal Navy.

After the differences with Portsmouth City Museum, the committee decided to set up its own conservation laboratory. Simon Aked was recruited from the City Museum to act as conservator and the structure of the project was further formalised with the incorporation of Invincible (1744–58) Conservations Ltd. The five members of the Invincible (1758) Committee and Simon Aked made up the board of the new company. Money was raised from the

directors' own resources and by bank loan. Premises at Kirkstall Road, Southsea, were bought. The workshop has facilities to conserve most of the types of material recovered from the wreck – wood, leather, metals, ceramics, glass, stone and textiles. Conservation work has been undertaken for other underwater sites such as the *Mary Rose*, the *Admiral Gardiner* and the Yarmouth Roads site, and this has brought some extra income to support the work on the *Invincible*.

The 1983 diving season was a little less intensive than 1981, with 192 underwater hours being logged. The 1981 trench was extended for $19\frac{1}{2}$ ft west so that it reached the side of the ship (then incorrectly believed to be the starboard side). Plans and drawings were produced and these gave the clearest view yet of the structure of the ship. New artefacts included military buttons, shoes, seals and part of a silver buckle.

Two main areas were explored in 1984. The excavation of the previous years was further extended, and more detailed plans were drawn of it, along with perspective views. In the early days of work on the structure, the divers had seen certain

Placing the wreck buoy on the site for the first time, with John Bingeman on the left, and John Broomhead on the right

timbers which they believed were part of the structure of the stern. As a result, it had always been believed that the wreck was facing south and lying on her starboard side, and that the ship had been turned around during her manoeuvres on the day she went aground. It was clear that the area being excavated was the boatswain's and carpenters' stores, hence the large quantities of rope, blocks and items associated with gunnery. French ships usually carried these aft, and it had been assumed that the *Invincible* would have continued this arrangement. During 1984 several divers, particularly those with experience on the *Mary Rose*, pointed out that the timbers being found looked much more like breast hooks than transoms, and this suggested that the area being worked on was in the bows of the ship. Almost simultaneously, research in the Plans Collection of the National Maritime Museum showed conclusively that British ships of this period invariably had gunners' and boatswains' stores in the bows, and it was certain, from the amount of work that had been done to the ship after her capture that she would have been fitted in standard British manner. It became clear that the orientation of the wreck had been misunderstood, not an uncommon mistake in the early stages of excavating a shipwreck, when comparatively little of the hull has been uncovered and conclusions have to be drawn from scraps of information. It was now certain that the wreck lay on her port side, the starboard side having been washed away, and excavations had taken place towards the bow of the ship.

The second task for 1984 was to examine the detached hull timbers to the east and north-east of the main site, probably the remains of the starboard side of the ship. A pre-disturbance survey of the area was completed and four main parts were identified. It had also been hoped to begin an exploratory trench in midships, but there was not time to attempt this.

In 1985 it was decided to resurvey the site, starting with the southernmost part. For the first time the season's excavation was done at the southern end of the site, now established as the stern of the ship, where a section of hull was uncovered, to show a complete gun-port, a transom knee and part of the inner hull planking. This area would have been used for the clothing stores, as well as providing accommodation for the surgeon, purser and the midshipmen. Numerous complete shoes and shoe fragments were found, as well as a shoe former, which was perhaps used by the ship's cobbler. A checker board, for draughts or chess, gives some insight into the leisure of the crew. Possibly it was used in either the gunroom or wardroom by the officers or midshipmen.

The southern part of the site was mapped in more detail and the timbers of the whole ship were individually numbered to give a frame of reference. Starting at the stern, most had a traffolite tally fixed to them. A grid was formed using $19\frac{1}{2}$ ft scaffolding poles placed in a line parallel to the main line of hull timbers, and a very detailed plan was drawn of the stern section to a scale of 1 to 50.

In 1986 there was further investigation of the hull

Five members of the *Invincible* team–from left, Simon Aked, Arthur Mack, John Saulet, John Broomhead and David Houghton

Of the ship as machine, there two different aspects, the hull and the fittings, including the rigging. Hundreds of rigging items have been recovered, largely because much of the excavation has been in the area of the boatswain's stores. There are rigging blocks of all kinds and sizes: single and double, fiddle blocks; rack blocks with several different sheaves in a single row, used to lead the ropes aft from the bowsprit; 'acorn' blocks, used for the main sheets, and many others. Length varies from nearly 3in to nearly 3ft. All the blocks are made of elm, with sheaves and pins of lignum vitae, and occasionally metal. Blocks are marked with the broad arrow and with their size, in Roman numerals for sizes above 10in. Much rope has also been recovered, including cables of $23\frac{1}{2}$in.

The more valuable navigation tools, such as dividers and compasses, were presumably removed before the ship was abandoned, but the ones which have survived are equally interesting. The sand-glasses were used for different purposes. The half-hour glasses, two of which were recovered, were used to mark the passing of time and to time the ringing of the ship's bell. The smaller glasses, 28 and 14 second, were for timing the running out of the log line to measure speed. The 14-second glasses, which may be the oldest surviving examples, were used to measure speeds in excess of 8 knots, and tend to confirm that the *Invincible* was regarded as a fast ship.

Many leather buckets have been found. These were stitched together with a reinforcement of hazel wood to make the top circular. They were used for fire-fighting. They are all marked with the broad arrow and some have the royal monogram and a number which may represent that of the gun they were placed beside. About 130 brushes have been recovered; records show that about 180 would be carried by a ship of this size. They were used for 'breaming' the ship. To clean her underwater hull, she was heeled over to one side and the brush was used to burn the weed off her bottom.

Some of the tools used about the rigging have also been found. A very large fid, known as an 'admiral', used for splicing cables, is more than $5\frac{1}{2}$in in diameter and 29in long. Among other tools found are copper adzes and 'drivers' used for hammering off the hoops of powder barrels. The miniature barrels, first recovered in 1980, were at first thought to contain fine powder for use with small arms. Chemical analysis has shown that they hold ink, with fine sand used for blotting. Nothing much is known about such barrels, but extensive research eventually found a shop sign of 1764 for the trade of colourman, which showed similar barrels. There was much clerical work involved in running the ship, with numerous logs, accounts and musters to be kept and letters to be written.

The hull itself is not easy to work on, but it gives plenty of new information. The iron knees seem to be the only surviving examples of this type of construction, for the French abandoned it for some reason in the second half of the eighteenth century, and later the British adopted a rather different form of iron knee which was used to brace a wooden one. There is some material on iron knees in the French archives and in contemporary books on naval architecture, but their importance was not fully appreciated until those found on the *Invincible* stimulated discussion.

The copper on the false keel is one of the most significant discoveries of all. Until it was found there was no known record of a ship being coppered before the *Alarm* in 1761. Further search in the archives shows that some ships were partly coppered during 1758, but the copper on the *Invincible* must have been fitted before that. It may be the very beginning of an experiment which, in the end, was to revolutionise naval warfare.

The material on the crew's living conditions is particularly rich. It is not difficult to find what seamen ate, how much they were paid and many other aspects of their life, for the records of these are copious. Very little had been known about their plates and eating utensils because they were not supplied from government stores. The purser of each ship was given a certain amount of 'necessary money', according to the size of the crew. With this he was expected to buy many items, including coal, wood and candles. He was also expected to provide the 'turnery ware', which meant the basic plates and mugs for the mess decks. Usually his provision was not very adequate and the seamen generally provided their own, either individually or as a mess. According to one seaman of fifty years later, some messes were 'well fitted up'. The table furniture found from the *Invincible* reflects this mixture of sources. Some items are marked with the broad arrow to indicate government property. Others have initials and some have symbols. One has a rough sketch which may show a gallows with the cage in which bodies were kept as a warning to others – perhaps it was owned by an illiterate seaman with a morbid sense of humour.

Bowls were round and wooden, probably turned on a lathe. One cup was made from half a coconut. A much more sophisticated tankard has been found, made up of staves like a barrel, with a handle and an opening lid. Several spoons have been recovered, some with the broad arrow, some marked with the owner's symbol, such as a row of crosses along the handle, and in one case the initials 'TH'. The only crew member with those initials was Thomas Hilliard, a captain's servant.

Among the most interesting items are the square plates. These are about 12in on each side, with the broad arrow on the underside. They have a wooden lip, known as a 'fiddle', around each side, and they have prompted two interesting suggestions about phrases in very common use. They might have inspired the term 'square meal'. The standard dictionaries can only trace the expression back to 1860 and believe it to be American in origin. It has also been suggested that 'on the fiddle' refers to a seaman having his food so heaped on his plate that it covered the rim.

Parts of shoes were among the first items recovered

from the wreck and they continue to be found. According to the Northampton Boot and Shoe Museum, they are very rare for the mid-eighteenth century and they raise some interesting points. Some are very small, suggesting that children were on board, or at least that some of the ship's boys were very small for their ages. Some are women's; this raises the question of whether there were any women on board at the time of the wreck. Log books offer no evidence of this, but they never do, even when it is known from other sources that they were on board. It is possible that some of the officers, either naval or military, arranged to have their families carried unofficially; it is also possible that the ship was merely carrying supplies for troops already in North America.

The military finds are perhaps the most surprising of all for they contradict several established assumptions. Again they can be divided into two categories: the items associated with the ship's own main armament on the one hand, and the small arms, used both by the ship's own marines and by any troops on board, on the other. As regards the main armament, there is almost a complete range of gunners' stores, for each of the three sizes of cannon on board. From these it is clear that, yet again, the Invincible was being used for experiments. In particular, her guns were among the first to be equipped with flint-locks for firing, instead of the old system of lighted matches. The locks were removed with the guns and no spares have yet been found, but many large flints have been recovered. The tin tubes, which carried the spark down into the powder, were not well liked at the time as they tended to fly out during action. It was largely because of this that the flint-lock was abandoned after this experiment, to be revived twenty years later with some improvements.

Powder boxes have also been found. These were hollow wooden cylinders, with lids and bases, used to protect the powder from sparks when it was being carried from the magazine to the individual gun. They were made of poplar, which has proved difficult to conserve. Tompions were used to cover the mouth of the gun when it was not in use. They seem to have been turned in batches and cut off as required. They were quite expendable and had none of the decoration associated with modern tompions.

Finally, the smaller military artefacts are examples of items not often found either by sea or land. Numerous hand-grenades have been discovered. Musket shot, found in enormous quantities, often had a small lip for fixing a paper cartridge to the rearmost part of the ball. An infantryman's cartridge box has been found. It was made of wood and drilled with holes to receive nine shot. It has a leather case and its stamped crest provided a vital clue in the identification of the ship.

Items of military and marine uniform provide some of the most puzzling features. A soldier's felt hat is thought to be from the 55th regiment, whose Colonel was Lord Howe and his brother was British Commander in Chief in North America during the War of Independence. A Howe family seal has also been found, although it is not clear what it was doing on board the Invincible. A great variety of military buttons had been uncovered, from no less than ten regiments, not counting the marines, whose 'foul anchor' button is also well represented. Obviously, the Invincible was not carrying troops from all these units, but there are two other possibilities. She had a notably large hold and perhaps she was supplementing the transports by taking some of the military supplies. The other possibility is that she was carrying staff officers from various regiments. Lord Amherst, the military commander of the expedition, later sailed in the Dublin, which eventually took the Invincible's place. It is possible that he had originally been intended to sail in the larger ship. The Invincible had been fitted out as a flagship, for she was to carry Hardy's flag again on arrival in North America. Perhaps her great cabin was to be used for Amherst and his staff. There is no sign that Amherst was on board when the ship sailed, although musters show that she carried fifteen supernumeraries 'belonging to no ship' who could have been staff officers. But, despite extensive research, the question remains unresolved.

However, the finds of buttons have proved conclusively that military buttons, and the naval foul anchor, were in use rather earlier than had been supposed. This has later been supported by evidence from other finds, for example on the site of the Battle of the Heights of Abraham, Quebec, in 1759, where numbered buttons have also been found. The Invincible's 'foul anchor' buttons have the name J. Nutting inscribed on the back.

The future excavations of the Invincible may have to be more intensive than originally planned. In 1985 it was learned that the Southern Water Authority was planning to build a sewage pipe which would discharge 1,300yds to the west of the Invincible site. A tidal atlas for the area was prepared by Hydraulics Research Ltd, and it showed that the sewage would be carried over the wreck on an east-going stream. Since there were eight hours of that stream, as against four hours of westerly stream, this did not look too hopeful. The water authority claimed that the site would not be greatly affected, but admitted that at low-water neaps some sewage would tend to accumulate over the wreck. Since this is obviously the best time for diving on the wreck, there was some cause for alarm. The authority also claimed that it had considered two other sites for the outflow, both to the east of the Invincible. These were rejected because they would cause an unacceptable build-up of sewage 5 miles away at Chichester Harbour. This did not augur well for the Invincible.

The Invincible project has tried to argue against these proposals. On taking legal advice, it was found that there was little chance of challenging the SWA through the courts, since it would be difficult to disprove their hydrodynamic tests. There remains the point that they may be breaking EEC regulations by not treating the sewage properly and merely passing it through 5mm grids. However, the directors of the project are preparing for the worst. They are seeking to increase the rate of excavation so that it will be able to complete the work on the wreck by 1990.

There is no doubt what contemporaries thought of the *Invincible*. To the French she was a ship which 'carried sail well, steered well and had a fine battery'. To Anson she was 'a prodigious fine ship and vastly large'. To Admiral Warren, who had the experience of sailing her, she was 'better in every way than any ship, and is in every shape a fine man-of-war'. Captain Keppel saw her and claimed that 'the *Invincible* outsails the whole navy of England'. To Boscawen 'the *Invincible* sails well, rather better than every ship'. The ultimate accolade was given by the Admiralty in London, who called her 'the best ship of her class, and answers all purposes that could be desired of a ship of war'.

Nearly two and a half centuries after her keel was laid at Rochefort, the story of the *Invincible* is not yet finished. She served in two different navies and had a profound effect on the ship design of both. She carried several famous admirals and thousands of seamen served in her over the years. She took part in two major wars at a time when the colonial rivalry between the powers of Western Europe was at its most intense. She saw a good deal of the world, on both sides of the Atlantic, from Haiti to Nova Scotia, from Madeira to Portsmouth. She survived one major battle and several violent storms. Much of the ship still exists beneath the waters of the Solent, forming a 'time capsule', and giving us a unique and fascinating picture of the life of seamen in those troubled and difficult times. Thousands of items raised from her have been conserved and should last indefinitely in museums throughout the world. No one knows what secrets she still holds.

Notes and Sources

Abbreviations

AN Archives National, Paris.
BL Addit. Additional Manuscripts in the British Library London.
MM *Mariners' Mirror*, Journal of the SNR.
NMM National Maritime Museum, Greenwich.
NRS Navy Records Society.
PRO Public Records Office, Kew and Chancery Lane, London.
SNR Society for Nautical Research.

Introduction

General

Mainly based on John Broomhead's dive logs, interviews with Arthur Mack, David Houghton and John Bingeman, and further comments by John Broomhead; John Bingeman's article in *Diver* magazine, August 1981; various press cuttings.

Chapter 1

General

Jean Boudriot, *The Ship of Seventy Four Guns*, in 4 vols. (The first two have been translated into English by David H. Roberts, 1986.) Numerous articles in *Neptunia* (published by the Association des Amis des Musées de la Marine, Paris) by Jean Boudriot.
Martine Acerra, *Rochefort, Rêve et Réalité*, in *Neptunia*, No 147, pp17–32.
Jean Meyer and others, *Rochefort et la Mer*, Jonzac, 1985.
Archives du Port, Rochefort, especially 1E series.

1 Rochefort archives, 1E 134. All the other information on the building of the ship comes from this series, unless otherwise noted.
2 See note by Boudriot in *Neptunia*, No 161 pp6–7.
3 Falconer, *Marine Dictionary*, 1769, p263.
Stalkaart, *Marine Architecture*, pp135–6.
Quoted in *Rochefort et la Mer*, p12.
4 British fleet from Charles Derrick, *Memoirs of the Rise and Progress of the Royal Navy*, London, 1806.
French fleet numbers from *Neptunia*, No 103, p37, and other sources.
5 Boudriot in *Neptunia*, No 137, pp1–2.
6 Archives National, Paris, Marine G 246 NMM, Greenwich, SPB/34.
7 Rochefort archives, 1E 134.
8 Based on Acerra and Meyer, above.
9 PRO Adm 106/3067.

Chapter 2

General

H. W. Richmond, *The Navy in the War of 1739–48*, 3 vols, Cambridge, 1920.
Archives National, Paris, Marine B⁴ 61 for accounts of the Battle of Finisterre.
AN, Colonies B⁴ 61, for letters on the voyage to the West Indies.
Anson's letters in PRO Adm 1/87.
Logs of ships in PRO Adm 51 series.
Lieutenant's logs in NMM ADM/L series.

1 AN files on Macnemara, Marine C⁷ 191.
2 Orders in AN Colonies B² 82.
3 AN Colonies B⁴ 67.
4 AN Colonies B⁴ 61.
5 PRO Adm 51/936, log of *Strafford*, 1/233, 9 March 1745–6, Admiral's letters.
6 PRO Adm 1/233, 15 May 1746.
7 Quoted in *Neptunia*, No 161, p.7.

8 NMM POR/D/9.
9 *Biographie Universalle*, Paris and Leipzig, 1843, Vol 37, pp317–21, biography of St Georges.
10 PRO HCA 32/118.
11 Rochefort archives, E 142, 26 January 1747.
12 PRO HCA 32/118.
13 *Ibid*.
14 Charnock, *Biographia Navalis*, London, 1794–8, Vol 4, p431.
15 PRO Adm 1/87.
16 St Georges' dossier, AN Marine C⁷ 293.
17 PRO Adm 1/87.
18 *Ibid*.
19 Richmond, Vol 3, p83.
20 *Gentleman's Magazine*, 1747, p276.
21 PRO Adm 51/135.
22 Unpublished journal of Robert Spotswood, p22.
23 PRO HCA 32/118.
24 PRO Adm 1/87.
25 PRO Adm 51/4286, log of the *Pembroke*.
26 PRO HCA 32/118.

Chapter 3

General

Logs of ships in the PRO, esp *Prince George*, Adm 51/4268.
Portsmouth Dockyard papers, NMM POR series.
PRO Adm 2 series for Admiralty orders.
For information on the defects of British ships, see Lavery, *Ship of the Line*, 2 vols, 1983–4.

1 N.A.M. Rodger, *Wooden World*, London, 1986, p30.
2 W. H. Long, *Naval Yarns*, 1899, reprinted 1973, p23–4.
3 Lieutenant's logs, NMM ADM/L/N 15.
4 Duke of Bedford's correspondence, ed Lord John Russell, London, 1842, Vol 1 p215.
5 Historical Manuscripts Commission, *Ducane* manuscripts, p64.
6 Hodges and Hughes, *Select Naval Documents*, Cambridge, 1922, p121.
7 NRS Vol 120, *Naval Administration*, ed Daniel Baugh, 1977.
8 NRS Vol 99, *The Vernon Papers*, p472.
9 MM Vol III, p50.
10 *Vernon Papers*, p348.
11 BL Addit. 15956.
12 Barrow, *Life of Anson*, London, 1839, p167.
13 *Letters of Horace Walpole*, ed Lewis, Vol 19, pp402–3.
14 Cobbett's *Parliamentary History*, XIV, 63.
15 Most of the information on the prisoners of war comes from NMM ADM/M/397–8.
16 BL Addit. 15957.
17 Barrow, p186.
18 Rochefort archives, 1E 145, f 553.
19 Hodges and Hughes, p121.
20 NMM POR/D/9.
21 Ordnance papers at Priddy's Hard, Portsmouth.
22 PRO Adm 1/2043.

Chapter 4

General

Richmond, as above.
Captain's letters, PRO Adm 1/2043.
Log, PRO Adm 51/477.
Warren's letters, PRO Adm 1/88.

1 N.A.M. Rodger, *op cit*, p19.
2 PRO Adm 2/71.
3 PRO Adm 3/57, 8 August 1747.

4 Dictionary of National Biography, Vol 59, p419, Warren.
5 NMM AGC/7/13.
6 BL Addit 15957.
7 NMM AGC/7/13.
8 N.A.M. Rodger, *op cit*, p352.

Chapter 5

General
Falconer's *Marine Dictionary*.
W. Mountaine, *The Seaman's Vade Mecum*, 1756, reprinted
  1971.
Admiralty Orders and Instructions, especially 1747 edition, in
  PRO Adm 7/202.

1 Falconer, p191.
2 Court martial report, Adm 1/5297.
3 PRO Adm 107/4.
4 PRO Adm 33/539.
5 NMM WQB/3.
6 PRO Adm 33/539.
7 Lloyd, Keevil and Coulter, *Medicine and the Navy*, 1956–63,
   Vol 3, pp84–5.
8 *Roderick Random*, Chapter XXV.
9 Burney, *Universal Dictionary of the Marine*, 1815, reprinted
   1970, p663.
10 PRO Adm 51/471.
11 PRO Adm 1/916, 2 December 1747.
12 PRO Adm 2/219, 21 October 1755.
13 *Medicine and the Navy*, Vol 3, p58.

Chapter 6

1 PRO Adm 2/72, 26 July 1748.
2 Baugh, *Naval Administration*, pp188–9.
3 *Naval Yarns*, p107.
4 PRO Adm 33/402, pay book.
5 PRO Adm 2/72, 1 July 1748.
6 Rodger, *op cit*, p271. Dictionary of National Biography, Vol
   4, p305, Bentley.
7 R. F. Mackay, *Hawke*, Oxford, 1965, pp102–4. MM Vol 47,
   p178 ff. NMM HWK/2.
8 PRO Adm 7/568.
9 PRO Adm 1/5294.
10 PRO Adm 95/25, f67.
11 PRO Adm 95/17.
12 NMM POR/A/17.
13 *Ship of the Line*, Vol 1, p94.
14 PRO Adm 180/10.
15 NRS, Vol 92, *Naval Miscellany*, Vol IV, p201.

Chapter 7

General
Sir Julian Corbett, *England in the Seven Years War*, London,
  1907.
Ship's logs, PRO Adm 51/471.
Boscawen's letters, PRO Adm 1/90.
Boscawen's letters to his wife in NRS Vol 92, *Naval Miscellany*,
  Vol IV, pp165–256, ed Peter K. Kemp, 1952.

1 PRO Adm 1/88.
2 *Ibid*.
3 Ordnance papers, Priddy's Hard.
4 Dictionary of National Biography, Vol 5, p415, Boscawen.
5 *Letters of Horace Walpole*, ed Cunningham, 1891, Vol II,
   p192.
6 *Life of Johnson*, p978.
7 *NRS Miscellany IV*, p199.
8 *Ibid*, p204.
9 *Ibid*, p214.
10 *Ibid*, p234.
11 *Ibid*, p235.
12 *Ibid*, p235.
13 *Ibid*, p238.

14 *Ibid*, p242.
15 *Ibid*, p241.
16 PRO Adm 1/90.
17 PRO Adm 1/1487.
18 PRO Adm 1/90, 1/1487.
19 PRO Adm 1/90.
20 *Ibid*.
21 *Naval Miscellany IV*, p229.
22 PRO Adm 1/90.
23 MM, Vol 62, p2.

Chapter 8

General
Falconer's *Marine Dictionary*.
W. Mountaine, *The Seaman's Vade Mecum*, 1756, reprinted
  1971.
Admiralty Orders and Instructions, especially 1747 edition, in
  PRO Adm 7/202.

1 NMM BEL/2a.
2 PRO Adm 95/15.
3 NRS, Vol 91, *Five Naval Journals*, ed Thursfield, p10.
4 Spotswood's journal, p33.
5 *Medicine and the Navy*, Vol 3, p84.
6 *Naval Miscellany IV*, pp182–3.
7 *Naval Yarns*, p63.
8 C.J. Marcus, *Quiberon Bay*, London, 1960, p189.
9 PRO Adm 7/202.
10 Spotswood p12.
11 PRO Adm 106/2508. (See *Ship of the Line*, Vol II. p177.)
12 Dictionary of National Biography, Vol 5, p415.
13 PRO Adm 106/2508, as above.
14 Cyril Field, *Britain's Sea Soldiers*, Liverpool, 1924, Vol 1,
   pp129–30.
15 Spotswood, p32.
16 *Naval Yarns*, p113.
17 *Five Naval Journals*, p25.
18 *Naval Yarns*, p86.
19 PRO Adm 106/2508, as above.

Chapter 9

General
Sir Julian Corbett, *England in the Seven Years War*, London,
  1907.
Holbourne's letters, PRO Adm 1/481.
Ship's log, PRO Adm 51/471.
Maritime Museum of Canada, *Occasional Papers*, No ii, ed
  Little.

1 *Augustus Hervey's Journal*, ed Erskine, London, 1953, p244.
2 PRO Adm 1/481.
3 PRO Adm 1/488.
4 NMM RUSI/90.
5 PRO Adm 1/481.
6 *Ibid*.
7 PRO Adm 51/471.
8 PRO Adm 1/481.
9 PRO Adm 51/471.
10 PRO Adm 52/863, master's log.
11 PRO Adm 1/481.
12 Maritime Museum of Canada, *Occasional Papers*, No ii, p27.
13 PRO Adm 51/471.
14 Maritime Museum of Canada, *op cit*, p20.
15 PRO Adm 1/1606.
16 PRO Adm 95/12, 21 May 1757.
17 *History of Marine Architecture*, London, 1800–2, Vol 3, p144.
18 NMM POR/D/12.

Chapter 10

General
Court martial minutes, PRO Adm 1/5297.

Bentley's log, PRO Adm 51/471. (The master's log is missing from the series.)

Lieutenant's logs, NMM ADM/L/J 87, especially the First Lieutenant's log, which is the clearest account of the incident.

NMM POR series, especially POR/F/11.

1 PRO Adm 106/1191, 18 December 1770.
2 NMM POR/F11.
3 PRO Adm 51/673.
4 PRO Adm 2/522.
5 PRO Adm 1/926.
6 *Lloyd's Evening Post*, 22–24 February 1758.
7 NMM ADM/Y/5.
8 NMM POR/D/13.
9 *Ibid.*
10 NMM POR/F/11.
11 NMM POR/D/13.

Chapter 11

General

Log and diary kept by John Broomhead.

Diving logs by John Bingeman and others.

Interviews with Arthur Mack, David Houghton, John Bingeman, Simon Aked.

Various press cuttings, etc.

Annual reports of the *Invincible* (1758) committee.

John Bingeman's articles in *International Journal of Nautical Archaeology*, 1982 and 1985.

Margaret Rule, *The Mary Rose*, London, 1982.

Keith Muckleroy, *Marine Archaeology*, 1979.